WORLD MISSION

An Analysis
of the World Christian Movement

SECOND EDITION
Full revision of the original work

The Strategic Dimension

Part Two of a Manual in Three Parts

Jonathan Lewis, Ph.D., Editor

WILLIAM CAREY LIBRARY
Pasadena, California

Published by: William Carey Library, P.O. Box 40129, Pasadena, CA 91114, telephone (818) 798-0819

ISBN 0-87808-238-7
Printed in the United States of America

Editor: Jonathan Lewis, Ph.D.
Assistant Editors: Meg Crossman and Stephen Hoke, Ph.D.
Technical Editor: Susan Peterson
Assistants: Joe Varela and Patrick Roseman
Illustrators: John Devine and Dawn Lewis

Acknowledgments

Many of the articles and excerpts in this manual are found in the mission anthology *Perspectives on the World Christian Movement: A Reader* (revised edition), edited by Ralph Winter and Steven Hawthorne and published by William Carey Library. We are heavily indebted to the editors of this anthology for their encouragement in the production of this course. We would especially like to thank Dr. Ralph Winter for his inspiration and genius as the originator of this course, and we recognize his tireless efforts on behalf of the unreached peoples of the world. A special note of appreciation also goes to the *Perspectives* course office in Pasadena, California, which has cooperated fully in the re-edition process, in the hope of greater compatibility with their popular extension course.

My heartfelt thanks go to my assistant editors, Meg Crossman and Dr. Stephen T. Hoke. Meg's advocacy and use of the *World Mission* manuals in the Arizona *Perspectives* courses provided a wealth of insights for improving the material. Her contributions are reflected primarily in the first two volumes. Steve Hoke, veteran missions lecturer, was of invaluable help in improving the third volume. His knowledge, insights, and ready assistance are very much appreciated. Most of the credit for the technical production of this work goes to Susan Peterson. Her long hours of formatting, proofreading, indexing, and producing the figures and tables speak eloquently for themselves. We gratefully acknowledge Joe Varela and Pat Roseman, who assisted Susan in these tasks. We have kept many of John Devine's and Dawn Lewis's illustrations from the first edition. Thank you all for your marvelous help. May it advance the expansion of God's kingdom to the ends of the earth.

Jonathan Lewis, Editor
January 1994

Other Course Materials by the Editor

- *World Mission Leader's Guide.* An aid to those who want to organize and conduct a study group utilizing these manuals. It includes suggestions for promotion and organization of the course, as well as sample answers to each of the questions in the texts. An appendix gives useful helps on group dynamics. Available from William Carey Library.

- *Misión Mundial: Un Análisis del Movimiento Cristiano Mundial* (3 volumes).

- *Guia para el tutor del grupo de estudio de: Misión Mundial* (3 volumes).

- *Video de Misión Mundial* (3 videos, 5 hours total).

  The Second Edition of the Spanish manuals, accompanying leader's guide, and the lecture videos are available from Unilit, 1360 N.W. 88th Ave., Miami, FL 33172.

  Please contact the publisher for other language editions under production.

- *Working Your Way to the Nations: A Guide to Effective Tentmaking.* A 12-lesson course for use by local churches in guiding the preparation of cross-cultural "tentmaking" missionaries. Available from William Carey Library. Editions of this strategic course in Korean, Spanish, and Portuguese are under production.

PART 2
THE STRATEGIC DIMENSION

	Page
Preface to the Second Edition	iv
Organization and Use of This Manual	iv
Chapter 6: Strategy for World Evangelization	**6-1**
I. Strategy and Prayer	6-2
II. History of Mission Strategy	6-14
III. Structures and Power	6-25
Chapter 7: The Task Remaining	**7-1**
I. The Great Commission Nations	7-1
II. Envisioning the Task	7-11
III. Major Blocs of Unreached Peoples	7-22
Chapter 8: To Reach the Unreached	**8-1**
I. Strategic Considerations	8-1
II. The Unique Solution Strategy	8-13
III. Putting It All Together	8-21
Chapter 9: Entry Strategies, Evangelism, and Church Planting	**9-1**
I. Entry Strategies	9-1
II. Evangelism	9-10
III. Church Planting	9-20
Chapter 10: Evangelism and Social Action: Two Partners in Mission	**10-1**
I. Holistic Mission	10-2
II. The World's Needy	10-11
III. Community Development	10-20
Appendix: Resources From Adopt-A-People Clearinghouse	A-1
Subject Index	A-9
Author Index	A-13

89995

Preface to the Second Edition

We live in a rapidly changing world. These changes affect the way the advancing World Christian Movement perceives its mandate and carries out its task. The Second Edition of *World Mission* has tried to analyze these trends and incorporate their discussion into the text. Two Thirds World missions, reaching rapidly expanding cities, mission to the world's poor and destitute, the 10/40 window, strategic partnerships, church/mission tension—these and other current issues are woven into the discussion of the biblical, historical, strategic, and cross-cultural foundation of missions, improving and strengthening these basic themes.

The editors have worked closely with the *Perspectives* office at the U.S. Center for World Mission in Pasadena, California, to assure that these manuals are suited for students participating in their extension courses. Questions have been improved, and the research assignment has been redesigned to enhance the application of the end-product. Useful indexes and an appendix have also been added.

Organization and Use of This Manual

World Mission: An Analysis of the World Christian Movement is a manual that can be used by study groups in a formal or informal educational setting. The manual is in three parts, each being a separate unit.

- **Part One, The Biblical/Historical Foundation**, examines the roots of world mission, including its origin and its development through the ages.

- **Part Two, The Strategic Dimension**, defines the remaining mission task and the strategies necessary to reach the unreached.

- **Part Three, Cross-Cultural Considerations**, explores the challenge of cross-cultural communication of the gospel.

Each of the 15 chapters of this manual is divided into three study units. Each unit develops a distinct concept and relates it to the material studied in preceding units. Questions interspersed throughout the text direct the reader's attention to key points and stimulate reflection on the readings.

Each chapter ends with two sections of questions. The first section, **Integrative Assignment**, is designed to help the reader assimilate the material studied. The questions invite the student to do further research and encourage the development of the student's abilities to communicate what is learned. Study groups should use these questions for group discussion. In Part Two of the manual, an "Unreached Peoples" research project is incorporated into the Integrative Assignment. This fascinating project will require extra time and effort from the student.

The second section of questions, **Questions for Reflection**, asks for a response to personal and spiritual issues raised by the readings. We recommend that each student enter his or her thoughts either in the workbook or in a personal diary. We also suggest that a devotional time be provided during each group session to share these comments.

CHAPTER 6

Strategy for World Evangelization

Seen from a mission perspective, history reveals itself in a unique and refreshing way. The kingdom of God, rather than the kingdoms of terrestrial potentates, is history's central theme. God's purpose to redeem a people and reestablish His rule upon the earth is the main plot. The "ten epochs" of mission history reveal that God's people have seldom been willing ambassadors of His kingdom's expansion. As the drama unfolds, exile, dispersion, persecution, and invasion have often been needed to cause believers to fulfill their covenant obligation. When God's people have set out willingly to share the gospel with the nations, God has greatly blessed and multiplied those endeavors. Although it has been only in the last two centuries that Protestants have taken their responsibility for world evangelization seriously, phenomenal growth and expansion have taken place.

This growth can be categorized into three distinct "eras" of expansion. The First Era was marked by an awakening of Protestants to the task and the sending of missionaries to the coastal areas of the unreached continents. The Second Era saw a movement towards the unreached interiors of Africa, Asia, and Latin America. The Third Era, the current one, is characterized by a movement towards unreached people groups. Most of these groups are no longer isolated geographically from the gospel but are isolated instead by social, cultural, and linguistic barriers. Such barriers have effectively prevented these "hidden" peoples from hearing and receiving the gospel, even though the church may exist nearby. Recent research, coupled with this clear understanding, demands a fresh, new, and culturally appropriate *strategy* for accomplishing the task of world evangelization.

As the Third Era unfolds, a flood of missionaries from the newer churches of the Two Thirds World has been added to the existing Western missions task force. Together, this broad, worldwide movement for world evangelization has the potential of bringing closure to the Great Commission!

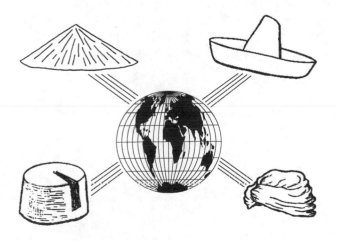

Figure 6-1. The "Together" Task Force

I. Strategy and Prayer

Some Christians believe that in performing God's work, strategy and planning conflict with prayer and the spontaneous leading of the Holy Spirit. If this were categorically true, a discussion of strategy would be useless. We are convinced, however, that when strategy is properly understood and implemented, it can work in perfect harmony with God's leading. We are aware of the dangers of merely applying human intelligence to the mission task, for "unless the Lord builds the house, they labor in vain that build it" (Ps. 127:1). God, however, does have a plan for building His house, the living temple of believers around the world, and historically He has provided strategic insight when His people are open to receiving it.

Consider again the parable of the talents in Matthew 25:14-30. Each servant was entrusted with a certain amount of money, and each one was expected to invest that money for the master's gain. The unfaithful servant was not judged for squandering his talent, but for failing to develop even the simplest investment strategy (such as putting the money in the bank), so that he could see growth for his lord. The other two servants used their investment skill, doubled their money, and were received "into the joy of [their] master" (Matt. 25:21, 23). It is this very matter of "investment skill" with which mission strategy deals.

Peter Wagner, Professor of Church Growth at Fuller School of World Mission, defines *strategy* as follows (emphasis added):

> Strategy is the means agreed on to reach a certain goal. Missionary strategy is the way the body of Christ goes about obeying the Lord and accomplishing the objectives He lays down. I contend that every Christian every day uses strategy of some kind or other in the attempt to do God's will. I also contend that some strategies are demonstrably superior to others, and that we do poorly if we do not examine them all and choose the best.... The best strategy is, first of all, *biblical* because God's work must be done in God's way. Secondly, it is *efficient*. Since our personnel, money, and time are all limited, we need to make decisions sooner or later as to what priorities to assign in their use. We can't do everything we would like to do, so we must on the basis of efficiency—do what will best accomplish God's objective. Third, strategy must be *relevant*. Missions is such a fast-moving field that strategy useful five years ago might well be obsolete today. It needs constant updating.*

GOAL

---

* Wagner, C. P. (1974). *Stop the world, I want to get on* (pp. 76-77). Glendale, CA: Regal Books.

1. How does strategy work alongside the leading of the Holy Spirit?

_____

_____

_____

Edward R. Dayton and David A. Fraser have written one of the most influential books on mission strategy in recent times, Planning Strategies for World Evangelization. In the following excerpt, they define the term and present a rationale for the use of strategy.

❑ Strategy *

Edward R. Dayton and David A. Fraser *

What does "strategy" mean?

In one sense, everyone and every organization has a strategy—a way of approaching problems or achieving goals. Many organizations do this quite unconsciously. Others have developed their strategies into almost fixed, standard approaches.

The Apostle Paul had a strategy. We read in Acts 17:2 that on the Sabbath he went into the synagogue *as was his custom.* Paul's strategy was to arrive at a major city, visit the synagogue if there was one, proclaim Jesus, and then let events take their course.

A strategy is an overall approach, plan, or way of describing how we will go about reaching our goal or solving our problem. Its concern is not with the small details. Paul's ultimate goal was to preach Christ throughout the world. His own calling motivated frontier evangelism, preaching Christ where there were no communities of Christians (Rom. 15:20). His day-to-day plans would differ, but his strategy remained the same.

Strategy looks for a range of possible "means and methods" and various "operations" that will best accomplish an objective. Strategy is a way to reach an objective. It looks for a time and place when things will be different from what they are now. For the military it might be capturing a key town or city.

> *A strategy is an overall approach, plan, or way of describing how we will go about reaching our goal or solving our problem.*

For a business person it might mean achieving a desired volume in a particular market. For a Christian organization it may mean everything from deciding in what country to serve to the overall approach to reaching a particular group of people.

---

* Dayton, E. R., & Fraser, D. A. (1990). *Planning strategies for world evangelization* (rev. ed.) (pp. 13-17). Grand Rapids: Eerdmans.

** Edward R. Dayton is a management consultant helping mission agencies. He served with World Vision International for 25 years, most recently as Vice President for Missions and Evangelism and as the founding director of World Vision's Missions Advanced Research and Communications Center (MARC). He has written extensively on management and mission strategy.

David A. Fraser is currently Chair of the Department of Biblical and Theological Studies and Associate Professor of Sociology at Eastern College in Wayne, Pennsylvania. He was formerly a professor at Columbia Bible College in Columbia, South Carolina.

2. What relationship exists between the terms "strategy" and "goal"?

_____

_____

_____

Why have a strategy?

As Christians, a strategy forces us to seek the mind and will of God. Strategy is an attempt to anticipate the future God wants to bring about. It is a *statement of faith* as to what we believe that future to be and how we can go about bringing it into existence.

Strategy is also a means of communication to fellow Christians so they can know where we think we should concentrate our efforts. It thus gives us an overall sense of direction and helps to generate cohesiveness. Because it tells us and others what we *will* do, it tells others what we have decided *not* to do.

3. How can planning a strategy be a "spiritual" exercise?

_____

_____

_____

4. What additional reasons are given for the importance of strategy? Can you think of any others?

_____

_____

_____

Types of strategies

There are many different approaches to strategies for evangelism. Some are based on past success. That is, a particular way of doing things worked so well in the past that the pattern became a *Standard Solution Strategy*. Standard Solution Strategies are assumed to be universally applicable. Their advocates use them in all parts of the earth with only cosmetic modifications.

The problem with these strategies is that they assume all people everywhere are basically the same. Cultural and social differences are not thought to play important roles in evangelism strategies.

Other strategies come from the notion that the Holy Spirit will provide serendipitous guidance in the moment of action. *Being-in-the-Way Strategies* assume that Christian partnership with God's activity does not require human planning. In fact, planning is sometimes seen as against the Holy Spirit.

The net effect of this approach eliminates failure. Whatever happens is God's responsibility. Anything that happens is God's will. But it runs into the problem that when two or more Christians appeal to the direct, inspired leading of the Holy Spirit "in-the-Way," they may be in each other's way. A hidden assumption of this approach is that proper spirituality cuts out the need for human forethought.

We are proponents of the *Unique Solution* approach to strategy. Like the Standard Solution approach, it recognizes that we learn from the way God has led people in the past. The successes of the Spirit are a real resource. We can and must learn as much as possible about what God has done and use it where it is indeed applicable.

But this approach argues that the differences between the situations and cultures of various people groups are also important. People and culture are not like standardized machines that have interchangeable parts. We cannot simply use an evangelism approach that has worked in one context in another and expect the same results. Strategies must be as unique as the peoples to whom they apply.

Further, the Unique Solution approach recognizes with the Being-in-the-Way Strategy that God has new surprises for us. Strategies must be open to new insight and new developments and cannot be rigidly standardized once and for all. Yet it also argues that we risk the sin of sloth (laziness) in not using all we have and are. We are to offer to God our best human efforts.

When God calls us to preach, we do not suppose we violate the leading of the Holy Spirit in carefully planning a sermon: researching the text until we have confidence we understand the author's intention, developing a clear outline to follow, praying for illustrations and examples that will communicate the point of God's Word in contemporary terms. We *plan* the sermon carefully *because* we seek to speak about and for God. We can take the Lord's name in vain by invoking the Holy Spirit over our inattention, lack of discipline and forethought, or even laziness.

Just so, while remaining constantly open to God's surprises and extraordinary leadings, the Unique Solution approach believes that we can sketch the outline of a well-thought-out "solution" to the question of how a given people could be effectively evangelized. We are not ruling out visions, dreams, or sudden convictions. Planning uses whatever resources are authentically given to us by the Spirit of God. The idea that the Holy Spirit does not use good human preparation in doing the work of the kingdom is inadequate to Scripture and experience.

Strategies must be as unique as the peoples to whom they apply. They must be open to new insight and new developments and cannot be rigidly standardized.

The Unique Solution Strategy thus seeks to avoid what we see as the two extremes in some Christian approaches to strategy. On the one hand, the Standard Solution approach supposes we need only one basic strategy, that God has revealed the universal pattern once and for all, that success is "in the plan." The Being-in-the-Way approach, on the other hand, turns out to be an anti-strategy dressed up in a rigid portrait of the Holy Spirit as guiding only when human beings do the least.

The Unique Solution approach argues that God has given us some universal *goals* and *guidance* as to what we are about in evangelism. Yet how and when and where and many other components are as variable as are the cultures and social groups God sends us out to evangelize. This is not to say that we do not use the experience of the past. Rather, we combine past experience with that which lies ahead.

---

5. *In what way is the Unique Solution Strategy a balanced perspective between the other two strategies described?*

Is our strategy "Western"?

If you are new to this idea of strategy, you may logically ask: "Isn't all this just a Western technological approach? Doesn't this substitute modern human methods for God's work?" These are valid questions.

We can never be complacent or arrogant about any of our approaches to doing God's will. There is a constant tension here. Often we do not know which ideas are purely our own and which indeed come from the wisdom of God. We never grow beyond the childlike dependence upon God, even when we have done our very best planning. However, childlike does not mean childish. When we act without forethought, we risk the sin of tempting God (Matt. 4:7).

Planning and strategies, while greatly refined and strengthened in the modern industrial world, are not a modern or even Western invention. Joshua followed a strategy in his capture of the city of Ai. The building of the Great Wall of China or the pyramids of Egypt shows the signs of careful planning and forethought.

However, in the most refined and technical sense of planning and strategy development (which we advocate in this book), we are following a pattern that has its roots and strength in Western developments. Yet it is also related to the Christian worldview. Because a loving and rational Creator created our world, early science was convinced it was a lawful world. And if the world is to some degree lawful,

then we can anticipate it and plan for its future. The more we understand how the world and history work, the more we can plan for the future.

So on the one hand we must say: this is a Western approach. Yet, on the other, we must say that developing strategies is not incompatible with the Christian mission. Planning is a way we can be "as wise as serpents, and as harmless as doves" (Matt. 10:16).

The more we understand how the world and history work, the more we can plan for the future.

Strategies take God's commission and goals seriously. They do so by showing how we plan to carry out God's commission. They also show how we seek to be wise in our evangelism. They help us insure that we are not harmful to God's intentions or to the people He sends us to evangelize.

In the 10 years since the concepts in this book were first developed, thousands of First and Two Thirds World missionaries have been exposed to them. Non-Western missionaries in Nepal, Indonesia, Chad, Taiwan, Singapore, Argentina, Chile, India, the Philippines, Kenya, Uganda, and a host of other countries have expressed joy in using them. They say that the Holy Spirit *focused* their thinking with these concepts and made them more effective for the Lord.

6. *How is strategy a concept which transcends time and culture?*

_____

_____

_____

As defined by Dayton and Fraser, strategy must have a goal. In the discussion of world mission, it is important that we know what the goal is and how to talk about it. While many good activities are undertaken in the name of missions, they are only strategic as they relate to the final goal.

❏ *Evangelism vs. Evangelization* *

Evangelism and evangelization share the same nature (communication of the gospel) and purpose (to give a valid opportunity to accept Christ), but they differ. Evangelism is an activity; evangelization adds the dimension of a goal.

"Evangelism" is making good news known. How it is made known (and with what aim it is made known) has been the subject of considerable debate. The following three "P's" denoting the types of evangelism should not imply that they are mutually exclusive. Indeed, the most effective evangelism consists of all three being employed simultaneously.

Presence. Presence evangelism is that which radiates the character of Jesus by the quality of Christian character and concern registered in the life of the evangelist. To be specific, it is the type of evangelism reflected in the Christian's care of the sick, his concern for the uneducated and poor, and his consistent godly life as a member of the community. In itself, "presence" evangelism does not denote a verbal witness as such, nor even close identification with the people.

Proclamation. Only the genuine good news of Jesus Christ can reproduce the church. Our task is to be sure we communicate the gospel and to select the appropriate means and media for this communication. At a minimum this is verbal proclamation by preaching or personal testimony.

Persuasion. To produce results, proclamation must intend to evoke a positive response from those who hear the gospel. The gospel confronts people with the necessity to make a commitment to Jesus Christ. People must be urged to make a decision. The goal of evangelism is the making of disciples.

Good evangelism is usually a balanced three "P" evangelism.

Evangelism is an activity; evangelization adds the dimension of a goal.

"Evangelization" is in fact the goal of evangelistic activity. Evangelization has preeminently a "closure" perspective since it aims always at a comprehensive goal, such as evangelism throughout a people group, city, country, or the world. Evangelization then adds two more "P's" to the list:

Planting. Those who believe the gospel and make a commitment to Jesus Christ must be incorporated into the body of Christ. They must become members of a local assembly of believers. This church is the context in which they can grow in Christ and in which they can properly serve Christ.

Propagation. Evangelization aims at the planting of churches that are able to spread the gospel throughout their own people group and also beyond to penetrate for the first time still other people groups. The ultimate goal is always to complete world evangelization. Take note of Brad Gill's challenge: "It is not enough for us today to go across the world and do a good job. We must work toward the goal of finishing the task of evangelization."** World evangelization should be the ultimate goal behind all mission activity.

---

* This section is excerpted from Hawthorne, S. C., & Winter, R. D. (1992). *Perspectives on the world Christian movement: A study guide* (1992 ed.) (p. 9-2). Pasadena: William Carey Library.

** Gill, B. A. (1979). A church for every people. *Church Growth Bulletin, 15*(6), 280.

7. Why is it helpful to keep in mind the distinction between evangelism and evangelization?

_____

_____

_____

_____

The preceding excerpts have helped clarify the concept of mission strategy. We know that all Christians have a strategy by which they operate, whether they are conscious of it or not. Strategy is defined as the way we approach the task that God has given us to do. Since some strategies are better than others, it is wise to examine critically a particular strategy before adopting it as the approach to a specific mission task God has given us. Many efforts among the unreached peoples will require a "unique solution" approach to strategy. We will examine this approach in chapter 8.

Setting forth a strategy is not an "unspiritual" activity but rather one which has a sincere quest for the will of God as its foundation. Much of God's will is already revealed to us in His Word. How to fulfill that will within a specific framework requires the use of our intelligence; it also drives us to our knees. Prayer and strategy are not at odds. In fact, any strategy which does not include prayer as a primary weapon is bound to fail.

> ### We must pray as if we could not plan, and plan as if we could not pray.

Are unreached peoples resistant to the gospel, or has so little prayer gone up for them that they are effectively held in check by the enemy? How prominent a role should prayer have in strategy for reaching the unreached? These and other important questions are examined by John D. Robb in the following article.

❏ *Prayer as a Strategic Weapon in Frontier Missions* *

John D. Robb

A revealing case study

One of the greatest illustrations of prayer as a strategic weapon in frontier missions is found in the experience of J. O. Fraser, the pioneer missionary to the Lisu tribe of southwest China. As a young missionary with the China Inland Mission in the early 1900s, Fraser preached Christ for several years among the far flung mountain villages of this people with almost no outward results.

His wife later wrote about the difference this prayer effort made in Fraser's work:

> He described to me how in his early years he had been all but defeated by the forces of darkness arrayed against him.... He came to the place where he asked God to take away his life rather than allow him to labor on

* Robb, J. D. (1991). Prayer as a strategic weapon in frontier missions. *International Journal of Frontier Missions, 8*(1), 23-31.

without results. He would then tell me of the prayer forces that took up the burden at home and the tremendous lifting of the cloud over his soul, of the gift of faith that was given him and how God seemed suddenly to step in, drive back the forces of darkness, and take the field.*

Breakthrough occurred when two things happened:

1. The Spirit of God enabled him to pray "the prayer of faith" for several hundred Lisu families to come to Christ.

2. He succeeded in forming a prayer support group of eight to 10 Christians in his home country to back up the work in ongoing prayer.

Fraser himself said:

> Work on our knees. I am feeling more and more that it is after all just the prayers of God's people that call down blessing upon the work, whether they are directly engaged in it or not. Paul may plant and Apollos water, but it is God who gives the increase, and this increase can be brought down from heaven by believing prayer whether offered in China or in England.... If this is so, then Christians at home can do as much for foreign missions as those actually on the field. I believe it will only be known on the last day how much has been accomplished in missionary work by the prayers of earnest believers at home....**

> I used to think that prayer should have the first place and teaching the second. I now feel that it would be truer to give prayer the first, second, and third places and teaching the fourth.... We are not dealing with an enemy that fires at the head only—that keeps the mind only in ignorance—but with an enemy who uses poison gas attacks which wrap the people around with deadly effect and yet are impalpable, elusive.... Nor would it be of any more avail to teach or preach to Lisu here while they are held back by these invisible forces.... But the breath of God can blow away all those miasmic vapors from the atmosphere of a village in answer to your prayers.***

It is after all just the prayers of God's people that call down blessing upon the work. If this is so, then Christians at home can do as much for foreign missions as those actually on the field.

In the years that followed, hundreds of families accepted Christ, and ultimately a people movement involving tens of thousands of Lisus ensued. Today in southwest China and northern Burma they are a missionary tribe taking the gospel to other tribes about them.****

Prayer, a linking activity

Prayer at its very heart is a linking activity. First, prayer links us with God to receive His power and direction as we pray for the world and carry out our own ministries. Secondly, as we pray for the unevangelized world, it links us with particular unreached groups and the Christian workers laboring among them. It links our efforts and their efforts to God in His almightiness, without whose help all such efforts ultimately are in vain. O. Hallesby writes:

> The work of prayer is prerequisite to all other work in the Kingdom of God for the simple reason that it is by prayer that we *couple* the powers of Heaven to our helplessness, the powers which can turn water into wine and remove mountains in our own life and the

---

* Fraser, Mrs. J. O. (1963). *Fraser and prayer* (pp. 11-12). London: Missionary Fellowship.

** Fraser (p. 26).

*** Fraser (pp. 46-47).

**** For further study, see Fraser, Mrs. J. O. (1963). *Fraser and prayer.* London: Missionary Fellowship.

lives of others, the powers which can awaken those who sleep in sin and raise up the dead, the powers which can capture strongholds and make the impossible possible.*

> **Every time the church has set herself to praying, there have been stupendous movements in the mission world.**

Yet having said this, prayer can often be the missing link in our efforts on behalf of the unevangelized world. As important as good organization, planning, and strategy are in world evangelization, in our busyness for God we may have neglected to link up with His power and direction to carry out that particular part of His mission given to us. And that is a crucial omission!

In musing over the failure of his generation to evangelize the world by 1900, A. T. Pierson attributed this failure not only to a lack of consecration in the church evidenced by a lack of giving, faith, and personal holiness, but most of all to the lack of prevailing prayer. He wrote:

> Every time the church has set herself to praying, there have been stupendous movements in the mission world. If we should but transfer the stress of our dependence and emphasis from appeals to men to appeals to God—from trust in organization to trust in supplication—from confidence in methods to importunate prayer for the power of the Holy Spirit, we

should see results more astounding than have yet been wrought.**

World evangelization above all is an issue to be decided by spiritual power, the power of the Holy Spirit released in response to the prayers of His people.

Arthur Matthews, the late former missionary of the China Inland Mission, put his finger on the reason that we often do not emphasize prayer enough:

> The concept that treats prayer as if it were a supplemental booster in getting some project off the ground makes the project primary and the prayer secondary. Prayer was never meant to be incidental to the work of God. It is the work.***

God requires intercession

Why does God desire and require His people's intercession? Most likely because God originally gave dominion of the earth to humankind. That dominion has never been revoked by God. Satan's dominion achieved through rebellion against the Creator is a false, illegitimate, usurped dominion. Redeemed through Christ, we can exercise our God-given right to influence the affairs of this world through the exercise of intercessory prayer. Prayer in the power of the Holy Spirit breaks through the false dominion of the enemy and clears the way for His deliverance and shalom to come to all peoples. He is seeking those who will stand before Him in the gap for the 2,000 major unreached peoples, the 1,000 unevangelized cities, and the 30 unevangelized countries.

---

* Hallesby, O. (1948). *Prayer* (p. 67). London: InterVarsity Press.

** Quoted in Johnson, T. (1988). *Countdown to 1900: World evangelization at the end of the 19th century* (p. 37). Birmingham: New Hope.

*** Matthews, A. (1978). *Born for battle* (p. 42). Robesonia, PA: Overseas Missionary Fellowship.

8. In what way is the "linking" nature of intercession a key strategic concept?

_____

_____

_____

9. Why is intercession a primary responsibility of Christians?

_____

_____

Victory in the spiritual realm is primary

King Jehoshaphat relied on the weapons of united fasting and prayer, public worship and praise which brought God's intervention against the invading armies of Israel's enemies. Bible teacher Derek Prince writes:

> These weapons, scripturally employed by Christians today, will gain victories as powerful and dramatic as they gained for the people of Judah in the days of Jehoshaphat.... *Victory in the spiritual realm is primary.* It is to be obtained by spiritual weapons. Thereafter its outcome will be manifested in every area of the natural and material realm.*

Prayer extends the outreach of the church

Prayer is mentioned over 30 times in the book of Acts alone, and generally it is mentioned as occurring just before major breakthroughs in the outward expansion of the early Christian movement. For the apostles, extended times of united prayer and waiting on God together were pivotal in their mission to the unreached.

The whole European side of the modern Protestant missionary enterprise grew out of Pietism, a revival movement that was steeped in earnest prayer. From its influence the Danish-Halle Mission to India went forth, and the Moravian movement under Count Zinzendorf emerged. The prayer meeting which the Moravians began in 1727 went on 100 years! This prayer effort kindled their desire to proclaim Christ to the unreached, and from this one small village, over 100 missionaries went out in 25 years.

> *Every fresh outbreak of missionary energy has been the result of believing prayer.*

Robert Glover sums up the role of prayer in the history of missions:

> From Pentecost and the Apostle Paul right down through the centuries to the present day, the story of missions has been the story of answered prayer. Every fresh outbreak of missionary energy has been the result of believing prayer. Every new missionary undertaking that has been owned and blessed of God has been the germinating of seed planted by the divine Spirit in the hearts of praying saints.**

Effective strategies come from research and prayer

Joshua was one of the original "researchers" who spied out the land of promise in Numbers 13. Because he knew the facts about the land and its peoples so well, he was prepared to be the great military strategist that he later became during the

---

* Prince, D. (1973). *Shaping history through prayer and fasting* (pp. 93, 95). Old Tappan, NJ: Fleming H. Revell.

** Glover, R. H. (1946). *The Bible basis of missions* (p. 178). Chicago: Moody Press.

conquest. However, in the book of Joshua, we see him continually seeking God for His guidance in the development of effective strategies. He did not lean on his own understanding, but relied upon God's direction given through prayer.

The principle is still the same. I am becoming more and more convinced that coupling research findings concerning the people group we are trying to reach with ongoing persevering prayer is an unstoppable combination in the process of developing effective mission strategy. John Dawson's recent book Taking Our Cities for God: How to Break Spiritual Strongholds insightfully ties together ministry related research and intercessory prayer.

Prayer is the supernatural way of sending out workers

Jesus did not tell the disciples to go all out and round up as many Christian workers as possible or to raise a million dollars for mission. Instead, He said that prayer to the One who owns the harvest was the priority, because He can call, equip, and send those workers who will be best able to reap the harvest.

I am convinced that the mightiest missionaries to the Muslims are not even converted yet. But God is waiting upon the prayers of His people to turn Muslim zealots around as He did the Apostle Paul, so they become missionaries to their people. I am convinced that as prayer networks are formed, focusing on particular peoples, cities, and countries, we will see God raise up armies of new workers.

In 1880, when the China Inland Mission had only 100 workers, and then again in 1887, when additional workers were required, Hudson Taylor and his associates spent protracted time in prayer until they received the assurance of faith that the number required would be granted. Both times, after an appeal for 70 new missionaries in 1880, and 100 in 1887, the full number reached China within the specified time and with all their support supplied.*

Prayer opens closed doors for Christian presence

Don McCurry of Ministries to Muslims International recently gave me a striking illustration in this regard. Six years ago he visited the West African country of Guinea. Sekou Toure, a Marxist leader, had just kicked out all the missionaries except two, and was busy torturing political prisoners. The two remaining missionaries, McCurry, and 12 national pastors met to intercede for the country.

First, they interceded with God for the removal of this Marxist tyrant who had closed the door to further mission efforts when most of the people groups still remained unoccupied by the church. Then they put up maps around the room in which they were meeting, and together laid their hands upon those areas of the country and groups that had no Christian presence. They prayed and agreed together for a breakthrough and the establishment of Christian ministries in them. Within a year, Sekou Toure was gone, replaced by a benign leader who opened the door to missions once again, and today every one of the people groups they prayed for is now occupied by a national or missionary effort!

Spiritual warfare breaks the control of darkness

Chains of spiritual darkness and bondage often link unreached peoples, cities, and countries to principalities and powers who seek to control the affairs of humankind. At present in the missions world, we are undergoing a rediscovery that the issue in reaching the unreached is one of spiritual power. If we are going to see missionary breakthroughs in peoples, cities, and countries, we will need to learn how to use the offensive weapon of prayer to dislodge the powers of darkness.

Francis Frangipane, writing about the strongholds the powers of darkness maintain over groups of people, takes a similar line of thinking:

---

* Glover, R. H. (1946). *The Bible basis of missions* (p. 183). Chicago: Moody Press.

There are satanic strongholds over countries and communities; there are strongholds which influence churches and individuals.... These fortresses exist in the thought patterns and ideas that govern individuals... as well as communities and nations. Before victory can be claimed, these strongholds must be pulled down, and Satan's armor removed. Then the mighty weapons of the Word and the Spirit can effectively plunder Satan's house.*

A study of the belief systems of pagan peoples attests to the reality of spirit beings portrayed in Ephesians 6, the book of Daniel, and elsewhere. The Burmese believe in supernatural beings called nats arranged hierarchically with control over natural phenomena, villages, regions, and nations. Their link with these beings is maintained through witches or mediums, at least one of whom is found in each village.

A book on the African country of Zimbabwe reveals that every region, city, and village is thought to be under the control of territorial spirits. In Nigeria an Assemblies of God leader, who formerly was a high-ranking occult practitioner before his conversion, said that Satan had assigned him control of 12 spirits, each of which controlled 600 demons. He testified, "I was in touch with all the spirits controlling each town in Nigeria, and I had a shrine in all the major cities."**

Could it be that whole peoples we have written off as being "resistant" are in themselves really not resistant at all but are in the grip of spirit beings that are the source of the resistance?

There are enormous prayer resources within the body of Christ that by and large are not being tapped for the unevangelized world because we have thus far failed to develop practical mechanisms to link these resources with the need of the unreached. Probably the most strategic thing we can do for frontier missions is to stimulate the formation of ongoing prayer and spiritual warfare networks focused on particular unreached peoples, cities, and countries.

> *The most strategic thing we can do for frontier missions is to stimulate the formation of ongoing prayer and spiritual warfare networks focused on particular unreached peoples, cities, and countries.*

David Bryant puts it this way:

> The greatest challenge any of us will ever face in the global cause of Christ [and] the greatest contribution any of us will ever make to the glorious task of advancing Christ's Kingdom among earth's unreached is... to grow as men and women of prayer and to mobilize others with us into a movement of prayer for the world. Other things wait to be done, but this is the greatest.***

Prayer and the Word of God are indispensable strategic weapons in combating the spiritual forces of darkness. No strategic plan for evangelism can succeed without them. The Word is a sword, and our prayers are arrows which can be launched at the enemy near and far. It has been truly said, "God's army advances on its knees."

---

* Frangipane, F. (1989). *The three battlegrounds* (pp. 15, 21). Marion, IA: River of Life Ministries.

** Wagner, C. P. (1988, December). *Territorial spirits* (p. 4). Paper presented at the Academic Symposium on Power Evangelism, Fuller Theological Seminary, Pasadena, CA.

*** Bryant, D. (1987, April). Prayer movements signal new light for the nations. *Evangelical Missions Quarterly,* 118.

10. *What strategic "functions" or "facets" does intercessory prayer have in the carrying out of world missions?*

_____

_____

_____

II. History of Mission Strategy

In formulating our own strategy, it is important to see how mission strategy has developed and to note success factors as well as actions which have led to failure. This evaluation should help us determine what to attempt, as well as what to avoid in our mission strategy. A naive urge to "reinvent the wheel" will only lead to a repetition of past mistakes out of ignorance or simplistic optimism. In our enthusiasm to finish the task, let's not "toss out the rice with the chaff."

In his excellent article, "The History of Mission Strategy," R. Pierce Beaver has noted: "Fifteen centuries of missionary action preceded the rise of Protestant world mission. Therefore, Protestant missionary action did not begin de novo, and with modern Roman Catholic theory makes up only the last chapter of a long story." The following summary and timeline are provided as the briefest of outlines in this fascinating history.*

Boniface

Some of the earliest intentional mission strategy can be traced to Boniface. His eighth century missions from England to the Continent were characterized by aggressive power encounters. Rather than accommodating the existing culture, his missionaries defied native gods, demolished shrines, cut down sacred trees, and built churches on holy sites. Boniface civilized converts through educational programs and the establishment of monastic centers of learning. He introduced the concept of women missionaries, using nuns in educational programs. The eventual failure of these missions to grow was due in part to their close association with imperial expansion. They were rejected by rulers because they were perceived as agents of imperialism, not because of the nature of their message.

---

* Beaver, R. P. (1970). The history of mission strategy. *Southwestern Journal of Theology, 12*(2), 7-28.

R. Pierce Beaver was Professor Emeritus from the University of Chicago until his death in 1982. He specialized in the history of missions in America and was for 15 years a formative director of the Missionary Research Library in New York City. He authored, among other books, *All Loves Excelling*, a description of the initiatives of American women in world evangelization.

The Crusades

The crusades to recapture Muslim-held lands can hardly be considered missions according to our current understanding of the word. The hatred and suspicion these wars created in Muslims towards Christians abide to this day. During this period, which lasted several centuries, there were only two prominent individuals whose efforts encompassed taking the gospel of love and peace to Muslims. The great monastic founder, Francis of Assisi, and the Spanish nobleman, Raymund Lull, both attempted missions to the followers of Mohammed.

Colonial Expansion

With the discovery of new continents, Catholic missions were given a great impetus. Missionaries were sent to all the newly discovered lands which came under the dominion of Spain, Portugal, and France. Since the Pope had a hand in dividing up these lands, he mandated that the natives must be Christianized. This was an obligation taken on by these governments. The natives were thus preserved, civilized, and Christianized. Although many of the early missionaries were sincerely interested in bringing the native peoples to faith in Christ, civilizing them was most often seen as the primary objective by colonial governments. Christianization was often equated with civilization. As with Boniface, aggression was often used, and the destruction of native culture was the primary objective. The annihilation of Mayan written records is still one of the most lamentable events in mission history.

CENTURY	
8th	BONIFACE
12th	CRUSADES
16th	COLONIAL EXPANSION
17th	MODERN MISSIONARY STRATEGISTS – Jesuits – Puritans
18th	DANISH-HALLE MISSION – Ziegenbalg MORAVIAN MISSIONARIES – Count Zinzendorf
19th	PROTESTANT MISSIONS – William Carey – Venn and Anderson – Paternalism and Colonialism – Evangelism, Education, and Medicine – Comity
20th	CONSULTATIONS AND CONFERENCES – Edinburgh Conference (1910) – World War II A NEW ERA

Figure 6-2. History of Mission Strategy

17th Century Missions

The Jesuits were the mission strategists of the 17th century. They were the pioneers of "cultural adaptation," or the practice of conforming to the host culture rather than trying to force the missionary's own cultural norms on the natives. These missionaries learned the native languages and used them for evangelism, teaching, and the production of literature. They also used native evangelists and catechists and even allowed some to become priests. In China, these intrepid missiologists used Confucian doctrine to teach Christian principles. Furthermore, they did not threaten the matrix of Chinese society by demanding that converts give up family and state rites, practices which they interpreted as civil rather than religious. In spite of the Jesuits' huge success in mission terms, their practices created opposition by those back home who could not separate European culture and forms from Christianity. Eventually, these progressive missiological practices were banned.

11. *What lessons in strategy can be learned from these earlier periods of missions efforts? List at least one from each period.*

_____

_____

_____

_____

Puritan Missions to Native Americans

Protestant strategy had its beginnings in 17th century efforts to Native Americans. These early missions aimed at evangelizing the Native Americans and civilizing them to become like the New World Puritans. Preaching, establishing churches, and founding Christian villages were all strategies employed. Christian villages were intended to isolate converts from the pagan influences in their own villages. While the strategy may have been effective to a degree in developing Christian character, it failed to allow new Christians to have a significant influence in converting their friends and family. Beaver summarizes the achievements of the Native American missions:

> Perhaps the most lasting effects of the Native American missions of the 17th and 18th centuries were two: first, they inspired numerous missionary vocations in a later day as men read the lives of [John] Eliot and [David] Brainerd; and second, they endowed the great overseas Protestant enterprise with its initial strategic program. This included evangelism through preaching, organization of churches, education aimed at Christian nurture and the attainment of civilization in European terms, Bible translation, literature production, use of the vernacular language, and the recruitment and training of native pastors and teachers.

The Danish-Halle Mission

The first missionaries sent from Europe were members of the Danish-Halle Mission. In 1705, a group led by Bartholomew Ziegenbalg went to the southern coast of India. Ziegenbalg stressed "…worship, preaching, catechization, education, translation work, and the reproduction of vernacular literature. He blazed a trail in the study of Hindu philosophy and religion, discerning the great importance of such knowledge for evangelization and church growth…." His most famous successor was Frederick Schwartz, who had a remarkable influence on both Indian and colonist alike. Schwartz adopted the form of a *guru* and was loved and respected by all as a spiritual teacher.

Moravian Missions

The Moravian church introduced the strategy of self-support as a policy for their missionaries. Under the direction of Count Zinzendorf and Bishop Spangenberg, Moravian missionaries were sent to the most despised and neglected people around the globe. Their self-support strategy served the double purpose of support and identification with the people. They used a variety of approaches. While most established businesses or small industries, others sold themselves into indentured servanthood to reach slaves in the West Indies!

These missionaries considered themselves "assistants" to the Holy Spirit. They were to recognize the people's God-given distinctive traits, characteristics, and strong points. Their primary role was as messengers, evangelists, and preachers. They were not to stress heavy theological doctrines but rather tell the simple gospel story and wait patiently for the Holy Spirit to do the work. They were very persevering and only left if severe persecution drove them out.

12. *What strategic emphasis led the Moravians to create businesses and industries, and what two advantages were gained through this practice?*

_____

_____

_____

Protestant missions in earnest did not really get underway until the early 19th century. It is important to recognize, however, that the earliest efforts did leave a legacy for William Carey, Hudson Taylor, and other pioneers. The following sections from Beaver's article examine Protestant mission strategy during the last two centuries of mission history.

The great century of Protestant missions

Out of all these earlier beginnings, there came the great Protestant missionary overseas enterprise of the 19th century. It took initial form in Britain with the founding of the Baptist Missionary Society by William Carey in 1792. Organization had begun in the United States in 1787, and a score of societies came into being, all having a worldwide objective. However, the frontier settlements and the Native Americans absorbed all their resources. At length a student movement in 1810 broke the deadlock and launched the overseas mission through the formation of the American Board of Commissioners for Foreign Missions. The Triennial Convention of the Baptist Denomination for Foreign Missions was next organized in 1814, followed in 1816 by the United Foreign Mission Society.

The new societies and boards began their work with the strategic presuppositions and methods inherited from the Native American missions and the Danish-Halle Mission. For many years the directors at home thought that they understood fully how the mission was to be carried out, and detailed instructions were handed each missionary when he sailed. After half a century or so, it was discovered that the experienced missionaries on the field could best formulate strategy and policy, which might then be ratified by the board back home. There was in 1795 a conflict over strategy in the London Missionary Society between two strong personalities. One man wanted well-educated, ordained missionaries sent to countries of high civilization and high religions. The other wanted artisan missionaries under an ordained superintendent to be sent to primitive peoples in the South Seas to Christianize and civilize them. Both objectives were accepted.

Even in countries with a high culture, such as India and China, European missionaries stressed the "civilizing" objective as much as their brethren in primitive regions because they regarded the local culture as degenerate and superstitious—a barrier to Christianization. During the early decades there was never debate about the legitimacy of the stress on the civilizing function of missions. Debate was only about priority; which came first, Christianization or civilization? Some held that a certain degree of civilization was first necessary to enable a people to understand and accept the faith. Others argued that one should begin with Christianization since the gospel inevitably produced a hunger for civilization. Most persons believed that the two mutually interacted and should be stressed equally and simultaneously.

During the early decades there was never debate about the legitimacy of the stress on the civilizing function of missions. Debate was only about priority; which came first, Christianization or civilization?

India was soon receiving the greatest degree of attention from mission boards and societies, and the strategy and tactics developed there were copied and applied in other regions. The Baptist "Serampore Trio" of Carey, Marshman, and Ward was especially influential in the early period. Although Carey sought individual conversions, he wanted to foster the growth of a church that would be independent, well sustained by a literate and Bible-reading laity, and administered and shepherded by an educated native ministry. This self-educated genius was not content with establishing elementary schools but founded a college. The King of Denmark (Serampore was a Danish colony) gave him a college charter which permitted the giving of even theological degrees. At Serampore there were schools for Indians and for foreign children. The vast program of Bible translation and printing, ranging beyond the Indian vernaculars even to the Chinese, established the high priority of such work among all Protestants. Other literature was produced for the churches. The Trio also demonstrated the importance of scholarly research for mission strategy and action, producing

linguistic materials needed by all and taking the leadership in the study of Hinduism.

Furthermore, this famous Trio worked for the transformation of society under the impact of the gospel, and they became a mighty force for social reform, bringing pressure on the colonial government and leading Hindus to enlightened views on old wrongs and their elimination. These men were influential in causing the abolition of *suttee* or widow-burning, temple prostitution, and other dehumanizing customs. Carey also introduced modern journalism, publishing both vernacular Bengali and English newspapers and magazines. He stimulated a renaissance of Bengali literature. It was a very comprehensive mission which was based at Serampore.

Much like Robert de Nobili before him, the Scotsman Alexander Duff believed that the Indian populace could be won for Christ only if the Brahmin caste were first brought to our Lord. He sought to win Brahmin youths through a program of higher education in the English language. Where he succeeded in large measure, others failed; but his venture led to tremendous emphasis being put on English language schools and colleges. They produced few converts, but they did give economic advancement which made for the welfare of the churches, and to the pleasure of the colonial establishment they produced English-speaking staff for the civil service and commercial houses. Such education soon consumed a large part of the resources of all the missions.

At the same time, without any strategic planning, there developed huge concentrated central mission stations where the converts clustered in economic and social dependence on the missionaries. Unless a convert came to Christianity with an entire social group, he was cast out of his family and lost his livelihood. Simply to keep such persons alive, they were given jobs as servants, teachers, and evangelists. The church became over-professionalized, laymen being paid to do what they should have done voluntarily. This bad practice passed on to missions in other regions. In such a main station there were the central church, the schools, the hospital, and often the printing press. A missionary was pastor and ruler of the community. Such a system had little place for a native pastor as William Carey had planned, and there were only preaching points, no organized churches, in the villages for 50 miles and more in the hinterland. Then in 1854-55 Rufus Anderson went on deputation to India and Ceylon. He caused the American Board missionaries to break up the huge central stations, to organize village churches, and to ordain native pastors over them. He decreed that education in the vernacular should be the general rule and education in English the exception.

13. *What strategic mistake did the new mission boards of the early 19th century make?*

_____

_____

_____

14. *How did the central mission stations develop, and what was their general impact on evangelization?*

_____

_____

_____

Mission strategists of the 19th century

The two greatest mission theoreticians and strategists of the 19th century were also the executive officers of the largest mission agencies. Henry Venn was general secretary of the Church Missionary Society in London. Rufus Anderson was foreign secretary of the American Board of Commissioners for Foreign Missions. Anderson's mission strategy dominated American mission work for more than a century, as did that of Venn in the British scene. The two men arrived independently at practically the same basic principles and in late years mutually influenced each other. Together they established as the recognized strategic aim of Protestant mission the famous "three self" formula to which British and American missions gave assent from the middle of the 19th century until World War II: the goal of mission is to plan and foster the development of churches which will be self-governing, self-supporting, and self-propagating.

Rufus Anderson was a Congregationalist and Venn an Anglican Episcopalian, but both would build the regional church from the bottom upward. Venn wanted a bishop appointed as the crowning of the process of development when there was an adequate native clergy and a church supported by the people. Anderson protested the great stress on "civilization" and the attempt to reform society overnight, holding that such change would eventually result from the leaven of the gospel in the life of a nation. He based his strategy on that of Paul as he found it recorded in the New Testament.

> *"Three self" formula: The goal of mission is to plan and foster the development of churches which will be self-governing, self-supporting, and self-propagating.*

According to Anderson, the task of the missionary was to preach the gospel and gather the converts into churches. He was always to be an evangelist and never a pastor or ruler. Churches were to be organized at once out of converts who showed a change of life towards Christ, without waiting for them to reach the standard expected of American Christians with 2,000 years of Christian history behind them. These churches were to be put under their own pastors and were to develop their own local and regional polity. The missionaries would be advisors, elder brothers in the faith to the pastors and people.

Social Darwinism had converted Americans to the doctrine of inevitable progress. This led to the idea that the kingdom of God was coming through the influence of Christian institutions such as schools.

Both Anderson and Venn taught that when the churches were functioning well, the missionaries should leave and go to "regions beyond," where they would begin the evangelistic process once again. The whole point of church planting was to be evangelism and mission. The churches would engage spontaneously in local evangelism and in a sending mission to other peoples. Mission would beget mission. In Anderson's view, education in the vernacular would be for the sole purpose of serving the church or raising up a laity of high quality and an adequately trained ministry. All ancillary forms of work were to be solely for evangelism and for the edification of the church.

The British missions resisted Anderson's views on vernacular education. American missions adopted his strategy officially and unofficially and in theory held to his system for more than a century. However, after his day they stressed secondary and higher education in English to an ever greater extent. This was partly due to the fact that social Darwinism had converted Americans to the doctrine of inevitable progress. This led to the replacement of the old eschatology with the idea that the kingdom of God was coming through the influence of Christian institutions such as schools. Also by the end of the 19th century a second great strategic objective had been more or less explicitly added to the three-self formula, that is, the leavening and transformation of society through the effect of Christian principles and the Christian spirit of service infused into the common life. High schools and colleges were essential to this aim.

John L. Nevius, Presbyterian missionary in Shantung, devised a strategy which somewhat modified that of Anderson, placing more responsibility on the layman. He advocated leaving the layman in his own craft or business and in his usual place in society. He was to be encouraged to be a voluntary, unpaid evangelist. Nevius advocated also constant Bible study and rigorous stewardship in combination with voluntary service and proposed a simple and flexible church government. His brethren in China did not adopt his system, but the missionaries in Korea did so with amazing success.

15. *Briefly describe Rufus Anderson's strategy.*

_____

_____

_____

16. *What influence did social Darwinism have on missions of the late 19th century?*

_____

_____

_____

A colonialist mentality

Despite the avowed continued adherence to the Anderson-Venn formula, there was a great change in missionary mentality and consequently in strategy in the last quarter of the 19th century. Under Venn, British missions in West Africa, for example, had aimed at (1) the creation of an independent church under its own clergy, which would evangelize the interior of the continent, and (2) the creation of an African elite, i.e., an intelligentsia and middle class, which would produce the society and economy which could support such a church and its mission. Almost immediately after Venn's termination of leadership, mission executives and field missionaries took the view that the African was of inferior quality and could not provide ministerial leadership, which consequently would be furnished indefinitely by Europeans. The African middle-class businessman and intellectual was despised. This imperialist viewpoint was an ecclesiastical variant of the growing devotion to the theory of "the white man's burden," and it reduced the native church to a colony of the foreign planting church.

A very similar development occurred in India in the 1880s. Americans and others caught this colonialist mentality by contagion from the British. German missions, under the guidance of their leading strategist, Professor Gustav Warneck, were simultaneously aiming at the creation of *Volkskirchen*, national churches, but until their full development had been reached, the churches were kept in bondage to the missionaries. Paternalism thwarted development. Thus all missions were paternalist and

> **The imperialist viewpoint reduced the native church to a colony of the foreign planting church.**

colonialist at the turn of the century. This unhappy state of affairs lasted until the studies and surveys made for the World Missionary Conference at Edinburgh in 1910 suddenly destroyed complacency and inertia. They revealed that the native church was really a fact and was restive under paternal domination. Consequently, following the conference, there was a tremendous drive for "devolution" of authority from the mission organization to the church, and practically all boards and societies gave lip service, at least, to this ideal.

17. What unbiblical assumptions were a part of the "cultural baggage" of the imperialist viewpoint?

_____

_____

_____

Evangelism, education, and medicine

Missionary strategy of the 19th century (down to Edinburgh 1910), in summary, aimed at individual conversions, church planting, and social transformation through three main types of actions, which became known as evangelism, education, and medicine. Evangelism included preaching in all its forms, the organizing and fostering of churches, Bible translation, literature production, and the distribution of Bibles and literature.

In the realm of education, industrial schools were stressed in earlier times but generally abandoned because of the desire for an academic education. By the end of the century, a vast educational system was in existence in Asian countries, ranging from kindergarten to college and including medical and theological schools. Africa, however, was neglected with respect to secondary and collegiate education.

The first doctors sent abroad were sent primarily to take care of the families of other missionaries, but it was soon discovered that medical service to the general populace brought good will and provided an evangelistic opportunity. Thereupon, it was made a major branch of mission work. It was not until the middle of the 20th century that it came to be realized that health services in the name and spirit of the Great Physician are in themselves a dramatic form of the preaching of the gospel. But at a very early date, even the rural evangelistic missionary had taken to carrying a medicine bag with him on his travels.

It was the same spirit of general helpfulness and cultivation of good will, as well as out of a desire to improve the economic base of the church, that missionaries introduced improved poultry and livestock and better seeds along with new crops. The great orchard industry and the big peanut industry in Shantung were introduced in this manner.

With regard to the other religions, mission strategy was aggressive, seeking their displacement and total conversion of the peoples. This aggressive spirit declined towards the end of the century, and something of an appreciation of the work of God in the other faiths grew slowly until by 1910 many regarded them as "broken lights" which were to be made whole in Christ and as bridges to the gospel.

Women as a strategic force

The customs of the Oriental peoples made it almost impossible for male missionaries to reach women and with them children in large numbers. Missionary wives endeavored to set up schools for girls and to penetrate the homes, zenanas, and harems, but they did not have enough freedom from homemaking and child care and they could not itinerate. Realistic strategy demanded that adequate provision be made for women and children, but the boards and societies were stubbornly resistant to sending single women abroad for such work. Finally, in desperation the women in the 1860s began organizing their own societies and sent forth single women. A whole new dimension was thus added to mission strategy: the vast enterprise to reach women and children with the gospel, to educate girls, and to bring adequate medical care to women.

When women came into the church, their children followed them. Female education proved to be the most effective force for the liberation and social uplift of women. The emphasis which the women placed on medical service led the general boards to

The boards and societies were stubbornly resistant to sending single women abroad for missionary work. Finally, in desperation, the women in the 1860s began organizing their own societies and sent forth single women.

upgrade the medical work, and greater stress was put on medical education. Out of these two great endeavors of American women, followed by the British and Europeans, there opened to women of the Orient what are today their most prestigious professions, medical service both as physicians and nurses, and teaching.

Comity

One more feature of 19th century missionary strategy must be listed. This was the practice of comity [mutual courtesy]. Southern Baptists were among the founders and practitioners of comity. Good stewardship of men and money held a high priority among boards and societies. Waste was abhorred, and there was a strong desire to stretch resources as far as possible. The practice of comity was intended to make some agency responsible for the evangelism of every last piece of territory and every people. It was further intended to prevent double occupancy of a region (excepting big cities) and overlapping of mission programs, so that competition might be eliminated along with denominational differences which would confuse the inhabitants and thus hamper evangelism. Prior occupation of territory was recognized; the newcoming missions went to unoccupied areas. This custom produced "denominationalism by geography," but the general expectation was that when the missionaries left for the "regions beyond," the nationals would put the several pieces together into a national church which might be different from any of the planting churches.

Missions agreed on recognizing each other as valid branches of the one church of Christ, on baptism and transfer of membership, on discipline, on salaries, and on transfer of national workers. These agreements led to further cooperation in the establishment of regional and national boards for the arbitration of conflicts between missions and to union Bible translation projects, publication agencies, secondary schools and colleges, teacher training schools, and medical schools. Effective strategy called more and more for doing together all things which could be better achieved through a united effort. City, regional, and national missionary conferences in almost every country provided occasions for common discussion and planning.

18. In what ways was mission strategy of the 19th century holistic in its theology and methodology?

_____

_____

_____

19. What were the "aims" of 19th century missions? How did missions try to achieve these aims?

_____

_____

_____

20. What key role did women play in the 19th century mission enterprise?

_____

_____

Consultations and conferences

Such cooperation on the mission fields led to increasing home base consultation and planning. The World Missionary Conference at Edinburgh in 1910 inaugurated the series of great conferences: Jerusalem 1928, Madras 1938, Whitby 1947, Willingen 1952, and Ghana 1957-58. In these the directions of strategy were largely determined and then applied locally through further study and discussion in national and regional bodies. The International Missionary Council was organized in 1921, bringing together national missionary conferences (such as the Foreign Missions Conference of North America, 1892), and national Christian councils (such as the NCC of China), and thus there was established a universal system at various levels for the voluntary study of problems and planning of strategy in common by a host of sovereign mission boards. In 1961 the IMC became the Division of World Mission and Evangelism of the World Council of Churches.

From 1910 to World War II the most notable development of strategy was increasingly putting the national church in the central place, giving it full independence and authority, and developing partnership between the Western churches and the young churches. "The indigenous church" and "partnership in obedience" were watchwords which expressed the thrust of prevailing strategy. The participants in the Jerusalem Conference in 1928 defined the indigenous church, underscoring cultural accommodation. The Madras Conference of 1938 restated the definition, emphasizing witness to Christ in "a direct, clear, and close relationship with the cultural and religious heritage of [the] country." Whitby 1947 held up the ideal of "partnership in obedience."

Since World War II

A radically different mission strategy, based on Paul, was expounded by Roland Allen in his books *Missionary Methods: St. Paul's or Ours?* and *The Spontaneous Expansion of the Church*, but he gathered no following until after World War II, when the missionaries of the faith missions especially rallied to his standard. In barest essentials this is his strategy: The missionary communicates the gospel and transmits to the new community of converts the

---

According to a radically different mission strategy expounded by Roland Allen, the missionary stands by as a counseling elder brother while the Holy Spirit leads the new church to develop its own forms of polity, ministry, worship, and life.

---

simplest statement of the faith, the Bible, the sacraments, and the principle of ministry. He then stands by as a counseling elder brother while the Holy Spirit leads the new church, self-governing and self-supporting, to develop its own forms of polity, ministry, worship, and life. Such a church is spontaneously missionary. Allen's theory applied to new pioneer beginnings. The old boards and societies were dealing with churches already old and set in their ways; they seldom sought untouched fields.

One after another the mission organizations on the fields were dissolved. Resources were placed at the disposal of the churches and missionary personnel assigned to their direction.

The Western boards and societies initiated very little that was new in the way of strategy, but much to develop new methods: agricultural missions or rural development, some urban industrial work, mass media communications, more effective literature. This was the final stage of a mission which had been in progress for 300 years. Now the world was no longer divided into Christendom and heathendom. There could no longer be a one-way mission from the West to the remainder of the world. The base for a mission was established in almost every land, for a Christian church and community with an obligation to give the gospel to the whole world existed there. The moment for a new world mission with a radical new strategy had arrived. The revolution which swept the non-Western portions of the world during and after World War II unmistakably put an end to the old order of Protestant missions.

A new age of world mission has arrived, one in which other religions are now engaged in world mission also. A new understanding of mission, a new strategy, new organization, new ways, means, and methods are the demand of this hour in the central task of the church which shall never end until the kingdom of God has come in all its glory. It will help as we pray, study, plan, and experiment if we know the past history of mission strategy.*

---

* *Editor's note:* Since this article was written, several major consultations on world evangelization have taken place in acknowledgment of "a new age of world mission." Four of the most notable ones are Lausanne (1974), Pattaya (1980), Edinburgh (1980), and Lausanne II in Manila (1989). These consultations have opened dialogue on the new "ways, means, and methods" to which Beaver alludes in his conclusion.

21. What contribution did Roland Allen make to mission strategy?

_____

_____

_____

22. What is the author's conclusion regarding current developments in world mission?

_____

_____

_____

III. Structures and Power

The preceding study makes it evident that mission structures have played an indispensable role in the spread of the gospel. The widespread use of mission agencies in the ongoing work of world evangelization continues today. Most Christians accept this phenomenon without a thought. Others are troubled by it. They question whether mission agencies are truly biblical. Do they perhaps usurp a role which rightfully belongs to the church? Shouldn't the church exercise its God-given authority in controlling the mission effort?

It is healthy to precede the discussion of mission agencies with the reminder that the church universal, the total body of Christ in all places (and in all times), is much larger than what we normally associate with the term "church." Most of us belong to a local congregation which is identified with a specific building in a specific location. Parachurch organizations with specialized functions in evangelism, missions, counseling, teaching, or other ministries are somehow disassociated in our minds from "church." These organizations, however, are certainly part of the church universal, and through their specialization, they help local churches carry out their God-given ministries and responsibilities. It is a symbiotic relationship, one of mutual interdependence, as it should be in the body of Christ.

In an address given to the All-Asia Mission Consultation in Seoul, Korea in August 1973, Ralph Winter described the forms that God's two "redemptive structures," existing in every human society, have taken throughout history. His thesis has two major implications:

1. We must accept both structures, represented in the Christian church today by (a) the local church and (b) the mission society, as legitimate and necessary.

2. Non-Western churches must form and utilize mission societies if they are to exercise their missionary responsibility.

The following sections summarize and excerpt some of the content of Winter's address.

Parallel Structures Throughout the Centuries*

Since the first century, God has always used two structures in carrying out His redemptive purposes. The first of these is a nurturing structure in which all believers can be included. The second is an outreach structure which calls for a greater level of commitment by those who participate. These two structures have emerged throughout the course of the expansion of Christianity.

During the first century, Christians borrowed the Jewish synagogue as their nurture structure. Paul's mission strategy was to preach in these Jewish "churches" all over the Roman Empire. He also organized believing communities into synagogue-type structures, ordaining elders and establishing norms for meetings (1 Cor. 14). When Paul set out on his first missionary journey, he was also following the tradition established by Jewish "missionaries," who Christ observed were "traversing land and sea to make a single proselyte" (Matt. 23:15). Paul used this known concept and practice and amplified it in the formation of his own mobile missionary band.

While neither of these New Testament structures was "let down from heaven," they did provide the basic pattern for the early church. It shouldn't surprise us that these forms were borrowed from existing cultural prototypes. As we have seen, cultural flexibility is one of the inherent premises of Christian expansion. These two prototypes, while not casting the *form* in stone, do provide the *functional* models for God's redemptive mission. The first focuses on nurture and incorporates all believers. The other focuses on outreach and incorporates selected members who have made a second, adult commitment commensurate with the purpose and demands of the structure.

As Christianity moved from being a primarily Jewish sect on to its conquest of the Roman Empire, two similar structures emerged, again borrowed from cultural models. The Roman *functional equivalents* of the two Jewish structures took preeminence as Christianity penetrated a larger world. While the *parish church* maintained much of the same nurturing function as the independent synagogues, a hierarchical structure borrowed from Roman civil government also emerged. Bishops were appointed to supervise a group of parish churches, giving rise to the *diocese*.

Roman military establishment provided an adequate model for the church's second structure. Calling men to a full commitment to a particular band or group, these structures eventually developed into a long tradition of monastic orders. The monastic movement was not entirely a "flee the world" tradition. Many orders were based on practical service to mankind and involved active mission outreach. The Irish *peregrini*, for example, were Celtic monks who "contributed more to the evangelization of Western Europe, even Central Europe, than any other force."

The two structures which emerged in the early Roman church were absorbed over time into Roman Catholic tradition and practice. In the 16th century, when Martin Luther and his followers protested the corruption which attended both structures during that time, they completely rejected the outreach

* Winter, R. D. (1992). The two structures of God's redemptive mission. In R. D. Winter & S. C. Hawthorne (Eds.), *Perspectives on the world Christian movement: A reader* (rev. ed.) (pp. B45-B57). Pasadena: William Carey Library.

After serving 10 years as a missionary among Mayan Indians in western Guatemala, Ralph D. Winter spent the next 10 years as a Professor of Missions at the School of World Mission at Fuller Theological Seminary. He is the founder of the U.S. Center for World Mission in Pasadena, California, a cooperative center focused on people groups still lacking a culturally relevant church. Winter has also been instrumental in the formation of the movement called Theological Education by Extension, the William Carey Library publishing house, the American Society of Missiology, the Perspectives Study Program, and the International Society for Frontier Missiology. Since March 1990 he has been the President of the William Carey International University.

(monastic) organization. As a consequence, for two centuries, Protestants did little in missions. It was William Carey's eloquent argument for *means* which finally provoked the emergence of Protestant outreach structures. Only through these second-commitment organizations, the mission agencies, could Protestants harvest and channel the tremendous volunteer potential for missions which, to that time, had lain dormant in the church.

TYPE OF STRUCTURE	FUNCTION	
	NURTURE	OUTREACH
New Testament	Synagogue	Missionary Band
Roman	Parish Church, Diocese	Monastic Movement
Protestant	Local Church, Denomination	Mission Agencies

Figure 6-3. Parallel Structures of God's Redemptive Mission

23. What functional differences do the two structures of God's redemptive mission have?

_____

_____

_____

24. How might you refute the assertion that mission agencies aren't "biblical"?

_____

_____

_____

Winter has coined two terms to distinguish between the two church structures: *modality* and *sodality*. *Modality* refers to the nurture structure in which no distinction of sex or age is made for membership. This fellowship is composed of the "modal" or conventional fabric of a given society. It grows biologically or through evangelization and incorporation of persons from the immediate society. The synagogue, parish church, diocese, and our own local congregation are all examples of modalities.

A second term, *sodality*, designates the outreach structure we have been discussing. Members of a sodality make a voluntary commitment to a particular group or agency and agree to abide by its regulations in the pursuit of a common objective. Paul's missionary band, monasteries, and mission agencies are all examples of Christian sodalities.

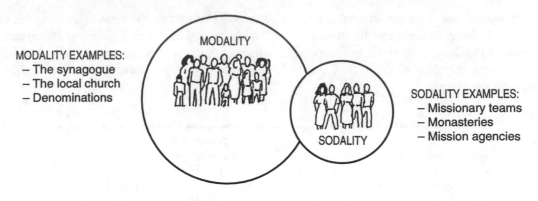

MODALITY EXAMPLES:
– The synagogue
– The local church
– Denominations

SODALITY EXAMPLES:
– Missionary teams
– Monasteries
– Mission agencies

Figure 6-4. The Two Structures

25. Using the concept of modality and sodality, explain why a mission agency is more like a professional football team, in some ways, than a local church.

_____

_____

_____

In the final portion of his Seoul address, Winter points out a contemporary blindness that needs to be corrected regarding the importance of outreach structures.

The importance of outreach structures

Protestant blindness about the need for mission sodalities has had a very tragic influence on mission fields. Protestant missions, being modality-minded, have tended to assume that merely modalities, e.g., churches, need to be established. Even in the case where mission work is being pursued by what are essentially semi-autonomous mission sodalities, it is modalities, not sodalities, that are the only goal. That is to say, the mission agencies (even those that have most independent from themselves been denominations back home) have tended in their mission work very simply to set up churches and not to plant, in addition, mission sodalities in the so-called mission lands.*

As we look back today, it is astonishing that most Protestant missionaries, working with (mission) structures that did not exist in the Protestant tradition for hundreds of years and without whose existence there would have been no mission initiative, have nevertheless been blind to the significance of the very structure within which they have worked. In this blindness they have merely planted churches and have not effectively concerned themselves to make sure that the kind of mission structure within which they operate also be set up on the field. As a matter of fact, many of the mission agencies founded after World War II, out of extreme deference to existing church movements already estab-

---

* See Winter, R. D. (1972). The planting of younger missions. In C. P. Wagner (Ed.), *Church/mission tensions today* (pp. 129-145). Chicago: Moody Press.

lished in foreign lands, have not even tried to set up churches and have worked for many years merely as auxiliary agencies in various service capacities trying to help the churches that were already there.

The question we must ask is how long it will be before the younger churches of the so-called mission territories of the non-Western world come to that epochal conclusion (to which the Protestant movement in Europe only tardily came), namely, that there need to be sodality structures, such as William Carey's "use of means," in order for church people to reach out in vital initiatives in mission, especially cross-cultural mission. There are already some hopeful signs that this tragic delay will not continue.

26. *Protestant blindness regarding sodality structures has led to what "tragic influence on mission fields"?*

_____

_____

_____

27. *Why are mission agencies so important to world evangelization? List several reasons.*

_____

_____

_____

_____

_____

Mission Power

The most clever mission strategy utilizing the most proven structures will not accomplish mission ends if there is no "mission power." The familiar text, "We wrestle not against flesh and blood, but against principalities and powers" (Eph. 6:12) takes on new meaning when applied to frontier mission work. This Third Era of Protestant mission has brought a renewed urgency in understanding the dynamic of spiritual warfare and God's use of the supernatural to bring men and women to Himself. Peter Wagner has traveled the world studying the most dynamic movements to Christ in recent time. In the following excerpt, he shares with us his insights regarding "mission power."

❑ *On the Cutting Edge of Mission Strategy* *

C. Peter Wagner **

A fresh look at God's supernatural

Jesus sent His disciples out with "power over unclean spirits, to cast them out, and to heal all kinds of sickness and all kinds of diseases" (Matt. 10:1). The Apostle Paul testified that he preached the gospel to the Gentiles from Jerusalem to Illyricum "in mighty signs and wonders, by the power of the Spirit of God" (Rom. 15:19). Hebrews records that salvation has come through God's witness "both with signs and wonders, with various miracles, and gifts of the Holy Spirit..." (Heb. 2:4).

Let people see Christian power displayed in relation to the spirit world in which they live with great fear, and they will "hear" the message more clearly than our words alone could ever make it.

While we do not deny the validity of the Word of God, many of us have not experienced this kind of New Testament power in our personal ministries. I for one never saw it at all during my 16 years as a missionary to Bolivia. To me the power of God was to save souls and help us live a good Christian life. I now see that as correct, but only a partial view of God's power. It is some consolation for me that all of my colleagues on the Fuller School of Mission faculty look on their missionary careers with similar observations.

As Timothy Warner of the Trinity School of World Mission and Evangelism says: "The issue of encounter with demonic forces is one which has understandably been avoided by large segments of the church. For most of my life, I was among those who steered clear of such involvement." But, he goes on to say, "We can no longer afford this luxury." Warner believes that power and the power encounter is a crucial factor in today's mission. As he looks out on the unreached peoples, he observes:

> In many parts of the world... people are much more power-conscious than they are truth-conscious. We may preach a very logical and convincing message by Western standards, but our hearers remain unimpressed. Let them see Christian power displayed in relation to the spirit world in which they live with great fear, however, and they will "hear" the message more clearly than our words alone could ever make it.

A similar concern is expressed by Richard De Ridder of Calvin Theological Seminary in his book *Discipling the Nations*. De Ridder reflects on his missionary experience in Sri Lanka in these words:

> One thing deeply impressed me: how irrelevant so much of traditional Reformed Theology was to these people and their situation, and how seldom this theology spoke to their real needs. For example, the questions that concern Satan, demons, angels, charms, etc., are not of great concern, nor do they receive much attention in the West. These are living issues to the Christians of these areas, sur-

---

* Wagner, C. P. (1992). On the cutting edge of mission strategy. In R. D. Winter & S. C. Hawthorne (Eds.), *Perspectives on the world Christian movement: A reader* (rev. ed.) (pp. D55-D59). Pasadena: William Carey Library.

** Peter Wagner has been Professor of Church Growth in the Fuller Seminary School of World Mission for over 20 years. Previous to joining the Fuller faculty, Wagner served the Lord in Bolivia in evangelism, church planting, seminary teaching, and mission administration. While there he began writing books and now has authored over 30 volumes on missions and church growth. Since 1980, Wagner has specialized in the spiritual aspects of church growth, writing such books as *Wrestling with Dark Angels, Spiritual Power and Church Growth,* and *Warfare Prayer.* In addition to teaching at Fuller Seminary, he coordinates the United Prayer Track of the AD 2000 Movement.

rounded as they were by animism and the continual fear of the spiritual realm. Among the greatest joys that we experienced was to proclaim to men the victory of Christ over the powers and see the shackles of slavery to elemental spirits broken by Christ. This is a chapter of Reformed Theology that has still not been written by the West. When the "Five Points of Calvinism" were preached to these people, they often responded with the question, "What's the issue?" Missionaries and pastors were scratching where it didn't itch.

How tragic when people get the idea that Christianity is a matter of mere intellectual conviction, a religion of words largely devoid of power.

I receive a large number of letters, both form letters and personal letters, from missionaries around the world. This personal letter is from a traditionally and impeccably evangelical mission executive:

> As you know, we are committed to planting churches in the Muslim world. We are face to face with a power encounter of gigantic proportions. I am convinced that there is a demonic base to Islam that is much greater than most of us have ever dared admit. Of course, it doesn't make good copy to say these things or write them, and we are all rather embarrassed by our ineptitude in facing Islam today. Why does the Christian church have to lie down and let the Islamic horde sweep over us as so many tanks?

This is an increasing cry. Large numbers of missionaries and international church leaders in our school at Fuller are asking the same questions, and we are beginning to provide them with some answers, however elementary at this stage. Two of our students, serving with the Latin America Mission in Costa Rica, wrote of several experiences with supernatural power in a recent newsletter. Among them was this:

> Since our return to Costa Rica in January, we have been operating in a new power we never knew in our previous six years here. We have ministered to a person that had been diag-

nosed to be epileptic, only to be freed by the expulsion of demons. This person had an experience early in life with witchcraft, through contact with a Ouija board. Her mother also had been very much involved in the occult. Now after 46 years of torment, she is totally free.

These missionaries lamented the fact that "Christianity has all too often been presented as a religion of the textbook and the head." They now see how distant this is from the Christianity of the New Testament, where "worship was alive and meaningful, prayer was an avid encounter, and signs and wonders drew people to faith."

An OMF missionary to Singapore recently wrote that he witnessed to a man there who said, "No point in becoming a Christian. My brother is a pastor. When my mother got ill, he couldn't do anything to help. We took her to the temple and she was healed." Another woman, a Hindu, said, "The trouble with you Christians is that you have no power!" My friend comments, "How tragic when people get the idea that Christianity is a matter of mere intellectual conviction, a religion of words largely devoid of power."

An increasing number of our evangelical seminary missions faculties and our evangelical mission agencies have begun to raise issues of spiritual power. I am convinced that it is an area which requires some fresh study and some discerning implementation if we are to participate fully in contemporary world evangelization.

A fresh awareness of worldview

Due to the pervasive influence of cultural anthropology in our current missiological research, the concept of *worldview* has gained a great deal of prominence. We are able to talk about worldview and to understand its implications in daily life much more freely and accurately than we used to. One of the more disturbing things we are beginning to discover is that, in more cases than we would care to think, our missionary message in the Third World has been having a secularizing influence.

I first realized this when I read an article by my colleague, Paul G. Hiebert, called "The Flaw of the Excluded Middle," in 1982. He begins the article by citing the question that John the Baptist had his disciples ask Jesus: "Are you the Coming One, or do we look for another?" (Luke 7:20). Hiebert emphasized that Jesus' reply was not a carefully reasoned argument, but rather a demonstration of power in healing the sick and casting out of evil spirits.

"When I read the passage as a missionary in India, and sought to apply it to missions in our day," says Hiebert, "I had a sense of uneasiness. As a Westerner, I was used to presenting Christ on the basis of rational arguments, not by evidence of His power in the lives of people who were sick, possessed, and destitute." He goes on to point out that the worldview of most non-Westerners is three-tiered. There is a cosmic tier on top, an everyday life tier on the bottom, and a large middle zone where the two constantly interact. This is a zone largely controlled by spirits, demons, ancestors, goblins, ghosts, magic, fetishes, witches, mediums, sorcerers, and such powers. The common reaction of Western missionaries, whose worldview does not contain such a middle zone, is to attempt to deny the existence of the spirits rather than claim the power of Christ over them. As a result, says Hiebert, "Western Christian missions have been one of the greatest secularizing forces in history."

The worldview of most non-Westerners is three-tiered. There is a cosmic tier on top, an everyday life tier on the bottom, and a large middle zone where the two constantly interact.

Most of us are aware that secular humanism has deeply influenced our culture in America. But relatively few of us have understood how profoundly this has permeated even our Christian institutions including churches, colleges, and seminaries. The more we realize it, however, and the more we recognize that our secularized worldview is significantly different from those of the Jews and the Greeks in the New Testament context, the more we can become open to what is called a paradigm shift.

Figure 6-5. Western vs. Traditional Worldviews*

This paradigm shift is very helpful in bringing missionaries more in touch with the worldview of the men and women to whom they are attempting to communicate the gospel.

A fresh examination of the theology of the kingdom

In the Lord's prayer we say, "Thy kingdom come, Thy will be done on earth as it is in heaven." I must confess that up until recently those words had very little meaning for my life. I repeated them by rote memory without much spiritual processing taking place as I did. For one thing, my understanding was that the kingdom was something that was future, so my assumption was that I was praying for the return of the Lord. An accompanying assumption was that, because God is sovereign, His will is in fact being done on earth today and that we can rather passively accept what happens as something which God directly or indirectly approves of.

I now see the theology of the kingdom in a different light. I now believe that when Jesus came, He introduced the kingdom of God into the present world.

This was a direct confrontation or invasion of the kingdom of darkness ruled by Satan, who is called

---

* This diagram was taken from Myers, B. L. (1991, June). The excluded middle. *MARC Newsletter*, 91-2, 3.

"the god of this age" (2 Cor. 4:4). I take Satan more seriously than I used to, recognizing that some things which occur today do so because of the will of the enemy, not because they are the will of God. The era between the first and second comings of Christ is an era of warfare between the two kingdoms. Two strong powers are occupying the same territory.

Let me say quickly that I still believe in the sovereignty of God who, for His own reasons, has allowed this spiritual warfare to take place for almost 2,000 years now. And there is no doubt as to the outcome. Satan and all his demonic forces were defeated by the blood of Jesus on the cross. His is, at best, a holding action, but a ferocious, destructive and dehumanizing action which God expects us, as His servants, to actively oppose.

What are some things clearly out of God's will which are happening today? In heaven there is not one poor, at war, oppressed, demonized, sick, or lost. As evangelicals we understand the last one best. Even though it is not God's will that any should perish according to 2 Peter 3:9, the world today is full of those who are perishing, as I have previously mentioned. There are three billion of them out there, and our task, as instruments of God's hands, is to reach out to them and bring them into the kingdom through the new birth (see John 3:3). This is the great missiological challenge.

We do the best we can to reach the lost for Christ, knowing full well ahead of time, on both biblical and experiential grounds, that we are not going to win them all. That knowledge does not discourage us, even though we know the reason why some do not respond. We learn from 2 Corinthians 4:3-4 that it is essentially because Satan has succeeded in blinding their eyes to the light of the gospel. We weep knowing that each year millions of people die and go into a Christless eternity, and we know that it is not God's will that they should perish.

If this is true about the lost, it may well be true about the poor, those at war, the oppressed, the demonized, and the sick. So long as Satan is the god of this age, they will all be with us. But meanwhile, as citizens of the kingdom of God, we must reflect the values of the kingdom and combat these evils as strenuously as possible. For example, we must heal the sick, knowing ahead of time that not all will be healed. I was pleased when this was recognized at a high level evangelical conference in 1982. At that time, the Lausanne Committee sponsored a Consultation on the Relationship of Evangelism to Social Responsibility in Grand Rapids and recognized in its report that among the signs of the kingdom were "making the blind see, the deaf hear, the lame walk, the sick whole, raising the dead, stilling the storm, and multiplying loaves and fishes."* The report mentions that "Demon possession is a real and terrible condition. Deliverance is possible only in a power encounter in which the name of Jesus is invoked and prevails." This is what missiologists, such as Timothy Warner, are also saying to us.

> *We can no longer afford to send missionaries and national church leaders to the missions field without teaching them how to heal the sick and cast out demons.*

At least two missiological faculties that I am aware of now consider this an important enough cutting edge issue to introduce it explicitly into their curriculum. Professor Warner of Trinity Evangelical Divinity School began a course on power encounter in the summer of 1991. In 1982 our Fuller missions faculty invited Pastor John Wimber to teach an experimental course on the miraculous and church growth, which he did for four years. It is now being reorganized under two of Wimber's disciples, Professor Charles Kraft and myself. I agree with Kraft, who once said in a faculty meeting, "We can no longer afford to send missionaries and national church leaders back to their fields or to send young people to the missions field for the first time without teaching them how to heal the sick and cast out demons." We are still at the beginning stages of this, and we are not yet satisfied with the way we are doing the job, but we are trusting God to continue to teach us so that we can in turn teach others.

---

* Lausanne Committee for World Evangelization. (1982). *The CRESR Report.* Charlotte, NC: Author.

I feel that one of the callings that God has given me is to be an encouragement to traditional evangelical non-Pentecostal and non-Charismatic institutions so that they will begin to take a new look at mission power—ministering supernaturally as we encounter the enemy.

28. *Why is "mission power" a strategic consideration?*

_____

_____

29. *What relationship does "worldview" have to "kingdom theology," and how does this relationship affect our mission strategy?*

_____

_____

_____

Summary

Simply stated, strategy is the means used in reaching a certain goal. All Christians operate with a strategy, whether they are conscious of it or not. Some strategies are better than others, however, and most often a "unique" strategy will have to be formulated to reach specific peoples. We don't have to think of strategy as unspiritual. Good mission strategy causes us to make a statement of faith regarding the establishment of God's kingdom among a particular people who are yet unreached. It forces us to depend on the Holy Spirit to meet the challenges of each unique situation. It drives us to our knees in rebellion against the status quo.

A look at the historical development of mission strategy reveals that strategy is not static. Strategy builds on strategy and is molded by the circumstances in which it finds itself. Principles for effective mission have emerged through trial and error and have been refined by time. As disciples of the kingdom, we do well to take from our treasure the old and the new in formulating strategy to meet the challenge of the present era of mission.

Historically, it is undeniable that God has used two structures with distinct functions in carrying out His redemptive plan. Modalities have functioned as the primary nurture structure; sodalities, as the primary mission structure. Both are needed to fulfill Christ's global mandate. It is also critical that mission be carried out in "mission power." Without such power, the most sophisticated strategies and structures will not accomplish kingdom ends.

Integrative Assignment

1. Outline a talk entitled, "Strategy and Prayer: A Balanced Approach to Mission."

2. Using the principles you gleaned from your reading of mission strategy, write down your own Ten Commandments of Mission Strategy. Use negative as well as positive commandments: "Thou shalt not...," as well as "Thou shalt...."

3. Outline a short talk entitled, "The Need for Mission Structures in World Evangelization." Give three reasons for such structures, and support your statements from Scripture or historical evidence.

Questions for Reflection

It is true that all of us who endeavor to do God's will use some kind of strategy. Even the lack of a conscious strategy is a strategy in itself—the "no strategy" strategy. But this lack of method in what we do often results in ineffectiveness for the Lord. What can you do to improve your personal strategy for doing God's will? Towards what goals are you working? What disciplines will help you to achieve those goals? Reflect on these matters and enter your thoughts below.

CHAPTER 7

The Task Remaining

It is important to know how far we've come in missions. To plan an effective strategy, however, it is also essential that we understand what's left to be done. What is the task remaining?

In 1974, Christians from all over the world met in Lausanne, Switzerland, for an International Congress on World Evangelization. This Congress, like its historic predecessor in Edinburgh (1910), attempted to analyze the current progress of world evangelization and to define the remaining task. One of the most significant addresses of the Congress was delivered by Dr. Ralph Winter, who convincingly demonstrated that there were 2.4 billion people still beyond the current reach of the gospel message. Building on research done by World Vision's Missions Advanced Research and Communications Center (MARC), Winter defined the task remaining in terms of "unreached" or "hidden" *people groups*. He proved conclusively that the "crucial need" in world evangelization today is for missions which will cross cultural frontiers with the gospel.

In this chapter, we will look at Winter's thesis, define his terminology, and examine the rationale behind his conclusions. We will also look at how other missiologists build on Winter's concept to define the remaining task. Finally, we will evaluate the current state of world evangelization and will delineate the task in terms of its highest priorities.

I. The Great Commission Nations

What did Christ mean when He commanded us to make disciples of all "nations"? Was He thinking of politically defined "countries," or did He have something else in mind? What was the common understanding of the term "nation" in Bible times? In the following excerpt, Winter defines this concept biblically and graphically illustrates how this term applies today.

❏ *The Task Remaining:*
All Humanity in Mission Perspective *

Ralph D. Winter

No perspective on the entire human race can be brief without tending to be simplistic. When God chose Abraham and his lineage both for special blessing and for special responsibility to share that blessing to "all the families of the earth" (Gen. 12:3; 18:18, etc.), Abraham mercifully did not understand how big and complex the task was.

Now, however, 4,000 years later, over half of "all the families of the earth" are at least superficially what Toynbee calls "Judaic" in religion and have certainly received at least some direct blessing through people with faith like Abraham's and through the redemptive work of the One to whom Abraham looked (John 8:56). If we take into account indirect influences, it would be possible to estimate that nine-tenths of all humanity has by now received

some of that blessing, even if mixed with other elements.

Nations and countries

In today's world we tend to think "political entity" or "country" when we see the word "nation." Unfortunately, this is not the concept expressed in the Bible. A closer translation comes directly from the Greek word *ethnos*, which has not only been translated "nation" but also "ethnic unit," "people," or (as in the New Testament) "heathen" or "Gentiles." In no case does it refer to a country as we think of a political unit today. A more correct usage would be as in the phrase "the Cherokee nation," referring to the tribe of American Indians known as the Cherokee. Even in the Old Testament this same concept

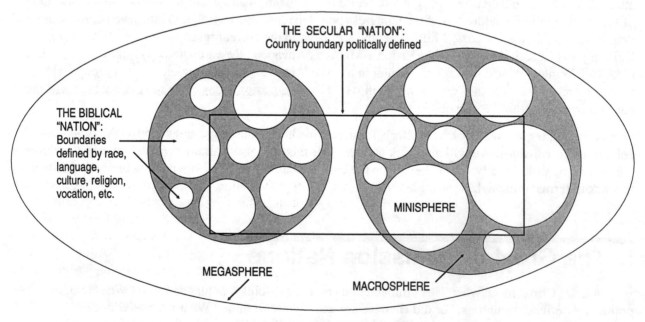

Figure 7-1. The Biblical "Nation"

---

* Winter, R. D. (1992). The task remaining: All humanity in mission perspective. In R. D. Winter & S. C. Hawthorne (Eds.), *Perspectives on the world Christian movement: A reader* (rev. ed.) (pp. B176-B181). Pasadena: William Carey Library.

holds true. Two words are used in the Old Testament. *Gam*, which occurs 1,821 times, refers to a people, a single race or tribe, or to a specific family of mankind, as in Deuteronomy 4:6 and 28:37. The other word, *mishpahgheh*, occurs only 267 times and is mainly used to refer to family, kindred, or relatives. This is the word used in Genesis 12:3, "In thee shall all the *families* of the earth be blessed." The concept of "country" or a politically defined nation is totally absent in both of these cases. The fact that not countries, but rather ethnic units or people groups is what is implied is made even more pointed when in a number of places (e.g., Rev. 5:9; 10:11, etc.) not only is the word "nation" used, but it is further spelled out as peoples, tribes, tongues, and kindred.

Paul knew himself as the apostle to the Gentiles (read "peoples" or "nations"). He was one of the first of the new church to conclude that God wanted to use the marvelous diversity of the cultural mosaic of mankind. He came to see that God did not require a Gentile to commit cultural suicide to become a believer. Paul spoke of this as a mystery long hidden, but now made plain (Eph. 3:4). There was nothing new about a Gentile becoming a Jew and joining the community of faith of the people of God. A few hardy proselytes in Paul's day did this, though they had a hard time. Most Gentiles would not have gone that far. (Did they sense instinctively that such a shift could not in itself be salvific?) They needed a Paul to establish a synagogue of, by, and for their own people, that is, a Gentile synagogue. The new thing was unity without uniformity. Gentiles could follow Jesus without becoming culturally Jewish.

Many Americans in particular tend to assume that all who live in China are racially Chinese, by which they probably mean "Han" Chinese. Or they may assume all the peoples of Russia are ethnically the same. However, even the unity-seeking government of the People's Republic of China recognizes a number of ethnic minorities, that is, distinctly non-Han groups of people who were born and have lived in China for hundreds of years. Furthermore, there are a great many varieties of Han Chinese. There are at least 100 mutually unintelligible varieties of the Chinese family of languages! India is a country of 3,000 nations, only 100 of which have any Christians at all. The Soviet Union also has widely diverse peoples with practically nothing in common except the political glue that binds them together.

For example, one major mission organization states its purpose as "multiplying laborers in every nation," yet it only keeps track of how many *countries* it works in, not how many biblical *nations* it is touching, nor whether such nations already have a well established work or not. Another outstanding mission agency has produced a book entitled *The Discipling of a Nation*, which speaks of needing one church for every thousand people in a "nation." The thinking of the leaders of that mission is clear, but the book title is ambiguous since most people would understand it to mean countries, not biblical nations. Yet, strange as it may at first sound, it is perfectly possible to reach the goal of having planted one church per thousand people in, say, the *country* of India and not have touched even half of the 3,000 different biblically defined nations in that country.

> *The "peoples" concept stresses the need to look at people as part of their own culture and to see them as strategic, natural bridges to the rest of their society.*

Thus to look at the world from the "peoples" concept is not only biblical, it is also highly strategic, for there is one kind of cross-cultural evangelism and church planting that is far more strategic than all the others. Moreover, the "peoples" concept stresses the need to look at people as part of their own culture, not merely as individuals, and to see them, when converted as individuals, as strategic, natural bridges to the rest of their society. To give a diagrammatic example of the significance of the "peoples" concept for mission strategy, let us look at one small sector of the world.

1. What is the difference between a "country" and the biblical concept of "nation"?

_____

_____

_____

2. What is the importance of this distinction?

_____

_____

_____

   The term "people group" has been coined to refer to the biblical concept of nation. People groups are sociological groupings of people, not political groupings. The Lausanne Committee for World Evangelization has defined a people group as "a significantly large sociological grouping of individuals who perceive themselves to have a common affinity for one another because of their shared language, religion, ethnicity, residence, occupation, class or caste, situation, etc., or combinations of these."

Megaspheres, macrospheres, and minispheres

Figure 7-2 shows some people groups within two large cultural blocs or "megaspheres"—the Muslim megasphere and the Han Chinese megasphere. Within these megaspheres we find three large circles filled with a number of smaller circles. Each large circle represents a "cultural macrosphere"—a group of societies that have certain cultural similarities both within and between them. The middle macrosphere consists of Cantonese-speaking people, most of whom are found in a single country, the People's Republic of China, and they number in the millions of people. The smaller circles, which I will call "minispheres," represent groups of people which speak divergent dialects of Cantonese mutually unintelligible to each other. People from two such subgroups can be understood by each other

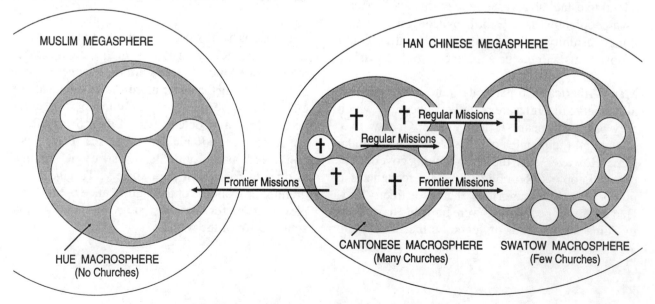

Figure 7-2. Regular Missions / Frontier Missions

only if they learn a "trade language" variety of Cantonese. Either the macrosphere or the minisphere could be considered a *nation* in biblical terms, but note that neither is a *country*. (Still

smaller "microspheres" could be defined by clan or family or vocational differences too small to require separate churches for maximally effective outreach.)

3. *How do the three "spheres" help us arrive at the biblical understanding of the term "nations"?*

_____

_____

_____

E-1, E-2, and E-3 evangelism

Note further that in some of the minispheres—the smaller circles—there is a cross, representing an indigenous church that has been planted within that culture sometime in the past. These churches, if they are vital and witnessing, are readily able to win the remaining non-Christians in that dialect group by normal, near-neighbor evangelism. We call this E-1 evangelism. There is only one barrier to be crossed in near-neighbor evangelism, the "stained glass barrier." Should that barrier get too thick, the believing community then becomes an enclave that is essentially a different minisphere and must be treated as such.

Some of the smaller circles, however, have no cross. Those minispheres obviously need someone from somewhere else to do that initial evangelizing and to plant the first church. That kind of evangelism from the outside is much more difficult than near-neighbor evangelism, for it requires the evangelist from the outside to learn another language, or at least another dialect of Cantonese. Also, he will find out that some of the cultural assumptions will be different. In other words, ordinary evangelism will not do the task that is required to pioneer in this frontier area. This type of evangelism we call E-2 or E-3. The evangelist must penetrate significant cultural barriers.

Looking again at Figure 7-2, you will notice that schematically we show only six of the many minispheres in the Cantonese macrosphere, and that five have a cross, meaning an indigenous church.

The Swatow macrosphere, by contrast, has only one minisphere with an indigenous church, and the Muslim Hue macrosphere, which pertains to an entirely different Muslim megasphere, has no Christian church at all in any of its minispheres. Each of these macrospheres numbers millions of people; indeed, even some of the minispheres may number over a million people. The job of the ordinary evangelist is to plant churches in his own minisphere. That we call E-1, near-neighbor evangelism.

> *There is only one barrier to be crossed in E-1 evangelism, the "stained glass" barrier. In E-2 or E-3 evangelism, the evangelist must penetrate significant cultural barriers.*

But where there is no church—no indigenous community of believers—there is not the evangelism potential to reach the entire minisphere. In fact, there may be a number of individual believers who (like the New Testament "God fearers") worship outside their culture. There may even be some believers from that group who have left their minisphere and become "proselytized" to another. But there is still no viable, indigenous church. By viable church we mean a minimum, yet sufficiently developed indigenous Christian tradition, capable of evangelizing its own people without cross-cultural help. This implies that there would be a cluster of indigenous evangelizing congregations and a significant part of the Bible translated by the people themselves. Minispheres which do not have that cluster of indigenous, growing, evangelizing congregations can be considered "unreached." These people groups require cross-cultural evangelism.

A people group can be considered "reached" if there is a body of Christians with the potential to evangelize its own people such that outside, cross-cultural efforts can be "safely" terminated. This potential may be roughly predicted by measuring the percentage of practicing Christians. The figure of 20 percent has been established by the Lausanne Committee for World Evangelization, to be on the "safe side," but this figure is not absolutely crucial if in a given case it is known that the indigenous church shows every indication that it can and will evangelize its entire minisphere. Where there is no viable church, it takes a Paul, or someone from outside that language group and culture, to go to that people and plant a church there. Or it takes a Luther within the culture to wake up and go indigenous. In any case, the Cantonese evangelist in Figure 7-2 who goes to a Swatow dialect where there is no church is doing a missionary type of evangelism. In Paul's words, he is "going where Christ is not named."

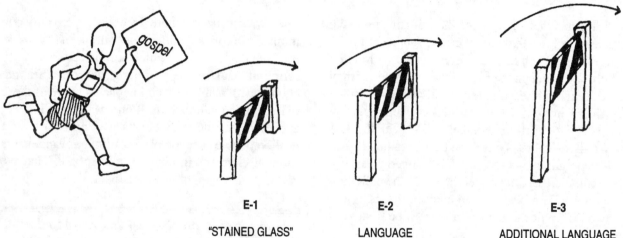

E-1

"STAINED GLASS" BARRIERS

E-2

LANGUAGE BARRIER

E-3

ADDITIONAL LANGUAGE OR CULTURE BARRIERS

Figure 7-3. E-1, E-2, and E-3 Evangelism

4. What are the main barriers to be crossed in each of the three kinds of evangelism?

_____

_____

_____

5. How do we know when a people group has a viable church?

_____

_____

_____

Evangelism and missions

If, however, a Cantonese evangelist goes from his Cantonese-speaking church to a Swatow minisphere where there already is an indigenous church, to help those believers to evangelize their own non-Christian Swatows, remaining in the same minisphere, he may very well be making a "missionary trip," but he is doing evangelism, not missions. We have defined as evangelism the activity of reaching out from an existing church within the same minisphere, working to its fringes. The people back home in his Cantonese minisphere may very likely call such a person their "missionary," but technically speaking, even in the biblical and classical sense, he is an evangelist who happens to be working at a cultural distance from his own background. The main point is that winning people into a church that is already within their own minisphere is the work of an evangelist, even if the "missionary" comes from a great distance. We must admit that this is the usual pattern of so-called "missions" today. Most "missionaries," whether from the U.S.A., Europe, Asia, or Africa, go from their own cultures to work in another culture where a church is already established. We may have to concede the term "regular missions" to such activity, just because of social pressure; in that case we fall back to the term "frontier missions" for the other activity. Some workers are incorrectly called "missionaries" even when they go to work with Christians from their own culture who have moved to a foreign country. In that case, such people are not even evangelists but rather "transplanted pastors."

Regular missions and frontier missions

We can distinguish "Frontier Missions" from "Regular Missions" by considering the matrix in Figure 7-4. The quadrants on the left side are concerned with *reached* people groups, and the quadrants on the right side are concerned with *unreached* or *hidden* people groups. Thus the horizontal axis effectively measures the *cultural* distance between the people and the culturally nearest potential witness embodied in a church, while the vertical axis is the *evangelist's* cultural distance from the potential convert. The bottom two quadrants designate *monocultural work*. The top two quadrants specify *crosscultural* evangelism.

Quadrant I is classic near-neighbor evangelism. An evangelist makes disciples within his own minisphere, where there is already a vibrant growing fellowship. But it is quite possible for this same Christian worker to work in what is for him a radically different culture (E-3 evangelism) and yet be working among an essentially reached group (Quadrant II). This is "missions" only in the sense that the worker is away from his own home. The converts have all the advantages of those in Quadrant I. But if our evangelist does E-3 evangelism in a people group without a viable church (Quadrant III), then he must work for the "missiological breakthrough" of establishing the first indigenous church. This is the crucial task of "Frontier Missions." We trust that the term "Regular Missions" highlights the strategic priority of "Frontier Missions" without diminishing the value of cross-cultural workers in reached people groups.

	Reached People Groups	Unreached People Groups
Cross-Cultural E2, E3	II. Regular Missions	III. Frontier Missions
Mono-Cultural E0, E1	I. Evangelism	

Evangelist's Cultural Distance From Potential Convert →

Convert's Distance From Culturally Nearest Church →

I. **Evangelism:** By a same-culture worker, where the missiological breakthrough of a viable church has taken place.

II. **Regular Missions:** Cross-cultural evangelism by a different-culture worker, in association with same-culture workers if possible, where a missiological breakthrough has taken place.

III. **Frontier Missions:** Here is where cross-cultural evangelism (by a different-culture worker) is essential, since no missiological breakthrough has yet been made.

Figure 7-4. Evangelism vs. Missions

6. What are the determining factors in identifying frontier missions?

_____

_____

_____

Cultural Barriers

When the biblical definition of "nation" is applied, Christ's words, "Go ye into all the world and make disciples of all nations" (Matt. 28:19), may take on new significance. Most of the world's *politically* defined nations have a viable church. But thousands of the world's *culturally* defined nations still don't have a viable Christian witness in their midst. These nations, or people groups, are isolated from the gospel by cultural barriers.

1. Linguistic Barriers

The most obvious cultural barrier which distinguishes one people from another is language. People who speak a language different from one's own are obviously foreign. To a slightly lesser degree, the same is true of those who speak a different dialect of one's own language. Dialects, or regional variations of a language, are distinguishable because of differences in accent, vocabulary, or grammar. Often these differences are so marked that it is difficult or impossible for people who belong to different dialect groups of the same language to understand each other. Because of these linguistic barriers, Bible translators have often identified a need for separate translations for different dialects. Currently, more than 4,500 linguistic groups need separate Bible translations.

Dialects may reflect geographical, economic, or social distance of members of the same tribe or ethnic grouping. Often, significant cultural differences beyond language exist. Most people think of the United States as a single nation, bound by a common language, English, which has only some slight regional differences. A study by Joel Garreau, however, identifies nine distinct regions in North America, each with its own economy and value system. Culturally and economically, these regions could well be considered as separate nations.* Even though most North Americans speak the same language, their regional culture may be sufficiently different that distinct strategies may be needed to communicate the gospel in each of these "nations."

In many countries, a national language is spoken for the purpose of trade, education, and government, but many local languages and dialects are spoken in the homes and in the localities where the languages originate. For example, in Cameroon, West Africa, English and French are spoken as national languages, but 183 distinct languages and dialects are spoken regionally. Cameroon must not be thought of as evangelized simply because French and English speaking congregations are established throughout the country. On the contrary, we can consider Cameroon to be "reached" only when its 183 linguistically defined "nations" have viable churches ministering to them.

---

* See Garreau, J. (1981). *The nine nations of North America.* New York: Avon Books.

2. Social Barriers

The cultural barriers to spontaneous evangelization are not simply linguistic. Some of the most significant barriers are social. Within most societies there are social classes which are defined along racial, occupational, educational, economic, hereditary, or religious lines. We give these classes designations such as "upper" and "lower" class, working class, professional class, ruling class, etc. In India, an intricate class or "caste" system has developed with hundreds of distinct classifications.

Perhaps because of a greater awareness of their own need and dependence on God, the poor "lower" classes have often been the most responsive to the gospel. But it is improbable, and in some cases nearly impossible, for upper class members or castes to become Christians if it means forsaking their own social position to become members of a "lower" class or caste church. For example, millions of Hindus in Southern India speak the same language. The church is well established there, but its membership is drawn from approximately five percent of the castes. We could not consider Southern India to be reached until viable churches are established which can minister effectively to the other 95 percent of the castes that are still unevangelized.

3. Rivalries and Prejudices

The barriers preventing the gospel from spreading spontaneously from one culture to the next are many and complex. Linguistic and sociological factors are the most significant, but there are also other factors which bar Christian neighbors from evangelizing peoples who are geographically, linguistically, and even sociologically similar. For example, herdsmen and farmers in the same region may speak a common language and may be considered on the same social level. A viable church may exist among the farmers, but age-old rivalries over land use will probably prevent the farmers from evangelizing the herdsmen. It may well require E-2 or E-3 evangelism from the outside to reach the herdsmen successfully.

In many countries, racial or class discrimination is widely practiced. Black/white tensions in the United States and the practice of apartheid in South Africa are perhaps the best known examples. But each part of the globe has its own racial prejudices. Native American populations of North and South America, Russian Jews, pygmies in Africa, Palestinians in Israel, tenant farmers, religious minorities in India, and powerless majorities elsewhere have all suffered tyranny and exploitation. The net result is that such mistrust and hate have built up over the years that it is highly unlikely that the dominant group will ever find a hearing among those who have been oppressed. Only E-2 or E-3 evangelists from the outside are likely to receive an open hearing.

7. To what "nation" do you belong? Describe it in terms of linguistic and social boundaries with near neighbors.

_____

_____

_____

_____

8. *What rivalries or prejudices exist between the group you are a part of and others in your community or general locality? How difficult is it to share the gospel across these barriers?*

_____

_____

_____

_____

Crossing Cultural Barriers

In Acts 1:8 Christ emphasizes the importance of cross-cultural evangelism. At first glance, it may seem that He is speaking simply of a geographical progression of the gospel from Jerusalem, throughout Judea, to Samaria, and from there to the uttermost part of the earth. Although geographic distance does figure into this expansion, the fact remains that this sequence reflects a cultural progression from the center of Jewish culture, Jerusalem, throughout the Jewish fringes of Judea, to the part-Jewish, part-Gentile Samaritans, and on to the larger Gentile world of the "uttermost parts," containing thousands of groups, each with its own cultural distinctives and barriers to be crossed.

The progression of the gospel in Acts was not as neat and simple as it might first appear; it did not simply flow from Jew to Samaritan to Greek. The Jews and the Samaritans, while culturally near, had no dealings with each other. The Jews despised the Samaritans for having defiled the Jewish race through intermarriage with Gentiles. Thus, although the Samaritans were at a close cultural and geographic distance from the Jews, long-standing prejudicial hatred was a difficult barrier to cross with the gospel. Indeed, when the Samaritans were reached, the contact was made not by an ethnic Jew, but by Philip, a Hellenistic Jew of Greek ethnicity (Acts 8). In this case, Philip may have been culturally more distant from the Samaritans than were the Jews, but it was this very distance which may well have given him a hearing among the Samaritans.

Paul himself, though ethnically a Jew, was raised in a Gentile culture. This heritage put him closer culturally to the Gentiles than the other apostles were, thus explaining in part why he was chosen to go to the Gentiles. Using Winter's terminology, we could say that Paul was at an E-2 distance from the Greeks, while Peter was at E-3 distance from them. Luke, who himself was Greek, was at E-1 distance. Likewise, Barnabas may have been sent to Antioch by the elders in Jerusalem because, being a native of those parts, he could minister on an E-1 basis.

There are many factors which determine cultural distance and the possible effectiveness of an evangelist. In today's complex world, there are many "Jerusalems," "Judeas," "Samarias," and "uttermost parts." One man's "Samaria" is another's "Judea" and a third person's "uttermost part." Figure 7-5 illustrates these relationships by showing the cultural distance between the Highland Quechuas of Peru and several other groups.

Farthest away culturally are the North Americans and the Koreans. They are clearly at E-3 distance because they must cross major linguistic and cultural barriers even to get to the Quechuas. Mestizos, the descendants of marriages between the Spanish conquerors and the Quechuas, are

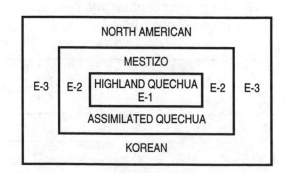

Figure 7-5. Cultural Distances

culturally closer, at an E-2 distance. The 500-year domination of the Quechuas by the Mestizos, however, has produced a "Jew/Samaritan" situation. Walls of prejudice in most cases inhibit effective evangelization of the Quechuas by the Mestizos because of the long tradition of exploitation.

At a closer E-2 distance are second generation urbanized Quechuas whose parents moved to the big cities to escape poverty and give their children greater opportunities. These ethnic Quechuas are being assimilated into Mestizo culture. Although the lifestyle and professions of these assimilated Quechuas have now distanced them from their Quechua heritage, they are barely beyond E-1 distance. Many understand their parents' Quechua dialect and may speak it as well.

9. *Based on the above information, which group is the best candidate to evangelize the Highland Quechuas? Why?*

_____

_____

_____

_____

II. Envisioning the Task

Understanding the complexity of cultural barriers allows us to see distinct groupings of people who, because of their affinities, consider themselves quite distinct from others, even their near neighbors. One of the best known of the missiologists attempting to quantify the number of these biblically defined groups is Patrick Johnstone, whose book Operation World has helped thousands to understand and pray for the unreached peoples. He describes the challenge involved in trying to compute the number of these groups existing in our world today.

❏ *Unreached Peoples: How Many Are There?* *

Patrick Johnstone **

The very term "unreached" is a challenge! Unreached peoples must be reached as soon as possible. The Church of the Lord Jesus must be mobilized to reach them. For this, we *must* know who they are, where they live, and how to reach them effectively.

For this we need to know how many unreached people groups (UPs) there are.

Yet after 15 years of talk and research, there is often more heat than light, confusion than clarity. Why? I see three basic reasons:

---

* Johnstone, P. (1992). Unreached peoples: How many are there? In S. C. Hawthorne & R. D. Winter (Eds.), *Perspectives on the world Christian movement: A study guide* (1992 ed.) (pp. G5-G6). Pasadena: William Carey Library.

** Patrick Johnstone has served as a missionary to southern Africa. He is presently the Director of Research for WEC International in England.

1. Differing goals

Christian anthropologists and *sociologists* are especially interested in defining our complex society. By this means, help can be given to churches struggling to find keys for evangelizing every section of the society in which they live. To such researchers, the actual number of people groups is not important, nor is the fact that in highly developed societies, any one person may be classified in a number of professional, occupational, residential, and social groups. Such a classification could mean an open ended total of millions of people groups in the world.

The command of the Lord Jesus that disciples be made of all nations or peoples must be bounded and completable.

Missionaries are primarily concerned for the fulfillment of the Abrahamic promise that all the families of the earth (implying peoples) might be blessed in the gospel, and that the vision of Revelation 7:9 might become reality—that there might be those redeemed of every race, tribe, people, and tongue. The command of the Lord Jesus that disciples be made of *all* nations or peoples must be bounded and completable. For world evangelization it is important that we define what we mean by a people group or people in this more limited sense. Revelation 7:9 gives us a good guide: these terms are predominantly ethnic and linguistic. This narrows down the number of peoples in the world to between 7,000 and 30,000, depending on the distinctions you make.

2. Differing definitions

So much depends on the ministry of an agency as to what definition is best for the chosen medium of outreach. Take language, for example.

Christian radio strategists tend to think in terms of using major languages, and covering small minorities in a commonly understood "trade" language. The world could be 99 percent covered by broadcasting in 400-500 such languages.

Bible translators have a stiffer criterion. Languages that already have some Scriptures or that might warrant a translation program may number 5,455 or more (the latest Wycliffe Bible Translators' *Ethnologue* figure).

Gospel Recordings, Inc., prepares tape and disk evangelistic messages and can refine the program to dialects. Dialects vary from a moderate change in accentuation to a high degree of mutual incomprehension. Who could ever define every dialect in the world—20,000; 40,000?

Social systems can be rigid. Many advocate that Hindu caste systems should be classified as ethnolinguistic peoples—there are over 3,000 castes in India speaking 14 major officially recognized languages!

So much, therefore, depends on our definitions and classifications. So any who propose a number for peoples and UPs for the world must also give their parameters.

3. Differing cut-off points

What is the minimal size of people that can qualify for inclusion in a world list? For instance:

Small tribes—At what size is a tribal group viable? Many of the Amerindian, Pacific, and African tribes are so small that they are unlikely to survive as a separate entity for long. Should they be included?

Migrant communities—At what size or level of integration should the many thousands of immigrant or refugee communities be recognized as unassimilated, viable, countable entities? Would, for instance, 15 migrant Uzbeks from the U.S.S.R. in Canada constitute a separate people? The total for Canada could be anything from 50 to 500 migrant ethnic communities.

The criteria for a suggested model

This is the model I used for *Operation World*:

1. Every indigenous people within a country for which a separate cross-cultural discipling and church planting ministry is required. This would generally mean that dialect and class distinctions are not made unless local knowledge justifies this. It may prove wise for separate and specific evangelistic and early discipling strategies to be developed for these, but an integrated church to be the goal.

2. All immigrant communities that retain a cultural and geographical cohesion requiring a church planting strategy in their own language. I have taken 3,000 migrants as a general lower limit.

3. The total of each country gives the number of "peoples within the country." The world total is derived by adding the totals for each country (i.e., any ethno-linguistic group found in a multiple number of countries will be included multiple times).

An estimation of the degree of reachedness of the world's peoples

Using the above criteria, these are the results from the information that we have in our files:

Total number of peoples within country boundaries	12,017
Total number of peoples over 50% Christian	6,000
Peoples with some viable indigenous churches	3,000
Peoples with missionary outreach; no viable churches	1,800
Peoples with neither missionary outreach nor indigenous churches	1,200

How does this compare to other estimates?

1. The famous 17,000 unreached people groups out of a total of 24,000 used by Ralph Winter has been a rallying cry for 13 years. I see it as a conceptual total based on theoretical assumptions which now needs updating and refining in the light of the more complete data becoming available. It can only be justified if all dialects, castes, etc. are included. To me, this makes the church planting task unnecessarily complex—let us not assume this addition until more detailed research obliges us to do so!

2. David Barrett's peoples database already had nearly 11,000 entries when I last heard. His cut-off points are higher than mine in large countries—possibly explaining some of the minor discrepancies with my world total.

3. Bob Waymire's (Global Mapping Project) total of 11,600 is very close to mine—but we have shared much of the definitions and data we use.

I therefore believe that the figure of 12,000 peoples is within 1,000 of the final total of peoples for which specific cross-cultural discipling in our generation may be required or already minimally achieved. This is a measurable, achievable goal—let's go for it, even by 2000 A.D.!

10. *Does Johnstone's figure of about 12,000 groups needing cross-cultural evangelization seem reasonable? Why or why not?*

_____

_____

_____

There are unreached peoples all around us. We find them in ethnic and social enclaves in cities and in the isolated countryside. These people have been "hidden" from the gospel because the church has not known about them or perhaps has not wanted to look for them. The church has often assumed that, as long as she keeps her doors open, it is the unreached who are at fault if they don't choose to walk through those doors. The "stained glass" barrier is a very real one, and it will continue to prevent the evangelization of these peoples unless the church is cured of her "peoples blindness" and takes the initiative to "*go*... and make disciples of all nations."

That Everyone May Hear

With thousands of unreached peoples left to hear, how do we go about defining the task? Ed Dayton has given a great deal of effort to helping Christians understand how the task can be managed.

❏ *The Task at Hand: World Evangelization* *

Edward R. Dayton

How do we think about evangelizing the entire world? Somehow that seems like too big a responsibility in a world that every day grows more complex, a world torn by disasters, political upheaval, and starving people.

How do you even think about a world like that?

The countries of the world

One way to think about it is in terms of the world's countries. While these countries are geographical locations, we are not really talking about the nations that the Bible describes; rather, we are talking about geographical territories that break up language groups and cultures. For example, the Kurdish nation is located in Iran, Iraq, Turkey, and the U.S.S.R. There is not a country called Kurdistan, but there is a nation that God desires to be with Him filled with Kurds.

In 1990 the United Nations said there were over 250 countries in the world. They come in all sizes. They range from an estimated 1 billion people in China, down to only 3,500 people in Niue, South Pacific. That tremendous variation shows the difficulty of talking about world evangelization in terms of countries. It is one thing to evangelize Niue; it is quite another to reach the 1 billion people of China.

11. Why is it difficult to conceive of world evangelization in terms of countries?

_____

_____

_____

The religions of the world

Another way to think about the world is in terms of its religions. Figure 7-6 shows the approximate distribution of the peoples of the world by different religions in 1990.

Those who acknowledge Jesus Christ number approximately 1.7 billion people. (This number includes many individuals who are Christians in name only, going to church once a year and never really knowing Christ.)

The second largest religion in the world is Islam, with an estimated 935 million Muslims. With the majority in India, there are some 705 million Hindus found all over the world.

_____

* Dayton, E. R. (1990). *That everyone may hear: Reaching the unreached.* Monrovia, CA: Missions Advanced Research & Communication Center.

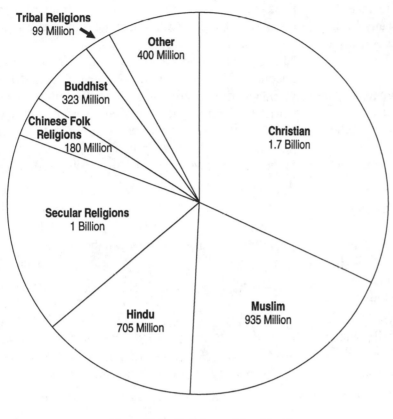

Figure 7-6. Religions of the World

"Secular religions" (such as Marxism, Communism, humanism, agnosticism, and atheism) include approximately 1 billion people. Chinese folk religionists are estimated to number 180 million. There are 323 million Buddhists (mostly in Japan, Thailand, Tibet, and Myanmar, formerly Burma) and 99 million tribal religionists (mostly in the South Pacific) who worship nature or the spirit world. All the other religions of the world make up the balance.

It is not so important how accurate any of these numbers are. In terms of proportions and magnitude, they are accurate enough to give us a picture of the challenge that approximately 68 percent of the world's people do not acknowledge Jesus Christ as the Lord. But it is obvious that, though this breakdown helps us, it still does not give us the basis for a workable strategy for reaching the world.

---

12. *What is useful about thinking of world evangelization in terms of other religions?*

_____

_____

_____

Three major tasks

Fulfilling Christ's Commission involves three major tasks for the Church today. They vary in complexity and difficulty. But all three are tremendously important:

1. First, we need to evangelize the millions of nominal Christians we have included in the "1.7 billion Christians." There are people all over the world, particularly in Western countries, who have been baptized and have joined a local church but have little understanding of the saving power of Jesus Christ, and even less of what it means to serve Him.

2. Second, we need to evangelize the 1 billion non-Christians with whom we are in immediate contact. We need to find ways to share with our non-Christian friends and neighbors the gracious love of their Heavenly Father and His desire to make them citizens of His kingdom.

3. Third, we need to discover the more than 2.2 billion people who are unreached by any Christian witness and to develop strategies for reaching them. This is the major task of the Church. Today less than 10 percent of all missionaries are attempting to reach these 2.2 billion people. To put it another way, we need to see churches planted among these 2.2 billion people, churches which can then get on with the responsibility of evangelizing people who speak the same language, people "just like them."

The challenge of unreached peoples

Of the approximately 3.6 billion people who are not Christians, only a little over 1 billion live within cultures where there are Christians who know Jesus and who can share His love. To put that another way, no matter how earnest all the local churches in the world are in reaching out to their near neighbors (people like them), only one-third of the non-Chris-

tians in the world can be reached by Christians who speak their language and understand their culture.

The other people of the world are not only unchurched, they are living in places around the world where there are no Christians to communicate Christ to them in their own language or culture. They live their lives every day without knowing or hearing about Christ, without any effective witness to the saving power of Jesus Christ. We need to say it over and over:

How, then, can they call on the one they have not believed in? And how can they believe in the one of whom they have not heard? And how can they hear without someone preaching to them? And how can they preach unless they are sent? As it is written, "How beautiful are the feet of those who bring good news!" (Rom. 10:14-15)

13. How does Dayton's "three task" categorization help us make decisions on how best to allocate workers in the field?

_____

_____

_____

How do you evangelize the world?

God is in the business of redeeming the world. This is His business. Our responsibility is to become involved with Him in carrying out His good purposes for the world.

One way of thinking about reaching the world is *one people group at a time*. Not one country at a time, because countries vary so much. India, with its over 853 million people, has 15 official languages and thousands of castes, tribes, and other social groups.

Certainly, reaching India is quite a different responsibility from reaching Niue with its 3,500 people.

Not one religion at a time. Not only are most of the major religions of the world huge in numbers of adherents, but they are also spread out through many different people groups. There are more Buddhists in the world today than the total population of the world at the time of Christ!

The term "people group" is a contemporary term for the biblical concept of "nation." Dayton's analysis points us back to the scriptural "all nations" mandate and allows us to see that the task, while huge in scope, has its bite size components. By thinking of the remaining task in terms of individual people groups, we are encouraged to believe that they can be won, one by one.

The 10/40 Window

Another mission strategist providing valuable insights into the remaining task is Luis Bush. At the second Lausanne Congress on World Evangelization (Manila, 1989), Bush, citing research also done by David Barrett and George Otis, Jr.,* drew attention to the fact that the majority of unreached peoples live in a geographical region identified as "the 10/40 window." Falling between 10 degrees and 40 degrees north latitude and stretching from North Africa and southern Spain to Japan and the northern Philippine islands, this window contains the vast majority of the world's unreached peoples.

❑ *The 10/40 Window: Getting to the Core of the Core* **

Luis Bush ***

The core of the unreached people of our world live in a rectangular-shaped window! Often called "The Resistant Belt," the window extends from West Africa to East Asia, from 10 degrees north to 40 degrees north of the equator. This specific region, which has increasingly become known as The 10/40 Window, encompasses the majority of the world's Muslims, Hindus, and Buddhists—billions of spiritually impoverished souls.

As we approach the end of this millennium, it is imperative that our evangelistic efforts be focused among the people who inhabit The 10/40 Window. If we are serious in our commitment to provide a valid opportunity for every person to experience the truth and saving power of Jesus Christ, we cannot ignore the compelling realities within this region.

The 10/40 Window confronts us with several important considerations: first, the historical and biblical significance; second, the least evangelized countries; third, the dominance of three religious blocs; fourth, the preponderance of the poor; fifth, the unreached ethno-linguistic people groups; sixth, the least evangelized megacities; and, seventh, the strongholds of Satan within The 10/40 Window.

The first and most fundamental reason why committed Christians must focus on The 10/40 Window is because of the biblical and historical significance of this area. Indeed, the Bible begins with the account of Adam and Eve placed by God in the heart of what is now The 10/40 Window. God's plan, expressed in Genesis 1:26, was that mankind should have dominion over the earth, subduing it fully. However, Adam and Eve sinned against God and forfeited their right to rule. Man's sinful behavior increased until God intervened and judged the earth with a cataclysmic flood. Then came man's futile attempt to establish new dominion in the building of the great Tower of Babel. That effort, which also occurred in the heart of The 10/40 Window, was an open defiance against God. Once again, God reached forth His hand in judgment. The result was the introduction of different languages, the scattering of earth's people, and the formation of the nations.

---

* David Barrett is the world's foremost authority on Christian demographics and is the author of the *World Christian Encyclopedia,* Oxford University Press. George Otis, Jr., has authored a book on the 10/40 window entitled *The Last of the Giants.*

** Bush, L. (n.d.). *The 10/40 window: Getting to the core of the core.* Colorado Springs, CO: AD 2000 and Beyond Movement.

*** Luis Bush, a citizen of Argentina, is the International Director of the AD 2000 and Beyond Movement. He was formerly the International President of Partners International. In 1987, he served as Director of COMIBAM, a continent-wide congress on world missions held in São Paulo, Brazil.

COUNTRIES IN THE 10/40 WINDOW

Afghanistan	Djibouti	Iran	Macau	Portugal	Turkmenistan
Algeria	Egypt	Iraq	Mali	Qatar	United Arab
Bahrain	Ethiopia	Israel	Malta	Saudi Arabia	Emirates
Bangladesh	Gambia	Japan	Mauritania	Senegal	Vietnam
Benin	Gaza Strip	Jordan	Morocco	Sudan	West Bank
Bhutan	Gibraltar	Korea, North	Myanmar	Syria	Western
Burkina Faso	Greece	Korea, South	Nepal	Taiwan	Sahara
Cambodia	Guinea	Kuwait	Niger	Tajikistan	Yemen
Chad	Guinea-Bissau	Laos	Oman	Thailand	
China	Hong Kong	Lebanon	Pakistan	Tunisia	
Cyprus	India	Libya	Philippines	Turkey	

Figure 7-7

In The 10/40 Window we can see clearly the crucial truth expressed in Graham Scroggie's book, *The Drama of World Redemption*: "A world having turned from God, He left it and chose a man through whom He would ultimately by Christ reach the world." Certainly we can see how ancient history ran its course in the territory marked by The 10/40 Window, from the cradle of civilization in Mesopotamia across the Fertile Crescent to Egypt. Empires rose and fell. The fate of God's people Israel varied in relation to their obedience to His covenant. It was here that Christ was born, lived a perfect life, died sacrificially on the cross, and rose triumphant over death. The church age was ushered in, and it was not until the second missionary journey of the Apostle Paul that events of biblical history occurred outside The 10/40 Window. Without question, this is an area of great biblical and historical significance.

14. *What biblical significance does Bush attach to the 10/40 window?*

_____

_____

_____

The second reason why committed Christians should focus on The 10/40 Window is because it is home to the majority of the world's unevangelized people. The "unevangelized" are people who have a minimal knowledge of the gospel, but have had no valid opportunity to respond to it.

While it constitutes only one-third of earth's total land area, nearly two-thirds of the world's people reside in The 10/40 Window. With a total population nearing 4 billion, The 10/40 Window includes 61 countries, both sovereign states and non-sovereign dependencies. Those countries with the majority of their land mass lying within the boundaries of The 10/40 Window are included.

Of the world's 50 least evangelized countries, 37 are within The 10/40 Window. Yet those 37 countries comprise 97 percent of the total population of the 50 least evangelized countries! Such a fact leaves no doubt that our challenge in reaching the unreached must center on the core—The 10/40 Window.

If we take seriously the mandate to preach the gospel to every person, to make disciples of all peoples, and to be Christ's witnesses to the uttermost part of the earth, we must recognize the priority of concentrating our efforts on The 10/40 Window. No other area is so blatantly in need of the truth that salvation is only in Jesus Christ.

15. *Why is the 10/40 window significant if we are thinking in terms of completing the Great Commission task?*

_____

_____

_____

A third reason we must focus on The 10/40 Window is evident in the fact that it contains three of the world's dominant religious blocs. The majority of those enslaved by Islam, Hinduism, and Buddhism live within The 10/40 Window.

In Figure 7-8, the Muslim world can be seen most prominently stretching in a wide band across the north of Africa into the Middle East, a bloc representing over 700 million persons. In the middle of the map, overshadowing the subcontinent of India, is the presence of Hinduism, also constituting a population of more than 700 million. On the right side of the map is the Buddhist world, encompassing the whole of China.

From its center in The 10/40 Window, Islam is reaching out energetically to all parts of the globe; in similar strategy, we must penetrate the heart of Islam with the liberating truth of the gospel. We must do all in our power to show Muslims that the highest prophet described in the Koran is not Mohammed, but Jesus Christ. And that He is not only the greatest prophet, but the Son of God Himself who died and resurrected in order that millions of Muslims may be saved.

Overwhelmed with poverty and ravaged by disease, India is victimized even more severely by the spiritual blindness of Hinduism. To a nation in which fattened cows roam freely among emaciated humans, we must proclaim the truth that Jesus came to give us life, and give it abundantly.

Although officially an atheistic country since the Marxist revolution of the late 1940s, China is nevertheless influenced deeply by its Buddhist roots. Some scholars, in fact, consider China's true religion to be a combination of atheism and Buddhism. In actuality, religion in China is a hodgepodge which includes folklore, mysticism, animism, and occult practices. Regardless of how one may assess the situation, the fact remains that 1.2 billion Chinese are in desperate need of Jesus Christ. They represent the largest identifiable bloc within The 10/40 Window.

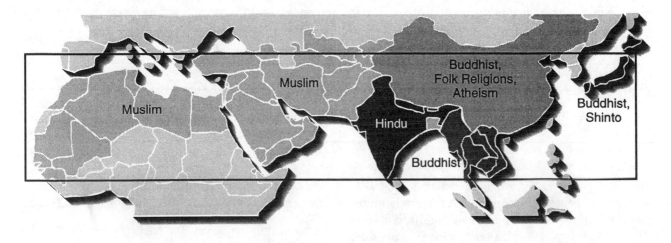

Figure 7-8. Religions Within the 10/40 Window

16. *In what ways is the predominance of other world religions in the 10/40 window significant to the missionary task?*

_____

_____

_____

A fourth reason we must focus on The 10/40 Window is because the poor are there. Of the poorest of the poor, more than eight out of 10 live in The 10/40 Window. On average, they exist on less than $500 per person per year. Although 2.4 billion of these people live within The 10/40 Window, only 8 percent of all missionaries work among them.

Bryant L. Myers, in his perceptive article entitled, "Where Are the Poor and Lost?" states that "the poor are the lost, and the lost are the poor." He arrived at this conclusion after illustrating that the majority of the unreached live in the poorest countries of the world.

When Christians from 170 countries gathered at Lausanne II in Manila in 1989, great concern was expressed for the materially poor. In the second section of the Manila Manifesto, that concern was recorded in the following declaration: "We have again been confronted with Luke's emphasis that the gospel is the good news for the poor (Luke 4:18; 6:20; 7:22) and have asked ourselves what this means to the majority of the world's population who are destitute, suffering, and oppressed. We have been reminded that the law, the prophets, the wisdom books, and the teaching and ministry of Jesus all stress God's concern for the materially poor and our consequent duty to defend and care for them."

Committed Christians cannot ignore the reality that there is a remarkable overlap between the poorest countries of the world and those which are the least evangelized.

The fifth reason we must address our concerns on The 10/40 Window is because it contains the largest spiritually bankrupt ethno-linguistic megapeoples (over 1 million). In fact, over 90 percent of the individuals in these people groups live in The 10/40 Window.

17. *How will the staggering poverty and quality of life indicators in the 10/40 window affect evangelistic efforts? What do you see the relation to be between poverty and lostness?*

_____

_____

_____

_____

_____

The sixth major reason we must focus on The 10/40 Window is because it contains the overwhelming majority of the world's least evangelized megacities—that is, those with a population of more than 1 million. Of the top 50 cities on this list, all 50 are in The 10/40 Window! This fact alone underscores the need for prioritizing our efforts to reach each of these great metroplexes with Christ's love and truth.

Reason number seven for focusing on The 10/40 Window is that it includes numerous strongholds of Satan. The billions of people who live in The 10/40

Window have suffered not only the ravages of poverty and disease, they have also been kept from the transforming power of the gospel. They are poignant examples of the truth expressed in 2 Corinthians 4:4, which states that "the god of this age has blinded the minds of unbelievers, so that they cannot see the light of the gospel of the glory of Christ, who is the image of God."

We must not view this situation with a fatalistic attitude, for we have been granted power to intervene. In a later passage of the same letter, the Apostle Paul declares: "For though we live in the world, we do not wage war as the world does. The weapons we fight with are not weapons of the world. On the contrary, they have divine power to demolish strongholds" (2 Cor. 10:3-4). Although Satan has established a territorial stronghold in The 10/40 Window, we must not concede one parcel of land nor one person. The gospel must advance!

Looking back across the pages of history, we discover a heartening story about spiritual warfare in the writings of the prophet Daniel. A fervent man of prayer, Daniel was highly esteemed by God and by the people of his generation. On one occasion, while waiting on God in prayer, Daniel fasted on bread and water for three weeks. Finally, a majestic angel whose appearance was as lightning brought an answer to his prayer. He assured Daniel with the promise that "… your words were heard, and I have come in response to your words" (Dan. 10:12). However, the angel then went on to explain how, en route to answer Daniel's prayer, he was detained for 21 days by the demon assigned to the Persian king (Dan. 10:13). It was only when the archangel

Michael arrived to help that he was able to free himself from the battle to go to Daniel.

This fascinating passage unveils the reality and territorial nature of the spiritual battle in the heavenlies. The angel who visited Daniel announced that he would have to return to the battle over the Persian kingdom. Apparently, that battle still rages, for ancient Persia is now modern-day Iran. Still a stronghold zealously held by Satan, Iran is situated at the center of The 10/40 Window.

If we are to storm the enemy's territory, we must put on the full armor of God and fight with the weapons of spiritual warfare described in Ephesians 6.

George Otis, Jr., has concluded that two powerful demonic forces, with great biblical significance, stand at the epicenter of the unreached world—the prince of Persia (Iran) and the spirit of Babylon (Iraq)—and both must be penetrated with the gospel before the Great Commission can be completed. Otis observes that this will occur in the region of the Garden of Eden, where the command to "subdue the earth" was originally given.

It is evident that the forces of Satan have great power and will resist all attempts to be overcome. If we are to storm the enemy's territory, we must put on the full armor of God and fight with the weapons of spiritual warfare described in Ephesians 6. To depend on anything less is utter foolishness.

18. *The six previous "realities" about the 10/40 window add up to one salient fact: it is the center of Satanic control and oppression. How does this fact affect our approach to evangelization of the unreached peoples of this region?*

The leaders of the AD 2000 Movement are in full agreement that our greatest challenge in the final years of this century is to provide a valid opportunity for every people, every city, every person to experience the truth and saving power of Jesus Christ. The goal of the AD 2000 and Beyond Movement is a church for every people and the gospel for every person by the year 2000.

The focus of the concerned Christian community 200 years ago was for the coastlands of the world. A century later, the success of the coastlands effort motivated a new generation to reach the interior regions of the continents. Within the past decades, the success of the inland thrust has led to a major focus on people groups. More recently, the world's burgeoning megacities have also become focal points of concern. Today, rapidly approaching the third millennium since Christ, we are wise to concentrate our efforts on The 10/40 Window.

Of course, this calls for some of us to reevaluate priorities. We must find the most innovative ways to reach the billions of people within The 10/40 Window with the love and truth of Jesus Christ. We must mobilize for a massive prayer focus on The 10/40 Window with the body of Christ worldwide.

However, it must be clearly understood that concentration on The 10/40 Window does not mean a curtailing of Christ's work going on elsewhere around the globe. Missionary endeavors in evangelism, training, relief, development, church planting, and mobilization for cross-cultural missions should go on unhindered.

If we are faithful to the Scriptures, obedient to the mandate of Christ, and unwavering in our commitment to plant churches within every people and city by A.D. 2000, then we will get to the core of the core—The 10/40 Window. May God grant each of us boldness and wisdom and energy to do our part in taking on this great and eternally significant challenge.

19. *Unlike Ralph Winter, who affirms unequivocably that we are in the third and last era of mission history, Bush suggests that the 10/40 window may be the challenge of a fourth era in world evangelization. Do you agree with this premise? Why or why not?*

_____

_____

_____

_____

_____

_____

III. Major Blocs of Unreached Peoples

Unreached or "hidden" peoples in need of cross-cultural evangelization can be found all over the world, perhaps even in your own neighborhood. Nevertheless, the vast majority of the unreached live in the 10/40 window and can be classified into five "megaspheres." These large, culturally defined groupings each contain hundreds of millions of peoples: Muslims, Chinese, Hindus, tribals, and Buddhists. In this section, we begin to gain an understanding of who these people are and the current state of their evangelization. For this purpose, we excerpt appropriate sections from Ralph Winter's and David Fraser's "World Mission Survey."

❑ *World Mission Survey* *

Ralph D. Winter and David A. Fraser

"Muslims for Jesus" strategy explored

Imagine you're a geographer. But in the world in which you live continents move several miles a year. Earthquakes weekly thrust up new islands or level mountain ranges. Lakes vanish overnight, their waters gulped by thirsty cracks in the earth.

What headaches in trying to draw a map! Every year the atlases and textbooks would have to be rewritten and relearned. A place known to be located at one point this year would have to be repositioned next year because of how much it had moved.

Such is the Muslim world. Not just because of the Gulf War. That brief war merely gives us a clue to what has massively modified the dynamics of the entire Middle East: oil. Titanic changes are affecting everything we thought we once knew about Islam's nearly one billion people. It is no longer the world Samuel Zwemer tried to reach with the good news. What used to be major features of its landscape are being transformed overnight. New maps must be drawn if the Christian is to discover passable highways to use in carrying the gospel to responsive Muslim peoples.

Muslims are on the move. While there are 42 countries with Muslim majorities, 40 other countries contain significant minorities. Petro-migration is thrusting Muslims out of traditional isolation. Six million reside in Western Europe. The U.S.A. boasts a dozen cities with more than 50,000 Muslims (and more than 70 Muslim sects competing for allegiance)! $15 million was spent on a mosque in Chicago. Yet the largest populations of Muslims are not found in oil-rich countries or the West but in Indonesia, Pakistan, Bangladesh, India, the People's Republic of China, and Turkey.

More Christians are flooding into the heartlands of Islam around Mecca than ever before. Professionals, technicians, and skilled laborers are being imported

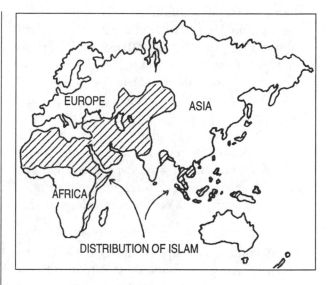

Figure 7-9. The Distribution of Islam

from dozens of countries to modernize sheikdoms and help the deserts bloom. Fifty thousand Arab Christians are employed in Saudi Arabia. Thirteen thousand foreign Christians work in Qatar. Foreigners outnumber the citizens in the United Arab Emirates (240,000 to 225,000), and no one has counted how many Christians there are among these Western technicians. Modernization is revolutionizing the atmosphere and opportunity for Christian-Muslim relationships.

There is a creeping optimism emerging in Christian circles. The long glacial age that began with the Christian Crusades in the Middle Ages appears to be thawing as traditionally icy attitudes towards Christianity seem to be melting. Not that there aren't places where Muslim conversion is met with death or where there are purgatories of hatred, such as Lebanon, with Christian and Muslim struggling in a death grip. But there are signs of new receptivity to the gospel. And promising developments are appearing on the horizon:

* Winter, R. D., & Fraser, D. A. (1992). World mission survey. In R. D. Winter & S. C. Hawthorne (Eds.), *Perspectives on the world Christian movement: A reader* (rev. ed.) (pp. B198-B210). Pasadena: William Carey Library.

1. The Ancient Christian Churches in Muslim lands (17 million members in the Middle East and Northern Africa) are being shown that they can break out of their ethnic and cultural defensiveness and win Muslims to Jesus. The Orthodox Egyptian Coptic Church has been undergoing a steady, massive revival for the past 30 years, and now it is resulting in 30 to 40 baptisms of Muslim converts a week. But this is still the exception rather than the rule. Centuries of turmoil and battering have made the ancient churches generally ingrown enclaves, whose cultural difference from the Islamic community is so great that it is almost impossible for a Muslim convert to join them without betraying his own cultural heritage or without remaining a "foreigner" to the Christian community with centuries of cultural divergence.

2. Cross-cultural ministry is finding explosive response where greater cultural sensitivity is being used in evangelistic approaches. The enrollment in one non-Arab country correspondence course added 3,900 Muslims in the first six months. A high percentage continued on to completion and advanced courses. Significant numbers evidenced new-found faith in letters and testimonies. Yet the Church is barely exploiting the tremendous opportunity of the Muslim world. There are about 500 North American Protestant missionaries engaged in Muslim evangelization, a bare 1 percent of the missionary force for 25 percent of the world's unreached population.

3. Secret believers and Christian sympathizers have multiplied. Muslim followers of Jesus still hesitate to take any step such as public baptism since it would send all kinds of wrong signals to their own people. Islam has formidable social and economic barriers for anyone leaving its fold. Apostasy is the supreme betrayal. Yet there are thousands secretly believing in Jesus who long for some new, creative form of Christian movement that would not appear to be treason to their own people and blasphemy to God.

4. New strategies are being explored to see if a "Muslims for Jesus" movement could not be a viable reality in a manner similar to the "Jews for Jesus" movement. Just as the Apostle Paul suggested that he be a Greek to the Greeks and a Jew to the Jews, so such principles might suggest being a Muslim to the Muslims. Some evangelical evangelists to Islam are saying that Muslims might truly become believers in Jesus Christ as Savior and Lord without calling themselves Christian, even as the "Messianic Jews" did. In some situations what may be needed is the encouragement of new Christian congregations with a Muslim cultural orientation, churches centered on Jesus Christ but with Islamic cultural forms, where, in fact, the word "Christian" is not even employed.

5. The old malaise and paralysis characteristic of Christian attitudes toward Muslim evangelization seems to be vanishing. Quiet conferences and consultations are forging new concepts and organizations. Hundreds of turned-on mission candidates ought to reconsider the enormous gap between the opportunity and the actual staffing of culturally sensitive approaches to Muslims. The believing followers of Christ are now at the very edge of what could be the most significant advance in reaching unreached Muslims in history—especially if we don't think we have to make them into "Christians" any more than Paul felt he had to make Greeks into Jews. In several places around the world there are movements running into the thousands which consist of blood-washed followers of Christ, whose Koran is now the Christian's Bible, but who do not refer to themselves as Christians.

We are at the edge of what could be the most significant advance in reaching unreached Muslims in history.

---

6. Some scholars feel that illuminating parallels can be drawn between the major cultural streams flowing out of the incarnation, death, and resurrection of Jesus Christ: Islam being an Arabic movement, but then there are the cultural synergies of Russian Orthodoxy, Greek Orthodoxy, Ethiopian Orthodoxy, Eastern-Rite Roman Catholicism, Latin-Rite Roman Catholicism, German Lutheranism, English Anglicanism, the variety of American sects. As well, thousands of even more strange cultural traditions have

evolved among the mission field believers of the world.

In each case, the gospel has put on "native" dress. The pre-Christian English sunrise service in honor of their spring goddess of fertility, named Eostre, is now our Easter service (which benefits only if we keep our minds and hearts on the biblical meaning assigned to it).

The pagan Roman practice of giving and receiving gifts on the 25th of December caught on in Latin-speaking countries but not in the Greek and Russian speaking countries, understandably. But the Christian adaptation of this pagan holiday, although the same day of the year, does not say anything about the meaning of Saturn, after which this day in the Roman pagan calendar was named (the Saturnalia).

The Assyrian Church of the East (hundreds of thousands of these Christians live in Iraq) had an interesting custom of praying seven times a day. It was borrowed by Mohammed for Islam (but he cut it down to five times a day so as to avoid awaking believers in the dead of night).

Even the Christian Syriac and Arabic word, Allah, which Christians had been using for God for centuries was adopted by Mohammed for Islam. It is still the word for God in the Christian Bibles in those languages.

20. From this brief review of Muslim evangelization, summarize the thrust of the most successful strategies for provoking larger movements of Muslims to Christ.

_____

_____

_____

_____

Bethlehem's star over China

The attics of Western memory are stuffed with an incredible array of pictures of China: weather-beaten junks, pagodas with upturned eaves on mist-enshrouded mounts, Dr. Fu Manchu, firecrackers and gaudy dragons, Kung Fu, Stillwell and Chiang Kai Shek, missionary graves, hordes of fanatics waving little Red Books. China has been one of the great obsessions of the West.

And well she might be! The major tides of history indicate that a major wave of the future may be from China. Across the centuries she has been weak only to have the tide of affairs reverse and carry her back to preeminence as the most advanced, powerful, albeit isolated nation on the face of the earth, a position she has held more often and longer than any other society. Christianity will have to sail that tide if she is to be part of China's future.

The church contemplates her more than a billion citizens as the largest single unified bloc of humanity, one which has a very widespread Christian element. At the height of missionary activity in Mainland China, nearly 10,000 Catholic and Protestant missionaries were active. When the Communists took over in 1949, one tangible result of a century and a half of effort was a formal Christian community of 3.2 million Catholics and 1.8 million Protestants, a bare 1 percent of the whole of China.

The Christian movement under the People's Republic has experienced a radical change and some shrinkage due to the loss of nominal members, some martyrdom, and minor migration. The pressures of successive waves of repression interspersed with brief periods of toleration for many years robbed the church of its more visible organized expressions.

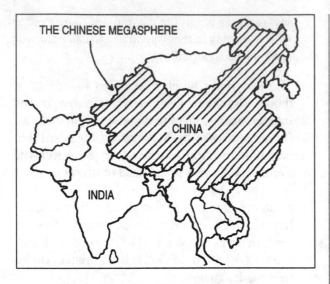

Figure 7-10. The Chinese Megasphere

"Institutionless" Christianity is what began expanding at an astounding rate. The Communists tried to rid China once and for all of Christians during the dread 10-year "Cultural Revolution," but only succeeded in refining and spreading the faith. Due to many factors, the government began to allow certain buildings to reopen as "official" churches, where the government could monitor events. One hundred were allowed. They were immediately but unexpectedly packed. Then, a few more, and more, and soon it was over 6,000 "official" churches. No one can hazard a guess at the church's real size, though one frequent figure quoted is that there may be more than 50 million believers and more than 50,000 "house" churches. The latter are without full-time clergy, denominational structure, church buildings, budgets, or seminaries. Their meetings are informal and semi-clandestine.

Some have held out hope that this scattered church under pressure will repeat the story of the early church, gradually leavening the whole of China. And the church is experiencing some growth through healings and exorcism, moving along the latticework of family relationships with which a Chinese screens himself in a hostile world.

Restrictions continue to be stringent so that open proclamation is forbidden. Those who believe missionaries or Chinese evangelists as such will soon enter the People's Republic cannot easily conclude this from current events in 1992. Millions of people go in and out of China each year but not openly as evangelists or Christian witnesses.

Radio waves do reach behind the Bamboo Curtain. Government presses actually print Bibles—perhaps due to outside pressures and the sheer economic profit from the world's most sought book. There are reports of greater Christian freedom and activity in southeast China and conversions in areas such as northern Thailand where crossing the border is possible. Despite the tightening following the Tienanmen Square incident, there is nothing so sure, so extensive, so durable, as Christianity in China.

Outside Mainland China the picture is even more hopeful. Overall 5 to 7 percent of some 40 million profess faith in Christ. Of course there are striking variations. In some cases there is burgeoning growth. Six hundred churches serve the one of eight in Hong Kong who follow Christ. Taiwan's AD 2000 Movement committee, the first to unite all of Taiwan's Protestants, has determined to go from 2,000 churches to 10,000 by the year 2000. About 10 percent of the 600,000 Chinese in the U.S.A. are Protestant or Catholic. In other instances the Christian presence has only begun to penetrate Chinese populations. Thailand's 3.6 million Chinese have only a tiny church among them with only 4,000 Protestants. Restaurant workers in Europe, such as those in the 50 Chinese restaurants of Vienna, are virtually without a Christian fellowship.

More importantly, there are indications that the Chinese church is taking major strides as a maturing body. Rapid and soaring increases are reported in many of the 70 countries with significant Chinese minorities. With that growth has come a new awareness of world mission. From Chinese churches and sending agencies there are now over 300 Chinese missionaries throughout the world. The majority of them, however, are not in cross-cultural ministry but are serving Chinese churches.

It may well be that this new movement of God's Spirit will equip the Christians of the diaspora for an as yet unforeseen opportunity to reach into Mainland China sometime in the near future, but it may also be that when that day comes, as in the case of the opening of the U.S.S.R., it will be a two-way street, as the believers whose faith has endured hardship become a blessing to those outside of their former prisons.

If the door to China were to open next year, what would happen? Many American-born Chinese Christians no longer speak any Chinese dialects. To evangelize in traditional fashion would require a relearning of their roots, their languages and cultures. English-speaking Chinese would be in real demand to again enter their homeland and through language teaching be ambassadors for Christ. Other parts of the Chinese diaspora are similar. Seventy percent of Indonesia's 3.6 million Chinese are Indonesian born. They speak Indonesian and live like Indonesians.

It is clear that China now contains one of the world's largest numbers of devout, praying Christians. Probably no people group, unreached or not, is very far removed, culturally, from another Chinese group within which the gospel is now strong.

21. *Keeping in mind the factor of cultural distance, who is most likely to evangelize the unreached peoples of China? Why?*

Any hope, India?

Remember "Wrong Way Corrigan"? He took off in a small plane from the New York airport and flew across the Atlantic in the repetition of Lindbergh's feat. He had filed a legal flight pattern to some nearby spot in the U.S. and then calmly flew across the Atlantic, pretending he had gone the wrong way. "They let Lindbergh do it. Why not me?"

God played a trick something like that with William Carey, that brilliant young rural schoolteacher in England in the late 1700s. He had plotted and planned for years to go to those islands in the Pacific newly discovered by Captain Cook. (Those islands today are 75 percent Christian in at least nominal church membership.) He landed instead in India, which is still 97 percent non-Christian. God had the best idea because East India is the closest thing to a crossroads of the world's great blocs of non-Christians—Chinese, Hindus, and Muslims. Hindus alone are over 750 million in 1992 and are mainly in India, that amazing country.

Why is India so amazing? Although smaller in size than Argentina, it has 25 times the population (more than the whole world in the days of Columbus), plus 800 distinct languages and dialects, and the world's largest democracy. It is the largest non-Christian country that is at all open to the gospel.

India is also amazing to even exist as a functioning nation. When the British were forced out in 1947, and literally millions were killed in the bloodshed that later separated Pakistan from a reduced India, many despaired that India could ever pull itself together and survive. Yet today India is in many ways doing magnificently. Only 25 percent literate, it nevertheless has 50 times as many radios as it did at independence and for many years has boasted the world's largest motion picture industry.

India is the largest non-Christian country that is at all open to the gospel.

What staggers the imagination is the human diversity of India. Most countries are stratified with layers of people ranging from the downtrodden to the aristocracy. But India is not merely vertically stratified by the world's most rigidly defined social caste system, it is also horizontally cut up due to the linguistic and racial differences that chop India into at least a thousand pieces. Nowhere in the world are cultural differences more difficult to ignore. The most astonishing thing of all is that the Christian church of India has valiantly tried to ignore those

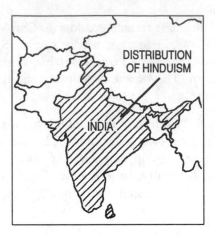

Figure 7-11.
The Distribution of Hinduism

distinctions. The church lives outside the caste system but almost entirely on the bottom level of society. Therefore, most Indians who join a Christian church must virtually part ways, downward from all their social and family relationships. Instead of determinedly taking the gospel into the thousands of social compartments of India, the prevailing strategy, insofar as there is one, at the grass roots level is to tear down the social fabric, not just the prejudices embodied therein.

Some estimates indicate that about 100 million Hindus would become Christians tomorrow if someone would take the necessary pains to establish a believing fellowship within their own social grouping.

Thus the Church of South India braved all prejudices by sending a lower class bishop to an upper class segment of their church in Kerala, thereby tweaking the nose of the caste system in India. This is all right for a bishop at his level, but the practical requirements of evangelism at the grass roots level of local churches are something else. This is a very delicate subject since at first glance there seems to be a collision between the demands of Christian unity and the freedoms of Christian liberty.

But do Hindus want to become Christians, if they are *not* forced to join a different caste? Some esti-

mates indicate that about 100 million Hindus—people who have been in contact with Christians of other castes for many years—would become Christians tomorrow if someone would take the necessary pains to establish a believing fellowship within their own social grouping. Isn't that a fantastic challenge?

What, pray tell, are missionaries and Indian Christians doing if they are not trying to penetrate one by one the thousands of subcultures of India? The answer is, they are doing other things. Aren't they evangelizing at all? Wouldn't it be great if the 25 million Christians in India would get out there and really evangelize? Yes, certainly, but two-thirds of the Christians in India need themselves to be evangelized, just as is true in America today. The real shocker is that according to one study 98 percent of the evangelism in India is devoted to rewinning nominal Christians rather than to penetrating the frontiers that effectively wall off 500 million people.

One of the great marvels of history is the impact of missions on the course of India. While less than 3 percent of the population is Christian, over half of all the nurses are Christian (it was once 90 percent); 600 hospitals are there because of missions, and thousands of schools of all kinds. Hinduism itself has significantly changed. The subtle impact of the missionary movement is a story that may never fully be told. Missionaries introduced not just hospitals and schools, but invented khaki colored clothing (it wouldn't show the village dust) and a special and superior kind of tile roofing used now all over India. They brought an end to the custom of widow burning. And the fact that many states of India even today prohibit all liquor is mute testimony of an impact far larger than church statistics. In south India, where most of the Christians are to be found, their presence is felt strongly. In the states of northeast India, where 50 to 70 to 95 percent of the population of the mountain peoples are Christians, the transformation is even more spectacular—from being headhunters as late as 1934, now to being devout Christians, some with Ph.D.'s. The stories behind all of these achievements almost defy comparison for sheer excitement.

For many years it was rare when mission agencies sprouted from Indian soil itself. Now there is the

India Mission Association which includes over 60 different mission agencies, although many others also exist to make India one of the leading countries for "Two Thirds World" mission societies.

The Indian Missionary Society followed by the National Missionary Society and then the Indian Evangelical Mission and the Friends Missionary Prayer Band (in 1903, 1905, 1965, and 1968, respectively) were early examples of the simple fact that Indians who believe the gospel are willing and able to do both home and foreign mission work. Three of these four early societies determinedly refuse to accept any foreign funds (one was offered a million dollars of foreign money), feeling that the development of sacrificial outreach among their people is as important as the outreach itself. India's strict rules against sending currency out of the country may require collaboration with other countries in order for some opportunities to be grasped. But the Friends Missionary Prayer Band sends its missionaries from south India to north India where there are very few Christians. Indeed, north India contains by far the largest bloc of reachable non-Christians. Pioneer missionary techniques are by no means out of date where the world's largest presently reachable mission field is still to be found.

22. **What are the significant social and cultural barriers that will have to be overcome if Indians are to become Christian in great numbers?**

_____

_____

_____

Tribes: An endangered species

The race is on! Tribes are vanishing faster than we are succeeding in translating Scripture into their languages. Technology is leveling the tropics, immobilizing the nomads, dispossessing the weak, deculturizing the alien, and decimating the primitive. Tribes fall prey to epidemics, economic exploitation, modern weaponry, and nationalism. In Brazil alone an Indian population of 3 million in 1500 A.D. at the first European contact was reduced to 200,000 by 1968 and to 80,000 since then.

> *In many areas of the world the strongest, most aggressive churches are found among tribal peoples.*

Yet, in many areas of the world the strongest, most aggressive churches are found among tribal peoples. At present, even excluding Africa, thanks in part to the world's largest mission, the Wycliffe Bible Translators, there are at least 10,000 Protestant missionaries who focus on tribal peoples.

It is virtually impossible to generalize about over 3,000 cultural groups ranging from several million people to minuscule groups of a few dozen individuals. Living in every imaginable habitat, following a mind-boggling array of different customs, and experiencing radically different fates, tribal groups vividly express the range and complexity of the unfinished task. But there are several patterns that are apparent from a broad, sweeping overview.

Receptivity

In general, tribal groups are refugees, living in perpetual fear of aggression from other tribes or more powerful civilizations. Often they are able to survive by finding out how to live where no one else would want the land, in incredibly mountainous areas as in west Cameroon, or south China, or northeast India, or the precipitous highlands (or gigantic swamps of the coastlands) of the great island of New Guinea, the tiny atolls of the South Pacific, or the swamps and jungles of the upper Amazon.

This is one reason they have been the most highly responsive peoples to modern missions, more so than the more secure peasant peoples which constitute the great world religions of Islam, Buddhism, Hinduism, and Confucianism.

Also, tribal peoples, characterized by beliefs called "animism" (each group having its own distinctive religious system and worldview) have found conversion to Jesus Christ and His book easier than those who already have their own religious book and literary tradition. Tremendous successes can be illustrated in Oceania, where 70 to 90 percent are Christian; Burma, where 97 percent of all Burmese Christians are tribal; and northeast India, where among the tribal peoples the Nagas are now 70 percent Christian, the Garos and Khasis, 50 percent, and the Mizos, virtually 99 percent! Though the tribal population is only 7 percent of India, it represents 15 percent of all Christians in India.

But it must be admitted that within certain types of tribal peoples the Church has made little impact. Nomadic peoples have almost never been reached until and unless they became settled. Hunters and gatherers, like the Pygmies of Africa and the pastoral peoples who exploit the enormous arid belt running from Morocco to Manchuria, still are solidly outside the faith. Bedouins, shepherds, reindeer and cattle herders await a new creative strategy to give the gospel mobility and vitality for them.

Privilege

At least with the major segments of tribal peoples, the Western Church and mission agencies have had the greatest interest and heaviest involvement. Where there has been receptivity and success, further resources and personnel have followed. Papua New Guinea boasted 3,388 missionaries or one missionary for every 800 people. The harvest gathered there has been great: 80 percent of the population of some 500 tribes profess Christ! It does not seem unreasonable to mount a parallel commitment to the major blocs of unreached peoples, the Muslims, Hindus, Chinese, and Buddhists. While those blocs are incredibly larger in the number of individual human beings, if you are counting the number of

missionary breakthroughs that are necessary, it is fascinating to note that there are only three or four times as many to deal with because each breakthrough is into a much larger group.

Of course we are not advocating any lessening of commitment to tribal peoples. But who knows what the impact might be and how the numbers of churches might multiply if those other parts of God's vineyard were to receive equal attention and care?

Change

It is impossible to keep tribal peoples isolated and "safe" from modern society. For good and mostly for bad, the tribal groups are being transformed. Where the faith of Jesus Christ has been potent, it has eased the impact of the modern world. Missionaries have been among the most ardent defenders of the rights and dignity of the tribals. Their voices have been heard against multinational corporation land seizures, local hostilities, and governmental neglect. Missionaries have been in the forefront of those resisting making tribal peoples into jungle slum dwellers. Where whole tribes have become Christian, economic and educational uplift has been enormous. But new problems of survival and finding a place in the modern world system put even greater demands on mission agencies.

Opportunity

Evangelization remains a basic task in many areas. India's 35 million tribals, concentrated in the north central hills, need to be evangelized. Indian Christians in the south and the tribal Christians of the northeast are beginning the task, just as Navajo Christians are sending missionaries to the Laplanders and to Mongolia (where the people have a number of similar customs!). Reconversion is needed in regions where second and third generation "Christians" are growing up with no vital experience with Christ or where tribes have left their first love for a syncretistic revival of traditional religion. Economic and educational developments cry out with enormous needs, which evangelical missions are now more responsibly meeting.

23. *What strategic implications does this analysis of tribal evangelization have for those seeking to reach the unreached in this megasphere?*

_____

_____

_____

350 million Asians: Latent or blooming

First, there are those who live in "Christianized" areas such as the Philippines and Oceania. Overall 80 to 95 percent of these regions would nominally claim to be Christians. Here the dominant problem is the need to convert "Christians" to Christ. That is quite a different matter from converting peoples with no professed allegiance or knowledge to the Savior. Missionaries tackle the situation in large numbers; although the population of the Christianized areas makes up only 15 percent of the 350 million people, fully 50 percent of the Protestant missionaries in these countries, as in Latin America, are seeking to make active believers out of nominal Christians.

Second, there are those who live in areas where vigorous, dynamic Christian movements are thriving. This brings us to the first law of these peoples: Where Buddhism has prevailed, the gospel has languished. Dynamic Christian movements are found largely in tribal animists, such as the 3 million Karen of Burma and Thailand, or among large ethnic

groups, such as the Koreans, where Buddhism is weak. But Korea shows that Buddhists can grasp the significance of Jesus. About one out of four people in South Korea are Christians. It is said that when the border to North Korea opens, there will be a million "evangelists" flowing northward to share their joy in Christ as at least that many split-up families attempt to reunite. With Billy Graham's visit, the beginning of the end of the hermit kingdom of the North draws closer, and sits astride a peninsula with the strongest concentration of active Christians anywhere in Asia.

> **Where Buddhism has prevailed, the gospel has languished.**

Third, there are those who live in areas with sizable Christian minorities that are currently static or stymied. These are the Roman Catholic showplaces of Sri Lanka (Catholics outnumber Protestants 9 to 1) and Vietnam (where the ratio is 13 to 1), with approximately 7 percent of the populace in each country professing some form of Christianity. Sri Lanka sees itself as the haven of "pure" Buddhism. Missions from the outside are limited. The Church is ineffective in reaching the Sinhala Buddhist majority and grows only out of biological necessity. Revival is the only hope at present. Vietnam's evangelical Church was experiencing significant growth, especially among the tribal peoples, when the war ended. Little reliable information is known, but the few indications coming out of Vietnam reveal the Church is continuing even though activities are greatly restricted. Vietnam's 3 million Catholics are a large and influential group, but their numbers were not growing by conversion before the war ended.

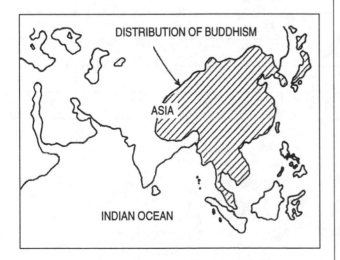

Figure 7-12. The Distribution of Buddhism

Fourth, there are those who live in areas where a tiny church is well established, the gospel is regularly proclaimed, but the growth of the Christian movement is negligible. Half of Asia's Christians live in this situation.

Burma exhibits such a pattern. Three percent profess Christ, but the majority of them are not the ethnic Burmese but the tribal animists who have come into the Church in large movements. They are of a different culture and social order than the Burmese Buddhists, who will not be easily or readily evangelized by them.

Japan is a unique case. The Western Church has sent large numbers of missionaries. Prominent and influential Japanese have followed Christ, resulting in major cultural impacts upon Japanese life. Popular surveys say Jesus Christ is the most admired religious leader in Japan. Yet a tiny percent of Japan's people is willing to identify with the well established but slow growing church. The one exception is among Japanese who have migrated to other countries. Brazil's nearly 1 million Japanese now profess Christ in the main, and best estimates indicate at least 8 percent regularly participate in Christian congregations.

Fifth, there are areas and peoples where the Church is at best precarious and where evangelization is either restricted or neglected. The tiny countries of Bhutan and Sikkim perched on the Himalayas have few known Christians. The only known church in Bhutan was established in 1971. Nepal suddenly turned a corner, and thousands of Christians greeted that change with new, bold plans. Cambodia's tiny church of 5,000 Protestants was exploding with growth when the country fell to the Khmer Rouge. Indications are not hopeful concerning the fate of that church.

Laos had a much larger missionary presence and church before it too closed to the West. But it was largely a tribal church and many members fled to Thailand. Mongolia, on the edge of China, has long been one of the few areas of the earth where there were no Christians present; now, like Albania, it is an almost totally new picture. Hundreds of English language teachers are being requested. These gospel-poor regions should drive the Church to her knees in prayer that the Lord of the universe will show His love to these long restricted areas.

24. *What seems to be the toughest religious group to evangelize in Asia? What are the indicators in this analysis that there is hope for reaching them?*

_____

_____

_____

_____

_____

_____

The Great Imbalance

Why have we focused on the five megaspheres having the smallest Christian populations? Don't the descriptions prove that these people are hard, resistant populations, nearly impossible to reach? This may be our initial response, but a further look at statistics will show that pathetically little has been done to reach any of these people. Take a look at Figure 7-13.

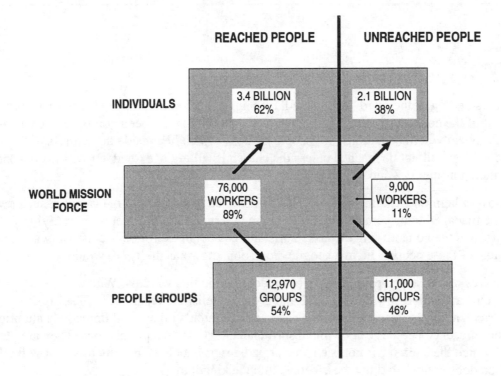

Figure 7-13. The Great Imbalance

These figures are a reflection of what Western missions have been doing for the last few decades. The statistics speak loudly for themselves. Only one missionary has been sent to work with unreached peoples for every nine who have been sent to work among peoples with an established church. When we consider that a large proportion of these have worked to reach tribal groups, the ratio of Western missionaries to the unreached among Buddhists, Muslims, and Hindus climbs to one in hundreds of thousands of people!

In light of these facts, we cannot lightly dismiss these people as unresponsive. They may not be easy to reach, but until the church makes a concerted effort proportionate to the vast need, she stands convicted of negligence in communicating the gospel to those who have never heard the saving name of Jesus Christ.

25. *Why is it important that the church work to correct this imbalance?*

_____

_____

_____

_____

Summary

A biblical understanding of the word "nation" will dispel the naive notion that, because the church is established in most of the countries of the world, the Great Commission has been completed. There are still thousands of biblically defined nations, or "people groups," which lie outside the witness of the established church. They will not be reached unless the church is willing to extend her witness beyond her own cultural frontiers through E-2 and E-3 evangelism.

With such an overwhelming task, missiologists have attempted to understand the world in such a way that the task can be managed to its completion. By thinking in terms of people groups, identifying who and where they are, and then quantifying the task, Christians can begin to work systematically at reaching the unreached. Most of these peoples lie in a geographic region known as the 10/40 window.

Huge megaspheres of unreached peoples have been identified in this window. Where there are so few Christians, it will take a massive new thrust of E-2 and E-3 evangelism to reach them. The Muslim, Chinese, Hindu, tribal, and Buddhist megaspheres deserve the church's urgent and immediate attention. Hundreds of other unreached peoples can be found surrounded by Christian populations. They are "hidden peoples" which the church has not been able or perhaps has not been willing to see. It will take more than an "open door policy" to draw these people into the kingdom.

Integrative Assignment

The integrative assignments in chapters 7 through 12 are intended to help you apply the principles you are learning to a practical situation. In essence, you are to target a people and develop a strategy for reaching them appropriate to their culture and situation. The end product of each assignment is a paper which integrates some basic research you will be doing with your own creativity in elaborating a strategic plan.

Purpose of the Project

The object of this exercise is to anticipate how God might work in a given situation if a sound strategy for evangelization were developed and applied. Some of you may already be burdened for a specific people group. For you, this activity may be a small step in fulfilling the desire which God has placed in you to reach this group of people. For others, this exercise will be primarily academic. In all cases, we hope the project will stimulate you to become a committed advocate for the redemption of a people group through intercessory prayer and through participation in efforts to reach the group.

Assignment Requirements

Each assignment in the series is intended to build on previous ones. For each assignment, you will be using worksheets to guide you in your research and creative thinking processes. The worksheets are comprised of a series of questions which you should attempt to answer through your own research and creative processes. Space has been provided under each question to jot your notes or short answers. Some of the questions on these worksheets may require information to which you cannot gain access. In such cases, supply information which seems realistic. We are more interested in the process of planning a strategy than we are with detailed accuracy of the information you use.

After you have answered all the questions, you will write a short essay on the topic that is covered. Your instructor or group leader will provide you with specific guidelines on length and other criteria for completing your report satisfactorily.

Getting Started

The first assignment is to answer the question: *What people?* If the priority today is the "hidden" or "unreached" peoples, then your selection should be made from the thousands of groups in this category. Three excellent resources which list unreached groups by countries are *Operation World* by Patrick Johnstone, *World Christian Encyclopedia* edited by David Barrett, and *A Church for Every People: The List of Unreached and Adoptable Peoples* edited by Frank Kaleb Jansen from the Adopt-A-People Clearinghouse. A listing of "Peoples Profiles" as compiled by the Adopt-A-People Clearinghouse is included in the appendix, together with information about other resources that are available. Ordering information is also included for your convenience.

The most difficult part of this particular assignment may be to narrow the field to just one people. Since your opportunities for research are limited and availability of information is a major consideration, try to pick a group that you have access to either through direct exposure, primary resource people, or literature.

- **Literature research**

  If you have access to a university or good public library, you may be able to select a people from books and magazines available about countries and their cultural groups.

- **Interview**

  If accessible, you may want to interview members of the group itself (perhaps foreign students), or those intimately acquainted with them.

- **Survey**

  If you have contact with a missionary or mission agency working among unreached peoples, they may be able to provide you with information in writing. A short questionnaire sent to several agencies or missionaries could provide very valuable data.

The key to selecting a group and successfully completing this assignment is to match your interest with a source of information which is readily available to you.

WORKSHEET #1: TARGETING A PEOPLE GROUP

As you begin considering a specific people group, answer the following questions. If you don't have enough information for some answers, attempt to make an educated guess.

A. Reachedness

1. Is there a "viable" church among this people, one which can adequately carry on evangelization?

_____

_____

_____

2. Is anyone currently attempting to reach this people group? If so, who? Are they being successful, or is a new effort desirable?

_____

_____

_____

_____

3. In your estimation, is this a reached or unreached group?

_____

_____

_____

4. To qualify for this project, the people selected must be "unreached," that is, without a viable church which can evangelize the group successfully to its cultural and geographic boundaries. If the group you selected is "reached," please choose another. If it is unreached, state what rationale you have used in reaching this conclusion.

_____

_____

_____

_____

_____

B. Receptivity

5. Is this people open to religious change of any kind?

_____

_____

_____

6. What is the current attitude of this people towards Christianity?

_____

_____

_____

7. Do you believe this people is or can become receptive to the gospel? Explain your reasoning.

_____

_____

_____

C. Strategic Considerations

8. Are there other strategic considerations related to the spread of the gospel in this area of the world that should be taken into account in targeting this people (i.e., location, social upheaval, political changes, etc.)?

_____

_____

_____

9. Are these other strategic considerations significant enough to override other factors such as apparent low receptivity?

_____

_____

_____

WRITTEN REPORT

After answering the above questions, write a short report. Name the group you will be targeting and provide the rationale you are using for selecting them.

Questions for Reflection

The introduction of terminology such as "hidden" or "unreached" people can dim the fact that the Bible calls these people "damned." Thousands of souls pass each day into a Christless eternity, never having had the opportunity to know their Savior. The horrible specter of masses of humanity passing into eternal punishment is something from which we all recoil. This grim reality should drive us to desperate efforts on their behalf. Unfortunately, the church's response is often tokenism or callous indifference. Does the plight of the lost make any difference to you? Meditate on John 3:16-18, 35-36. Record your thoughts below.

_____

_____

_____

_____

_____

_____

_____

_____

_____

_____

_____

CHAPTER 8

To Reach
the Unreached

In the last chapter we looked at the mission task remaining. We understand that only by considering the world in light of the biblical definition of nations can we get an accurate picture of what remains to be done. Such a view shows us a world with thousands of culturally defined nations or *people groups* which have not yet been discipled. It also shows us the priority of cross-cultural, *pioneer* missions in fulfilling the Great Commission.

Our previous study gave us a general idea of how to approach groups within the Buddhist, Chinese, Hindu, Muslim, and tribal megaspheres. Now we begin to focus on the specifics of strategy. To do this, let us consider what factors must be evaluated in targeting a people to be reached, how to define our objectives, and how to determine what methods we should use to reach those objectives.

The first part of this chapter looks at the general framework in which strategy must be formulated. Peter Wagner points out four major considerations, while Donald McGavran drives home the need to think in terms of reaching specific people groups. Next, we will look at an approach to formulating a strategy for reaching an unreached people. Finally, we will illustrate these principles through case studies of successful church planting efforts.

I. Strategic Considerations

In his popular book, *Stop the World, I Want to Get On*, Peter Wagner points out four areas for consideration when discussing strategy.* He lists these as:

1. The Right Goals
2. The Right Place at the Right Time
3. The Right Methods
4. The Right People

---

* Wagner, C. P. (1974). *Stop the world, I want to get on* (pp. 77-87). Glendale, CA: Regal Books.

We will use this helpful outline to summarize Wagner's thoughts and to lay out some other strategic considerations in choosing a people to "engage" and putting together a missionary team.

The Right Goal

In order for any endeavor to be counted successful, it must aim at the right goal. The achievement of misunderstood or wrong goals counts for little. To understand what the goal of missions is, we must look at Christ's foremost mission command known as the "Great Commission" (Matt. 28:18-20). In these verses we find not only the principal goal we seek, but also a suggestion of the methods and people to use in reaching that goal.

Although several verbs are used in the translation of the Great Commission (go, make, baptize, and teach), only one of them is imperative in the original Greek—"make disciples." Going, baptizing, and teaching are participles in the Greek and suggest activities by which disciples are made.

The first of these activities is "going." Remember that this command was given to "apostles," men who were already "sent ones." To reach the "disciple" goal, the disciple maker must continually be on the move, not in a random fashion, but towards the "all nations" parameters of the command. Witness must be extended beyond the circle of those who already know the gospel.

The second activity, "baptizing," represents the act of bringing people to repentance and faith in Christ as symbolized by the exercise of water baptism. Obedience to the whole command of disciple making implies starting with unbelievers.

The third activity is "teaching them to observe all that I have commanded you," which is the life-long endeavor of "discipling" as popularly understood. Wagner contends that even this activity is aimed primarily at unbelievers, who must be made to understand that "observing" Christ's commandments, i.e., obedience, is at the heart of becoming a disciple.

In Wagner's judgment, "The greatest error in contemporary missionary strategy is the confusion of *means* and *end* in the understanding of the Great Commission." Wagner's point is well taken. Many missionaries confuse the activities related to making disciples with the goal. Tract distribution may be a *means* of gospel proclamation, but if it does not result in disciples, the goal has not been reached. We cannot measure the success of mission simply by the fact that workers have blanketed an area with tracts, broadcast so many hours of gospel messages, held so many evangelistic campaigns, or engaged in a quantity of other good and measurable activities. Only as these methods can be demonstrated to work effectively with others, leading to the *making of disciples*, can the work be evaluated.

There is a tremendous amount of activity being done in the name of the Great Commission. Most of it is good, sound enterprise carried out by sincere people. In the final analysis, however, by Great Commission standards, much of the activity is focused on the methods and not the goal. This is reflected in the fact that less than 10 percent of the total resources allocated to missions is spent on reaching beyond the present boundaries of Christianity, i.e., to the "uttermost parts."

How do we know if a mission is measuring up? Wagner suggests the following criteria:

> If a mission society moves into a pagan village one year and moves out three years later leaving a group of 250 people who declare that Christ is their Lord, who meet together regularly for worship, who read the Bible and pray—they have made 250 disciples and to that degree have fulfilled the Great Commission.

1. *What is the goal of the Great Commission? How should this goal affect our choice of a people to engage in mission?*

_____

_____

_____

The Right Place at the Right Time

Related to the right goal is the concept of planning activities so as to be in the *right place* at the *right time*. Wagner illustrates this point with the analogy of a farmer.

No farmer works his field for the fun of it—he works for the payoff, which is the fruit. A man buys a farm with the anticipation that it will produce fruit. He may enjoy mechanics, but he works on his machinery only because it will help him get the fruit. He sows his seed and cultivates his crops, not because he thinks it's fun to ride tractors, but because if he doesn't there will be no fruit. "He that soweth and he that reapeth rejoice together" (John 4:36). Why? Because they gather fruit together.

Sound missionary strategy never loses the vision of the fruit. In missionary work this fruit is *disciples*. Keep this vision foremost in sowing, pruning, and reaping.

The vision in sowing

The Parable of the Sower appears in Matthew, Mark, and Luke. The briefest summary is in Luke 8:4-15. It tells of a farmer who sowed seeds on four different parts of his farm, but got fruit on only one.

Anyone with the vision of the fruit will instantly ask, "Why?" Jesus' disciples undoubtedly asked the same thing when they first heard it.

According to Jesus' interpretation, the variable factor was not the sower, nor was it the seed (which is described as the "word of God"), nor was it the method. It was the soil. No matter how good the seed is, any farmer knows it will not bear fruit on roadways, on rocky soil, or among thorns. In order to produce fruit, good seed must be sown in fertile soil.

The obvious lesson for missionary strategy is that the seed of the Word must be concentrated on fertile soil if fruit is to be expected. Some peoples of the world are receptive to the gospel while others are resistant. The world's soils must be tested. Concentrating, come what may, on rocky soil, whether or not any disciples are made, is foolish strategy. Farmers who have the vision of the fruit do not make that mistake too often, but some missiologists unfortunately do. This is the "right place" aspect of strategy.

2. *How does the vision in sowing apply to targeting unreached peoples?*

_____

_____

_____

The vision in pruning

The Parable of the Fig Tree in Luke 13:6-9 is seen as a threat by some missionaries. If they are guided by the vision of the fruit, however, it should not be.

The farmer who came along and saw a beautiful fig tree was forced to look a little deeper. The problem there was comparable to many mission fields. The fig tree had grown well, but there were no figs! Much missionary "work" has likewise developed to a high degree, but there is no fruit—there are no disciples. The farmer in the parable is a good strategist. When there is no fruit after much work and a prudent time lapse, he says cut it down—change your program. He operates on the basis of the vision of the fruit. His hired man does not share the vision because his income depends not so much on the harvest as on a salary. His strategy is to continue the work as long as he can. He, like many missionaries, is program-centered, not goal-centered.

Missionaries who are comfortably settled into a certain "program" or "missionary work" would do well to examine what they are doing in terms of the vision of the fruit. It is not easy to change a program, especially when you have been hoping against hope that in a year or so it will begin bearing fruit. But too often these years have stretched out into lifetimes. Missionaries who could have spent 10 years making disciples spend the same 10 years simply doing "mission work" because they lack the courage to cut the barren fig tree down and change their program.

3. How does the vision in pruning affect our methods as we seek to make disciples?

_____

_____

_____

The vision in reaping

When Jesus talks to His disciples about reaping, for the first time He mentions the need for praying that the Lord of the harvest will "send forth laborers into His harvest" (Matt. 9:37-38). When the "laborers are few," the farmer runs the risk of losing some of the harvest. The strategy aspect in this case is the "right time." Laborers are not needed when the harvest is still green, nor are they needed when the harvest has passed. Timing is of utmost importance in any harvest.

> *No one who takes strategy seriously would advocate a massive labor force in green fields.*

Suppose, for example, that you owned an apple orchard. In Field A, a worker could harvest five bushels in an hour. In Field B, it would take him five hours to harvest just one bushel. In Field C, he couldn't harvest anything because the apples are all still green. If you had 30 workers today, where would you send them? I think I would send 29 of them to Field A so as not to lose the fruit there. I would send the other one to do what he could in Field B and also to keep his eye on Field C. His job would be to let me know when those fields were ripe so I could redeploy the personnel.

Parallel situations arise time after time in missionary work. Some peoples are ready to be harvested today, some are not yet ready. These "unresponsive peoples" should not be neglected—someone should be there who is expert enough to tell when they are becoming ripe for the gospel. In one sense you need the very finest workers in the unresponsive fields. But no one who takes strategy seriously would advocate a massive labor force in green fields. Jesus wouldn't. He does not tell us to pray for more laborers to go to green fields or to fallow fields. The laborers are needed for the *ripe* harvest fields.

Right after Jesus says that in Matthew 9, He sends His own harvesters out in Matthew 10. There were three fields in those days: Jews, Gentiles, and Samaritans. Only the Jews were ripe at the time. Jesus specifically tells His disciples not to go to the Gentiles and Samaritans (Matt. 10:5, the green fields), but to go to the Jews (Matt. 10:6). Later on, both the Gentiles and the Samaritans ripened and bore much fruit, but not at that time.

Granted, it is not always the easiest thing to tell which soil is most fertile or just when a particular harvest is going to ripen in missionary work. Agricultural testing methods are much more advanced today than missiological testing methods. But missiologists are improving their methods all the time and making encouraging advances. A good deal is now known about testing peoples as to their degree of resistance or receptivity to the gospel. Up-to-date missions will take full advantage of such expertise, thus applying these aspects of strategy—the right place at the right time.

Figure 8-1. The Vision in Reaping

4. How is the vision in reaping related to strategy?

The Right Methods

Wagner continues his discussion of strategy by emphasizing the importance of using appropriate methods for making disciples.

When there is much work and little or no fruit, something is wrong. Careful analysis will usually pinpoint the trouble as either working in unripe fields or working in ripe fields but using wrong methods. You can go into a perfectly ripe field of wheat and work your head off, but if you are using a cornpicker, you will get nothing. Potato diggers are useless in apple orchards.

Around the world there are peoples who would gladly receive the gospel and become Jesus' disciples, but missionaries among these people are not making disciples because they are using inappropriate methods.

The wrong language is one of the common methodological mistakes. In many cases on record, the missionary thought that preaching in the trade language would be adequate for making disciples. Only when he switched to the local dialect, the language of the heart, however, did the fruit begin to come. If he had refused to change his methods, no amount of hard work would have done the job.

Mixing peoples has often proved to be another wrong method. For many years, for example, the Oregon Friends were reaping a great harvest among the Aymaras of Bolivia, while others working equally as hard were not. It was then discovered that the Friends insisted on keeping their churches purely Aymara, while others thought it well to mix mestizo believers with Aymaras. Missiologists call this *the principle of homogeneous unit churches*. Churches of one kind of people only are more effective in winning others of the same people. In Bolivia the method made the difference.

Methods must be selected on largely pragmatic factors, since the Bible does not pretend to give 20th century instruction. Therefore, it is good strategy not only to set measurable goals, but also to build in from the start of the effort instruments for measuring its success or failure. Only by doing this will it be possible to look back and know which methods God has blessed and which methods He has not blessed. One of the most curious facts in modern missions is that this simple procedure is so seldom carried out.

5. Why is it so important that an evaluation of the methods used in trying to make disciples be undertaken before writing off a people as "unresponsive"?

_____

_____

_____

The Right People

The last strategic consideration Wagner presents is the need for Spirit filled workers.

Some things God does by Himself; some things He does by using human beings.

It seems, for example, that the difference between fertile and barren soil is basically a matter of divine providence. The ripening of certain harvest fields at certain times can be attributed only to the sovereignty of God. "I have planted, Apollos watered," writes Paul, "but *God gave the increase*" (1 Cor. 3:6).

God brings the harvest to ripeness, but He does not harvest it. He uses Christian people to accomplish that task, and He is glorified when His people "bear much fruit" (John 15:8). He is particularly interested in "fruit that remains" (John 15:16). But how does this fruit come? The servant of God can only bear fruit if the branch abides in the vine. Jesus is the vine, and Christian people are the branches.

This strategy, then, stresses the right people. The right person is the person entirely filled with the Holy Spirit. He abides in Jesus. He is fully committed. He takes up his cross daily and follows his Master. Without this strategy, the first three strategies are dead letters. That is why Jesus insisted that His disciples not begin their missionary work until they were "endued with power from on high" (Luke 24:49).

6. *Why does the success of the first three strategies hinge on the fourth strategic consideration?*

_____

_____

_____

The right people are those who go, baptize, and teach with the clear goal of making disciples of the nations. The promise is that Christ will be with those who do this till the end of the age (Matt. 28:20).

Unreached Does Not Mean Unreachable

Because some megaspheres of unreached peoples have developed a reputation for being resistant, it is easy to conclude that these peoples represent "unripe" fields, and therefore should be bypassed for riper fields. The assumption is that the right strategies have always been used in attempting to reach such people. Well documented cases have shown, however, that failure to reap a harvest has often had more to do with wrong goals, methods, or personnel than with lack of a receptive target group. Frequently, a conscious effort to employ the right strategy among people believed to be "unreceptive" has resulted in a fruitful harvest.

One such case was an outreach effort to the Tonga tribe in Zambia, Africa. In 1967, Phil and Norma Elkins along with two singles and two other couples determined to target an unreached people group. They spent three years in study and preparation before being sent out in 1970 by their church. The following describes the results of their efforts.

Early decisions and convictions *

As the team searched for an unreached people (two years), they concluded the Holy Spirit was leading them to a segment of the Tonga tribe (one of the largest in Zambia, numbering over 300,000) called the Toka-Leya. Ninety-five percent of these people were adherents of an ethnic, or localized, folk religion (some would use the term animistic). Within a 12-mile radius of where the team settled (the primary target area) were 100 villages with four small congregations that had not grown for several years (a total of 75 Christians).

The team spent most of the first two years (1970-71) learning the language and culture, without engaging in overt evangelistic activities. By the end of 1973 there were four times as many churches (16) and six times the membership (450). Beyond this immediate 12-mile area, completely new movements were started. For example, in the Moomba chieftaincy, 70 miles to the north, newly trained national Christians planted six churches with 240 members within a few months. This was done in 1973 and involved winning the chief, a third of all the village headmen, and both court judges.

I mention this early rapid response to show that we were indeed led to a "ripe pocket" in God's mosaic of peoples. We knew that the national church, motivated and trained, had to be the vehicle to gather the harvest. By 1974 we felt most of the American team could pull out. By 1979, the last two "foreign" families felt they could responsibly move on to

* Elkins, P. (1992). A pioneer team in Zambia, Africa. In R. D. Winter & S. C. Hawthorne (Eds.), *Perspectives on the world Christian movement: A reader* (rev. ed.) (pp. D163-D164). Pasadena: William Carey Library.

another new people to begin the process again. Today a national church continues the process of winning and discipling "to the fringes."

"Methods," "approaches," and "strategy" may be "unspiritual" words in some Christians' vocabulary. I feel in the context of this effort there was validity in the strategy and specific methods followed by the team. In addition to what has been described, I think the first two years in which we were involved as in-depth "learners" of the Tonga world view (language, lifestyle, values, politics, social structure, beliefs, educational systems, and other aspects of culture) were essential to our efforts as church planters. My wife and I lived in a village of 175 people and followed a lifestyle closely identified with that of other Toka-Leya families. We learned to "hurt" where they hurt and "feel" what they felt. We identified, not so much to be "accepted," though that is important, but to understand and appreciate their culture for its finest and best dimensions. We had to know what parts were already functioning positively within the will and purpose of God. We needed to know what had to be confronted and changed to fit the demands of the kingdom of God.

Perhaps most critical was the need to learn where people had "felt needs" through which God's message of redemption could be accepted as good news. The message that had been proclaimed as "gospel" by earlier Christian efforts was in fact perceived as "bad news." The gospel was perceived as God calling men to have one wife and not to drink beer. Though Christians were saying many other things, this was perceived as the "banner" of the message. Because missionaries showed a major interest in setting up schools for children, the adult population found the message all right for children but almost unthinkable for adults.

7. Why was the Tonga Team's approach to reaching the Tongas more effective than previous efforts?

_____

_____

_____

_____

People Movements

We have stated that the goal of the Great Commission is disciple making. It is clear that correctly applied strategy may produce results even among people who are considered unresponsive by some. As we conclude this section, we want to consider a subject which is often misunderstood, the "homogeneous unit principle" as defined by Donald McGavran.

McGavran spent many years in India serving as a missionary and mission executive. From what he observed in India and subsequent travel to many fields around the world, he concluded that even when the right goal is attempted, a fundamental ignorance of *how churches grow* has relegated many missions to sterile efforts. In the following excerpts, McGavran outlines several important concepts related to this important subject.

❏ *A Church in Every People:*
Plain Talk About a Difficult Subject *

Donald A. McGavran **

In the last eight years of the 20th century, the goal of Christian mission should be to preach the Gospel and by God's grace to plant in every unchurched segment of mankind—what shall we say—*a church* or *a cluster of growing churches*? By the phrase "segment of mankind" I mean an urbanization, development, caste, tribe, valley, plain, or minority population. I shall explain that the steadily maintained long-range goal should never be the first but should always be the second. The goal is not one small sealed-off conglomerate congregation in every people. Rather, the long-range goal (to be held constantly in view in the years or decades when it is not yet achieved) should be *a cluster of growing congregations in every segment.*

As we consider the question italicized above, we should remember that it is usually easy to start one single congregation in a new unchurched people group. The missionary arrives. He and his family worship on Sunday. They are the first members of that congregation. He learns the language and preaches the Gospel. He lives like a Christian. He tells people about Christ and helps them in their troubles. He sells tracts and Gospels or gives them away. Across the years a few individual converts are won from this group and that. Sometimes they come for very sound and spiritual reasons; sometimes from mixed motives. But here and there a woman, a man, a boy, a girl do decide to follow Jesus. A few

employees of the mission become Christian. These may be masons hired to erect the buildings, helpers in the home, rescued persons, or orphans. The history of mission in Africa is replete with churches started by buying slaves, freeing them, and employing such of them as could not return to their kindred. Such as chose to could accept the Lord. A hundred and fifty years ago this was a common way of starting a church. With the outlawing of slavery, of course, it ceased to be used.

The long-range goal should be a cluster of growing congregations in every segment.

One single congregation arising in the way just described is almost always a conglomerate church—made up of members of several different segments of society. Some are old, some young, orphans, rescued persons, helpers, and ardent seekers. All seekers are carefully screened to make sure they really intend to receive Christ. In due time a church building is erected, and lo, "a church in that people." It is a conglomerate church. It is sealed off from all the people groups of that region. No segment of the population says, "That group of worshipers is *us*." They are quite right. It is not. It is ethnically quite a different social unit.

---

* McGavran, D. A. (1992). A church in every people: Plain talk about a difficult subject. In R. D. Winter & S. C. Hawthorne (Eds.), *Perspectives on the world Christian movement: A reader* (rev. ed.) (pp. D100-D105). Pasadena: William Carey Library.

** Known worldwide as perhaps the foremost missiologist of his generation, Donald McGavran was born in India of missionary parents and returned there as a third-generation missionary himself in 1923, serving as a director of religious education and translating the Gospels into the Chhattisgarhi dialect of Hindi. He also founded the School of World Mission of Fuller Theological Seminary. McGavran died in 1990 at the age of 93. He is the author of several influential books, including *The Bridges of God, How Churches Grow,* and *Understanding Church Growth.*

8. From the point of view of the target people, what is the problem with the conglomerate church?

_____

_____

_____

If we are to understand how churches grow and do not grow on new ground, in untouched and unreached peoples, we must note that the process I have just described seems unreal to most missionaries. "What," they will exclaim, "could be a better way of entry into all the unreached peoples of that region than to win a few individuals from among them? Instead of resulting in the sealed-off church you describe, the process really gives us points of entry into every society from which a convert has come. That seems to us to be the real situation." Those who reason in this fashion have known church growth in a largely Christian land, where men and women who follow Christ are not ostra-

cized, are not regarded as traitors, but rather as those who have done the right thing. In that kind of a society, every convert usually can become a channel through which the Christian faith flows to his relatives and friends. On that point there can be no debate. It was the point I emphasized when I titled my book _The Bridges of God._

But in tightly structured societies, where Christianity is looked on as an invading religion, and individuals are excluded for serious fault, there to win converts from several different segments of society, far from building bridges to each of these, erects barriers difficult to cross.

9. On what grounds might some people try to defend the concept of the conglomerate church?

_____

_____

_____

The concept of the conglomerate church is defended heatedly by some who feel a targeting of a specific element of society implies making distinctions among people. It is true that in Christ no differentiation is made between male or female, Jew or Greek, slave or free. Thus, some have labeled the _homogeneous unit principle_ as discriminatory and unbiblical.

To achieve a balanced perspective, it is important to understand that McGavran espouses this approach only where Christianity is considered a foreign religion and is heavily stigmatized. In many societies, where the church has achieved a certain level of maturity and Christianity has gained an acceptable status, this principle may be counter-productive.

The homogeneous unit principle emphasizes the need to be *focused on a specific target group* so that the gospel enhances the natural relationships in the society. This principle is an element of strategy to be applied when targeting specific unreached peoples. McGavran outlines seven steps to follow in applying this important concept:

1. Be clear about the goal. The goal is not one single conglomerate church in a city or a region but a cluster of growing churches.

2. The national leader, or the missionary and his helpers, should concentrate on one people, caste, tribe, or segment of society.

3. Encourage converts to remain thoroughly one with their own people in most matters, following their traditions and customs. Believers should not flaunt their new-found freedom in Christ. They should continue to eat what their people eat, dress as they dress, and follow socially correct conduct. They should strive to be better sons or daughters, better husbands or wives, better fathers or mothers, better employees or employers, etc., than they were before. They should be taught to bear cheerfully any exclusion, oppression, and persecution they are likely to encounter. While believers should be encouraged to remain loyal to their people, there may be areas in which they will have to take a stand. They cannot participate in idolatry, drunkenness, or other obvious sins. Where they can, though, new believers should make every effort to continue to identify with their people.

4. Try to get *group decisions* for Christ. Don't baptize a lone convert immediately. Instead, say, "You and I will work together to lead another five, or 10, or God willing, 50 of your people to accept Jesus Christ as Savior so that when you are baptized, you will be baptized with them." Remember that ostracism is very effective against one individual. However, when exercised against a dozen people, ostracism loses its power, and when exercised against 200 it has practically no force at all.

5. Aim for scores of groups of that people to become Christians in an ever-flowing stream across the years. This principle requires that from the very beginning the missionary keeps on reaching out to new groups instead of becoming entrenched in a teaching role. A church dependent on missionary teaching soon becomes ingrown and sealed off from its own

people. Risky as it sounds, the primary responsibility for teaching must be left to the Holy Spirit if spontaneous, ongoing growth is to occur.

6. The converts, five or 5,000, should feel that they are the vanguard of their segment of society. They are pioneers, showing their relatives and neighbors a better way of life. They are leading their people into the "promised land."

7. Constantly emphasize brotherhood. In Christ there is no Jew, no Arab, no slave, no free, no barbarian, no sophisticated person. We are all one in Christ Jesus. The way to achieve this unity is not by attacking all imperfect social institutions. Paul did not denounce slavery; he told the slave to be a better slave and the slave owner to be a better slave owner. The most effective way to achieve brotherhood is to lead ever-increasing numbers of men and women from every *ethnos*, every tribe or segment of society into an obedient relationship to Christ.

10. *What might we expect if the previous seven principles are applied faithfully in evangelizing a people?*

_____

_____

_____

Planning for People Movements

Historically, most observable people movements seem to have happened almost by accident. Sometimes a missionary "accidentally" stumbles on a key cultural concept whose long-awaited fulfillment is embodied by his own coming and presenting the gospel. This happened to Albert Brant, sent to the Dorsa tribe in Ethiopia. Upon arrival, he decided to camp under a certain sycamore tree. Little did he know that Dorsa tradition stated that someday God the Creator would send a messenger who would camp under that very tree, a fact which established immediate credibility for Brant's gospel message. Within a few years, hundreds of churches were established among the Dorsas.

Other people movements have been started by a convert who is won through the "one by one" approach. Then, quite apart from the missionaries' efforts, the convert returns to his own people with a message presented in a manner uniquely suited to the people's needs. The story of pioneer missionary Adoniram Judson is a perfect example of this. While Judson struggled to win the Burmese, his houseboy, who was a member of a tribal group, was converted and quietly began to lead his tribe's people to a knowledge of Christ. Within a few decades, the vast majority of his tribe had become Christians.

God desires that the nations be discipled. People movements reflect the fulfillment of that desire. In recent years, missionaries have begun to pray, plan, and purposefully work towards starting people movements among specific peoples. The results have been rewarding. Without minimizing the patient work of evangelism which has already been accomplished through a "one by one" approach, let us trust God for people movements among those peoples who have yet to be reached.

II. The Unique Solution Strategy

Our mission objective has a profound effect on the methods we employ for evangelization. If our objective is to see a people movement for Christ, we must understand that each group is unique and will therefore require a unique approach. How do we go about formulating a unique strategy? Edward Dayton has outlined a five-step process which should help us begin to answer that question.

❏ *How Do We Reach Them?* *

Edward R. Dayton

The world we are concerned with is the world of unreached people. Some of these groups are large. Some are small. The point is that we need to discover God's strategies, His best way for reaching these people. Certainly if the God of the universe is capable of being concerned with each individual in the world, He is just as concerned for the peoples of the world.

How do we reach them? Through their need.

- By trying to know them as God knows them.

- By attempting to meet their need as they see it.

- By communicating the saving power of Jesus Christ in their language and in their cultural understanding and in terms of where they are.

Too often some forms of evangelism have been carried out by people who had a solution and were looking for a problem. In other words, they assumed that there was one particular evangelistic method that would be appropriate in every setting. Evidently, God has not ordained it so. God's great love for humanity is expressed by His willingness to accept people wherever He finds them.

In order to communicate to people, we have to begin where they perceive their need. We have to reach them through their need. We need to know them as God knows them and to begin by attempting to meet their need as they see it. When we have done this, we will have the potential for communicating the saving power of Jesus in their language, and their

cultural understanding, and in terms of where they find themselves. Understanding a people through their need is basic to the strategy that we are presenting here, a strategy that is useful anywhere in the world.

> *In order to communicate to people, we have to begin where they perceive their need.*

How do we discover their needs? What do we need to know about them?

- Where they are.

- Why they should be considered a people group.

- Where they are in their movement toward Christ.

- Their potential receptivity to the gospel.

- Their perceived spiritual needs.

Where they are geographically is, of course, of first importance. But we need to go further and understand why they should be considered a people group. We need to put some boundaries around them.

A group of people is not static. Even in so-called traditional societies there is always movement. So we need to understand where this people is in terms of their movement toward Christ. Are they on the brink of receiving Him, or are they completely

---

* Dayton, E. R. (1978). To reach the unreached. In C. P. Wagner & E. R. Dayton (Eds.), *Unreached peoples '79* (pp. 25-31). Elgin, IL: David C. Cook.

unaware of His existence? The situations within which people find themselves will have a great deal to do with their receptivity to new things and thus their receptivity to the gospel. We need to make some statements about that.

Finally, we need to understand their perceived spiritual needs. Jesus Christ is the answer to everyone's needs. But people have different needs at different times, and we must begin where they presently are.

---

11. *Why are the needs of a people the key to developing a strategy for reaching them?*

_____

_____

The Engel scale

In recent years some new tools have been developed to help us to better describe and thus better understand a people. One of these tools helps us to understand where people are in their movement toward Christ.

Notice that this scale shows a progression from no awareness of Christianity to being an active propagator. The scale is not special or peculiar to religion or Christianity. All of us, in making major decisions, go through some steps like this. And if we think back on our own conversion experience, we will discover that there were different people, different situations that moved us toward Christ.

There was a day when, either because of ignorance or because of our extreme youth, we had absolutely *no awareness of Christianity* (-7 on this scale).

Most Westerners are aware or have some *awareness of Christianity* (-6 on our scale), and most Americans have *some knowledge of the gospel* (-5). The day came when some of us had an *understanding of the fundamentals of the gospel* (-4). What happened next and in what sequence is very difficult to tell. It varies tremendously from individual to individual. But in addition to an intellectual understanding, each of us had to understand that this gospel was meant for us; we had to *grasp the personal implications* (-3). But even that is not enough. We must also have a *recognition of personal need* (-2) that we think the gospel can meet. Only then are we ready to have a *challenge and decision to receive Christ* (-1).

THE ENGEL SCALE*

No awareness of Christianity	-7
Awareness of the existence of Christianity	-6
Some knowledge of the gospel	-5
Understanding of the fundamentals of the gospel	-4
Grasp of the personal implications	-3
Recognition of personal need	-2
Challenge and decision to receive Christ	-1
– Conversion –	
Evaluation of the decision	+1
Incorporation into a fellowship of Christians	+2
Active propagators of the gospel	+3

* This scale was originally proposed by Dr. James Engel of the Wheaton Graduate School in 1973.

Figure 8-2.
Where Is This People in Their
Movement Toward Christ?

What takes place next is, in purely religious terms, called "conversion." In more biblical terms we would call it regeneration, a new birth.

But as is the case in most major decisions, there is almost always an *evaluation of the decision* (+1). Research has shown that this is the key time in the life of a new Christian. How we minister to people as they go through this evaluation will have a major impact on their future.

Once this decision is past, people move on to being *incorporated into a fellowship of Christians* (+2) and then become *active propagators* (+3).

We have described this decision-making process in terms of individuals. Actually, groups of people go through this same type of group process, and so this scale becomes even more useful to us. Let's look at some examples, using the following illustration.

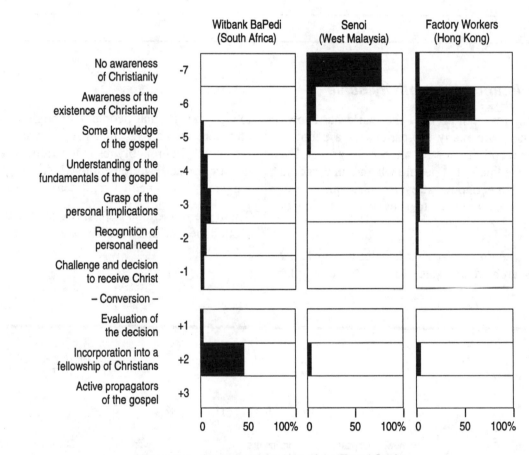

Figure 8-3. Example of the Use of the Engel Scale

Here are three different groups of people: Witbank BaPedi in South Africa, the Senoi in West Malaysia, and factory workers in Hong Kong.

The people in the first group are almost all Christians. Only a small percentage are still back in that category of having not moved beyond some knowledge of the gospel (-5). Approximately 45 percent of them have been incorporated into a fellowship of Christians (+2). This is a *reached people*.

The Senoi are at the other extreme. As best we can tell, about 80 percent of them are absolutely unaware of any existence of Christianity. True, there is a very small church (+2), but there is very little movement towards Christ.

The factory workers of Hong Kong, on the other hand, are surrounded by Christian symbols. Large numbers of them have an awareness of Christianity (-6). But the church is very small, although it appears that there are numbers of people who are moving towards Christ.

Now the advantage of these descriptions of people is that it helps us to *tailor our message*. We are much like the manufacturer of a product or a provider of a service. They have to know where the people are in order to do a good job of marketing. In the best sense of the word, we want to be outstanding marketers of the gospel! But still another factor must be considered. What is the *potential receptivity of a people to the gospel*?

12. Why is the Engel scale useful in planning strategy?

_____

_____

_____

The resistance / receptivity scale

Missionary research all over the world has shown us that there are many indications of a people's potential receptivity or resistance to the gospel. For example, we know that people who are undergoing a great deal of economic stress or upheavals in their way of life are more open to a new understanding of the world.

The *resistance/receptivity scale* helps us know how much research we are going to have to do in order to reach a particular people. Although it is a generalization, we can say that people who are highly receptive will probably respond to almost any evangelistic method, while people who are highly resistant are going to need a great deal of special care.

There are tremendous opportunities for the gospel around the world! These are listed on the next page.

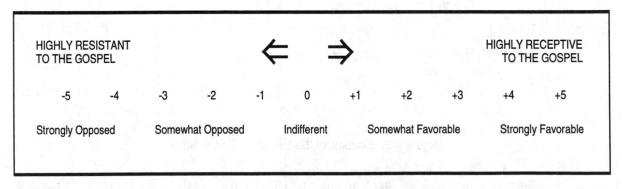

Figure 8-4. The Resistance/Receptivity Scale

COUNTRY	GROUP	POPULATION	PERCENT CHRISTIAN
CHINA (TAIWAN)	HAKKA	1,750,000	1%
INDIA	KOND	900,000	3%
PHILIPPINES	COTABOTO MANOBO	10,000	1%
THAILAND	LEPERS OF NORTHEAST	390,000	0.5%
INDONESIA	SUNDANESE	25,000,000	1%
BENIN	BOKO	20,000	2%
ETHIOPIA	SHANKILLA	500,000	1%
KENYA	FISHING TURKANA	20,000	4%
GERMANY	KOREANS	10,000	8%
U.S.A.	RACETRACK RESIDENTS	50,000	10%
MEXICO	AZTECA	250,000	2%
BELIZE	BLACK CARIBS	10,000	1%
COLOMBIA	COREGUAJE	500	1%
GUATEMALA	QUICHE	500,000	7%

Figure 8-5. People Known to Be Open to the Gospel

13. *How will the resistance or receptivity of a people to the gospel affect our strategy?*

_____

_____

_____

Designing keys and unlocking doors

There are peoples all over the world who are "locked out" from the gospel; they are hidden people, because no one has really found a key to open the door of their understanding to Christ's love for them. They will be reached only when they are approached as unique people groups with their own culture and sense of unity.

With God's help you can design keys which will unlock the door for a particular people to whom God has called you.

There are some obvious questions that can be asked that will enable the Holy Spirit to give us the mind of Christ:

1. What people does God want us to reach?
2. What is this people like?
3. Who should reach them?
4. How should we reach them?
5. What will be the result of reaching them?

These five steps can be thought of as a planning process. The emphasis is placed on asking the right questions, for as each people is unique before God, so will be the answers to the questions.

The five steps we have just listed are all intertwined: what people we want to reach, what the people are like, the means and methods we would use to reach them, and who should reach them are not questions that can be asked one at a time. That is just not the way we think. Obviously, our ability to reach a people will have something to do with which people we try to reach. If we cannot discover God's way of reaching them, then we will have to search for a different people.

A much better way to think of these questions would be to see them arranged in a circle. Each question leads to the next, with the last leading back to the first. It is a process that needs to be repeated over and over.

So although the questions are presented in a sequence, you will discover that you will often be asking many different questions at the same time. Don't let the sequence of the questions keep you from allowing the Holy Spirit to lead your mind and heart.

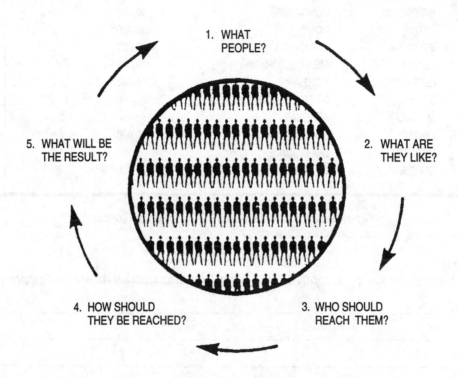

Figure 8-6. Steps for Reaching a People Group

14. Why are the five questions in this section better placed in a continuous circle than in a list?

_____

_____

_____

The mystery of evangelization

Planning strategies for evangelization is no substitute for the powerful presence and action of the Holy Spirit! If anything, the more carefully and prayerfully we try to think through the evangelization of a specific group, the more keenly we feel our dependence upon God.

There is a *mystery* to evangelization. The Spirit moves as He sees fit (John 3:8). It is God who is at work to do His perfect will. In ways that we cannot understand, He uses imperfect, sinful men and women to communicate His love and the good news of salvation through His beloved Son to all who will receive Him.

There is a *mystery* to what happens as the Holy Spirit transforms lives of individuals and nations. We can many times see only the results of the Spirit's work. The finger of God writes across the pages of history, and we can see what He has done. But so often we are unable to understand fully what has happened.

But there is *mystery* too in the fact that God has charged His church to go into all the world to preach and make disciples, trusting Him for results and yet at the same time praying, dreaming, anticipating, longing into the future. And as we respond to the command of God's Word and the prompting of His Spirit within us, we are expected to bring our *total being* to bear on the task before us, to think, to pray, and to plan. Jesus spoke to this when He said that a man should not start to build a tower or engage an enemy without first considering the possible outcomes (Luke 14:28). It was said of the early church that they outlived, outdied, and outthought the Roman Empire.

There is a *mystery* about God's action in society through the society itself. Many times God uses changes in the society to prepare people to receive His Word.

Finally, there is *mystery* about the person of the evangelist. The Word of God has as much to say about what we are to be as what we are to do. The gospel is proclaimed through the spoken word. People cannot come to a knowledge of the Savior unless they hear (or read) that He is. But they are often attracted to Him by the love they find among His disciples.

The more carefully and prayerfully we try to think through the evangelization of a specific group, the more keenly we feel our dependence upon God.

Remember, each disciple is called upon to see himself or herself as part of a larger body (1 Cor. 12:12). Within that body each has a special place, and in the process of evangelization different persons play their special role at different times. "I sowed, Apollos watered, but God gave the increase" (1 Cor. 3:6, RSV).

Let us then use all the gifts that God has given us, both individually and corporately. Let us try to think God's thoughts after Him. Let us attempt to uncover God's strategy—to think about the people to whom we may be called, to earnestly consider their needs, to take into account all that God might do to reach them. Let us make certain that we are clean vessels, fit for His use. And then let us go forward believing that God will be faithful, and GIVE HIM THE GLORY.

---

15. How should the "mystery of evangelization" affect our attitude towards planning strategy?

_____

_____

The Tonga Team in Zambia used an approach similar to the one Edward Dayton suggests to determine the best way to present the gospel to the Tongas. They spent two years learning the language and culture in an effort to understand the people and their view of the world. During this time they discovered that Tonga culture is permeated by fear of evil spirits. The Tongas feared the *isaku* in particular, evil spirits commanded by humans who had won their allegiance through a gruesome ritual involving, among other things, the head of a human corpse.

In the following excerpt, Phil Elkins describes how presentation of the gospel from an understanding of the people's needs produced the desired result.

Responding to felt needs *

From all of the above insights a picture of *felt needs* emerged to which God could speak meaningfully. The first *Good News* from God for the Tonga was that He had given to us a *Holy Spirit*. The Tongas knew nothing of a good spirit, much less a *Holy Spirit* from God Himself as a gift. We shared that we were not afraid, as they were, of *isaku* spirits because we had residing in us continually a *Spirit* that would not tolerate other spirits. The Spirit in us was more powerful than any other spirit. This explained the lack of fear they had seen in our lives, the joy, the confidence, and hope.

> *The Word is not confined to the printed page. The Word was communicated daily by a God who was willing to reveal Himself in the people's lives.*

The second part of our *Good News* was that the God, which they already knew by name, had *not abandoned them*. The Tonga had left God, but He was willing to live among them again. He had already proved His willingness by sending a Son who lived as a human and showed humans how to really live. We explained that one can now talk directly to God about their needs and that this *Son* also serves as a person's special advocate before God. We further explained that God's Son was so concerned to remove the sin and guilt for all of the offensive ways that we live that He Himself accepted the punishment on our behalf.

The Tongas began to realize the verification and proof of what we said was the *Holy Spirit* which lived in us. Lest I be misunderstood by a reader of this, I am not talking about a special gift of speaking in tongues. I am speaking of that which every Christian receives at his *new birth*.

We also spoke of the verification that would come from knowing the Bible. This had little immediate impact, as most of the people could not read. However, the Word is not confined to the printed page. The Word was communicated daily by a God who was willing to reveal Himself in their lives. He revealed Himself one day as we went to a village where we were stopped by a drunken woman who forbade us to come into her village. She said they followed Satan and not God. That night she died and the next day hundreds of people came wanting to know more of God's will for their lives.

The major political leader of our area had been leading the people to the graves of their ancestors annually to solicit rain. When he accepted the *Good News*, he demonstrated his faith by leading his people in a new way. When the first drought occurred he called the people together to spend a day calling to God to give them rain. This was a bold move which exceeded the faith of some of the missionaries. But God honored the boldness, and before the sun set the earth was drenched in rain.

In the village where we made our home, almost half of the adult population accepted baptism. At their

---

* Elkins, P. (1992). A pioneer team in Zambia, Africa. In R. D. Winter & S. C. Hawthorne (Eds.), *Perspectives on the world Christian movement: A reader* (rev. ed.) (pp. D167-D168). Pasadena: William Carey Library.

initiative we all spent a night in prayer before going out as a group to share our faith with another village.

As our team of American missionaries saw more and more churches planted, we began to modify our role as leaders in evangelism and church planting. I believe it was a good strategy for us to identify with the Tongas physically and to provide a physical and spiritual model for evangelism. I know this is a concept that is considered "past" in many circles, but I feel it should still be an emphasis in pioneer mission efforts.

To train an indigenous leadership we set up 16 extension centers for training every Christian in the basics of the Christian faith and instituted a special course for those who emerged as church leaders. This was done with the new Christians bearing the cost of the courses. We followed the practice of not subsidizing the construction of buildings or providing funding for those who entered the preaching ministry.

16. *In the preceding account, why was understanding the people's felt needs essential to effective communication of the gospel?*

_____

_____

_____

III. Putting It All Together

In the final section of this chapter, we will look at three case studies which have applied to some degree their own versions of the "unique solution" strategy. As you read these, try to pick out the application of the principles set forth by Wagner, McGavran, and Dayton in the previous readings. At the end of each case study, you should be able to discuss what elements of strategy were used in each case.

❏ *South Asia: Vegetables, Fish, and Messianic Mosques* *

Shah Ali with J. Dudley Woodberry **

My Muslim father tried to kill me with a sword when I became a follower of Jesus after comparing the Qu'ran and the Bible. He interpreted my decision as a rejection not only of my faith, but of my family and culture as well. Historically, Christians were largely converts from the Hindu community and had incorporated Hindu words and Western forms into their worship.

---

* South Asia: Vegetables, fish, and Messianic mosques (1992, March). *Theology, News and Notes* (pp. 12-13). Pasadena: Fuller Theological Seminary.

** Shah Ali is the pseudonym of a follower of Christ from a Muslim family in South Asia. His identity is being concealed—currently, there is persecution of Christians in his country. He translated the New Testament into his national language using Muslim terms and is training leaders of Messianic mosques. J. Dudley Woodberry is Associate Professor of Islamic Studies and Dean of the School of World Mission at Fuller Theological Seminary in Pasadena, California. He has wide experience in church and mission work and has served as a government consultant on Middle East matters. He is the third generation of his family to serve in missions.

In trying to express my faith, I encountered two sets of problems. First, as indicated, Christianity seemed foreign. Secondly, attempts by Christians to meet the tremendous human need in the region had frequently led to the attraction of opportunistic, shallow converts and the consequent resentment of the Muslim majority.

Christian faith in Muslim dress

I was able to start dealing with the foreignness of Christianity when a missionary hired me to translate the New Testament using Muslim rather than Hindu vocabulary and calling it by its Muslim name, the *Injil Sharif* ("Noble Gospel"). Thousands of *injils* were bought, mostly by Muslims, who now accepted this as the "Gospel" of which the Qu'ran spoke. This approach may be supported not only pragmatically by the amazing results but, more importantly, theologically as well. Unlike the Hindu scriptures, the Qu'ran shares a lot of material with the Bible. In fact, most Muslim theological terms were borrowed from Jews and Christians.*

Subsequently, a graduate of Fuller's School of World Mission asked me to train 25 couples to live in villages and do agricultural development. Only one couple was from a Muslim background. All the others had problems. Muslims would exchange visits with them but would not eat their food until they began to shower in the morning, hence were ceremonially clean by Muslim law after sleeping with their spouses.

The Christian couples were called angels because they were so kind, honest, and self-sacrificing, and they prayed to God. However, they were not considered truly religious because they did not perform the Muslim ritual prayer five times a day. Thereafter, we only employed couples who followed Jesus from a Muslim background, and we developed a ritual prayer that retained all the forms and content that Muslims and Christians share but substituted Bible passages for Qu'ranic ones. Little adaptation was necessary, because early Islam borrowed so heavily

from Jewish and Christian practice in the formulation of the "pillars" of religious observance (the confession of faith, ritual prayer, almsgiving, fasting, and pilgrimage).**

Our Muslim neighbors defined "Christianity" as "a foreign religion of infidels"; so we often referred to ourselves as "Muslims" (literally, "submitters to God"). The necessity of submitting to God is certainly Christian (see James 4:7), and Jesus' disciples call themselves "Muslims" according to the Qu'ran (5:111). In this context, however, they demonstrated their submission by believing in God and His apostle (apparently Muhammad, who had not yet been born).

> *Our Muslim neighbors defined "Christianity" as "a foreign religion of infidels"; so we often referred to ourselves as "Muslims" (literally, "submitters to God").*

When villages have decided to follow Christ, the people continued to use the mosque for worship of God but now through Christ. Where possible, the former leaders of mosque prayers (imams) are trained to continue their role as spiritual leaders.

Persuasion, power, and people

God used other means as well as contextualization to bring Muslims to faith in Christ. On several occasions I have had public discussions with Muslim teachers (*malvis*) and have been able to show that, contrary to popular belief, the Qu'ran does not name Muhammad as an intercessor. Rather, it states that on the judgment day "intercession will not avail, except [that of] him to whom the Merciful will give permission, and of whose speech He approves" (5:109 Egyptian ed./108 Fluegel ed.). But the *Injil* ("Gospel"), which is from God according to the Qu'ran (5:47/51), not only states that God approves

---

* See Jeffery, A. (1938). *The foreign vocabulary of the Qu'ran.* Oriental Institute.

** For the details of this argument see Woodberry, J. D. (1989). Contextualization among Muslims: Reusing common pillars. In D. S. Gilliland (Ed.), *The Word among us* (pp. 282-312). Waco, TX: Word.

of Jesus (e.g., Matt. 3:17), but that He is the *only* intercessor (1 Tim. 2:5).

God has also shown His power through answered prayer—the recovery of a three-year-old girl who, the doctors said, would die in a few hours; the sending of rain and the stopping of flooding; and the appearance of an unknown man to stop a crowd bent on killing an *imam* who followed Christ.

A conscious effort has been made to foster the movement of groups rather than just individuals to Christ. People have only been baptized if the head of the family was baptized. Effort was made to see that leaders understood the message. A Muslim mystic (Sufi) sheikh, upon learning that the veil of the temple had been rent from top to bottom, threw down his Muslim cap, followed Christ, and brought his followers with him.

Since illiteracy is high, the Bible and training materials are recorded on cassettes, and inexpensive cassette players are made available to the villagers.

There has been persecution. Our training center was closed down. A court case was made against me and three fellow workers. Likewise, there has been friction between the leaders and misunderstanding by other Christian groups. But the movement of people to Christ continues. Most new believers remain in independent Messianic mosques, but some contextualized congregations have joined the major denomination, while still other individuals are absorbed into the traditional, Hindu-background church.

Toward responsible self-help

Besides trying to express our faith in meaningful cultural forms, we have been trying to meet the tremendous human need around us. We want to proclaim the Kingdom and demonstrate its values. Trying to do both presents certain problems. First, there is the problem of using human need for evangelistic purposes—of manipulating people and attracting the insincere. Consequently, we help all the villagers despite their religious affiliation and give no financial help to Jesus mosques or their *imams*.

Secondly, the former colonizer-colonized dependency easily gets transferred to donor-recipient dependency. Thirdly, even the distribution of donated

food from abroad may only help in the city, because of the difficulty of distribution, while giving little incentive to the peasants to produce more because of the artificially reduced price. Fourthly, the introduction of technology may only help those with the skills or the finances to make use of it, while the poorest can just watch the gap between the haves and have-nots widen.

Trying to proclaim the kingdom and demonstrate its values presents the problem of using human need for evangelistic purposes—of manipulating people and attracting the insincere.

To deal with these problems, we have followed such common development practices as loaning planting seed to be replaced at harvest time and providing pumps that are paid for from increased productivity. Now, however, we are adapting a program developed in Southeast Asia which should express holistic Christian concern, deal with the problems outlined, and ensure that the indigenous church remains self-supporting.

The program is training national workers in contextualized church planting and an integrated fish and vegetable cultivation system. The workers are, in turn, sent to needy districts where they are responsible for training local farmers in the easily transferable technology so that they can become self-sufficient. Increased population means less land is available for cultivation, and a poor transportation infrastructure means food must be produced near its consumption.

The intensive food production system was developed elsewhere. In that system, fish ponds are dug and the excavated dirt used for raised vegetable plots. Excess stems and leaves from the vegetables are used to feed the fish, and the waste from the fish is used as fertilizer for the vegetables. These food production centers are within walking distance of regional urban centers for daily sales and provide space for training of regional farmers and leaders of the Jesus mosques.

The concept of Messianic mosques and completed Muslims (following the model of Messianic synagogues and completed Jews) still causes considerable misunderstanding among other Christians. The combining of evangelism and humanitarian ministries by the same people also raises concerns among those who feel Christian agencies should only focus on one or the other. Nevertheless, the models we are developing have been used by God in the raising up of many new disciples and expressing His concern for total persons with physical and spiritual needs. Likewise, the Messianic Muslim movement has spilled over into a neighboring country through the normal visiting of relatives; when colleagues and I visited a Southeast Asian country recently, a whole Muslim village began to follow Jesus.

17. What strategic principles were used in this case study?

_____

_____

_____

In the case study just considered, the context was a mixed Hindu, Muslim, and Christian society in which Muslims were being targeted for evangelization. In the following case, it is a predominantly Roman Catholic society where social stratification is very strong. Consider how the Lord led in this movement to reach members of the traditionally unresponsive upper class.

❏ *An Upper Class People Movement* *

Clyde W. Taylor

In recent months I have become acquainted with a fascinating movement in Latin America where the Gospel is spreading by a pattern as close to the New Testament pattern as I have ever seen. I'll not name a country, for the leaders do not want any publicity. But what is happening is to the glory of God and represents a quite significant breakthrough.

I learned of it when I was invited to hold a missionary conference in that country a couple of years ago. I was not prepared for what I encountered. I understood the missionary involved had a small work, but I discovered the Gospel was spreading in a way that Dr. McGavran would call a "people movement."

The unusual aspect of this movement is that its faith is spreading almost exclusively among the upper middle and upper classes of the nation. Furthermore, the number of converts involved is relatively high for the size of the segment of society involved. Since the movement is intentionally not highly structured, it is difficult to get accurate statistics; but my extensive conversation with leaders lead me to conclude that a minimum of 2,000 converts were actively involved. The number could easily be as high as 5,000 or more.

Beginnings

The work of the missionary, whom I'll call "John Swanson," began in the 1950s in somewhat typical fashion as he witnessed and evangelized among the responsive lower classes. After several years of ministry in the capital city, he had some 20 to 25 converts whom he was training in his home. He came to realize that he was really not a pastor and preacher—his skills were in music and teaching and so asked another mission to shepherd his little flock.

---

* Taylor, C. W. (1980). An upper class people movement. *Global Church Growth Bulletin, 17*(2).

In 1962, Swanson moved to the second largest city in the nation where—after studying the methods of Paul in the book of Acts—he changed his approach. He went to the university and started witnessing to students. Within a few months he won 12 of these to Christ, whom he then began to train in discipleship. For seven years he led them in their spiritual growth and trained them also in theology, church history, books of the Bible, and so on.

While Swanson was writing, translating, and mimeographing materials for the daily sessions with his disciples, they were out witnessing to other students. By 1964 they had won and discipled about 300 others. These were all baptized in and some became members of various churches in the city. (At present about a dozen of these early converts are full-time workers in some of these churches.) The movement at this point was focused in small groups meeting in private homes and university lounges.

Churches grow and multiply

These early converts, it should be remembered, were all students and therefore single. In time, when some of them graduated and got married, they began thinking in terms of their own church. In 1969, therefore, the first church with five couples was organized in a home, and a second church was organized three years later.

In 1977 the first house church, which had grown to 120 members, divided into two separate churches of 60 members each. The second church grew to 160 members and in 1978 divided into two congregations of 80 each. In February of that year, another church was formed bringing the total to five house churches with a combined membership of about 500.

This gives a partial picture only of the work, for, in addition to the many who joined existing churches, the leaders of this new movement to Christ estimate that at least 50 percent of their members have scattered to other sections of the country and even the U.S. In many cases they begin the process of witnessing, training new converts, and establishing house churches all over again.

Furthermore, cells of believers have been established in many of the universities of the region. I was told, for instance, of a type of church meeting for 35 medical students, another for 15 in the biology department, and another for 12 in the technical institute of one university.

In 1964 one of the original 12 leaders graduated and returned to the capital city and began a work along the same lines he had come to know the Lord in and been trained in. Swanson followed him a few years later.

When I visited there in 1979, I was told that there may be as many as 100 Christian cell meetings among the upper classes in the city. These seem to be spreading on their own. The churches (cells) directly identified with Swanson and his workers, however, have grown to 15 with a total membership approaching 1,000. They told me about a number of similar house churches in other cities as well.

An inside view

One of the unique features of these house churches is that they are made up of members from the upper middle and upper classes of people. The churches in the capital city in particular are made up primarily of those from the highest circles of society. This is not to say that they are unconcerned about the poor and less educated. They have evangelized among them and gained many converts. They discovered, however, that as soon as people from the lower and middle classes began attending their churches, ingathering from among the upper class ceased.

> *They concluded that if they were going to win upper class people, they were going to have to win them with Christians who were likewise from the upper classes.*

Taking Paul's statement that he became all things to all men, they concluded that if they were going to win upper class people, they were going to have to win them with Christians who were likewise from the upper classes. As soon as they gain enough converts from the lower classes, therefore, they organize separate churches for them. For these leaders, it is not a matter of not wanting to associate with those on lower rungs of society, but a matter of how best to win the most people to Jesus Christ on all levels.

The growth of this cluster of congregations looks a lot like that of New Testament congregations. The converts meet in homes where they worship, fellowship, study the Word, and are sent out to bring others to Christ. Each convert is not so much "followed up" but receives the Gospel in a very personal context to begin with. For example, the group has printed and distributed millions of tracts, but none of them have a name and address printed on them. Instead, the one passing out the tract gives his own name and address. When someone comes to know the Lord, he is immediately given training in discipleship.

I talked with one girl, for example, who meets with four new converts at six a.m. They pray, have fellowship, and study the Word until breakfast at seven. She meets for lunch with three other girls who are older Christians. They pray and discuss problems together.

Each church is completely independent, though they all carry the same name. They do not keep any membership lists, but they do seem to know everyone who belongs. They baptize, serve communion, and train and ordain their own pastors, whom they call "elders." They are not highly structured, but their high level of caring and training binds them together.

It is an interesting paradox that these converts are wealthy, but they can expand indefinitely with almost no funds, since they meet in their large homes and ordain their own lay and unpaid elders (pastors). But they do give 20 percent of their incomes on the average. With these funds they send out missionaries to other parts of Latin America and even Europe.

Money is never mentioned until someone is ready to go to the field and needs support. Then it is not uncommon for someone to say, "I'll give $200 a month" and another to say, "I'll give $150," and so on. Support is thereby raised very quickly.

I heard of one missionary lady who is supported by four of her friends, all executive secretaries. They give her full personal support which is equal to what she would earn as an executive secretary in her home country. They also pay her transportation to and from the field and her ministry needs as well. One of the girls gives 80 percent of her salary, another 60 percent, another 50 percent, and another 30 percent. Altogether, the fellowship of house churches fully supports 16 missionaries.

Disciple making and church planting are now spreading quickly through a segment of society that has been heretofore unreached. If it can happen in one nation of Latin America, it can happen in others.

The exciting thing about this Christward movement is not just that millionaires, government officials, and leading businessmen are becoming believers. The Lord loves the poorest beggar, and his conversion is no less precious in His sight. It's significant that disciple making and church planting are now spreading quickly through a segment of society that has been heretofore unreached. If it can happen in one nation of Latin America, it can happen in others. The Lord of the harvest—of all kinds of crops—will be pleased when it does.

---

18. Identify at least five distinctives of the church described above and explain how these qualities are beneficial for evangelizing others.

_____

_____

_____

_____

In this final case study, we will look at a strategy used to reach a nomadic Muslim tribal group, one of the most challenging of all missions scenarios.

❑ *Ann Croft and the Fulani* *

Fatima Mahoumet

Although Ann Croft's father had planted many churches in the U.S. Midwest during her childhood, she wasn't thinking of herself as a missionary when she went to Nigeria. She was simply a teacher of English as a Second Language.

She was able to get to know some of them better, joining them for some meals, and eventually reading and discussing stories from the Bible. One student expressed an extraordinary interest in the Bible.

Open doors

As their friendship grew, her student opened doors for her into the labyrinth of extended family life among the Fulani people in her area. He had many sisters who had married into a number of families in the area. When her student visited them, Ann accompanied him and met each family member.

As a teacher, Ann was also respected by the male leaders of the community. At their request, she spent many hours answering their questions about the Bible, helping them to understand more fully the biblical events and characters, including Jesus, which they had encountered in the Quran. In preparation, she had done a comparative study of the Quran and Bible, noting their uniqueness, differences, and similarities. She used their folk tales as bridges for discussing Scripture.

Soon, Ann had access to every part of the Muslim community. As a woman, she was able to meet the women related to all of her male contacts, even those in the strictest *purdah* (seclusion) who would otherwise be well beyond the sphere of married, let alone single, Christian men. One of the women was especially drawn to Ann. She took her to all the special ceremonies, such as naming ceremonies, weddings, and funerals. She helped her with the language and provided many needed bridges of communication and explanations as Ann continued to learn about the Muslim way of life. Ann also learned the traditional stories of her new people and grew to deeply love and appreciate the rich fabric of their lives.

She discovered that being a single woman had its advantages too. In response to questions as to why she was not married, Ann referred to 1 Corinthians 7 and a comparable passage in the Quran about single women being able to be totally involved in the work of the Lord. She added that the Bible, unlike the Quran, allowed her to do so well past her 20th birthday. Besides, she remarked, how could she otherwise teach their children and always be available to them any time they were having trouble, day or night? She wasn't subject to the demands of marriage or the constraints of *purdah*. She was always free to help.

Caring for cattle

Ann continued her efforts among the Fulani people of northern Nigeria.

The Fulani are a largely nomadic people, whose search for good pasture for their cattle has scattered them throughout sub-Saharan West Africa. Strong clan fidelity and six centuries of Muslim evangelism have made them the most effective champions of Islam in West Africa. Of 6.7 million Fulani, only 400 are known Christians.

As Ann studied more about the people to whom God had sent her, she discovered ways of showing the Fulani cattle-herders that they are very special to God. In the Bible she found numerous references to nomadic cattle-herding peoples who played special roles in biblical history.

* Mahoumet, F. (1992). Ann Croft and the Fulani. In R. D. Winter & S. C. Hawthorne (Eds.), *Perspectives on the world Christian movement: A reader* (rev. ed.) (pp. D198-D199). Pasadena: William Carey Library.

Knowing the great importance of cattle to them, Ann began to help upgrade the health of the cattle with veterinary medicine and so helped the Fulani begin to cope with some of the economic problems they faced with the growing pressure of urbanization.

Caring for cattle was the way to the Fulani heart. On one occasion she helped a Fulani elder get tuberculosis medicine for his son and worm medicine for himself. But it was not until she gave him medicine for his cows that he said, "Now I know you really love us!"

Ann was able to join forces with another mission agency in a distant city that was planning an evangelistic three-day "conference" especially for Fulani. Fulani people were told that it would be a religious conference studying one of the prophets—Abraham, a super-herdsman who had cows and sheep and donkeys and goats and camels. This was a big event for the Fulani, not accustomed to special events just for their people.

At the end of the evangelistic conference, the chief of the area said to Ann that he wanted his people to become part of the Christian community. He had seen that Christians and their Holy Book cared about the needs of his people. Some of the greatest prophets, after all, like Abraham, were cattle-herders too! He also told her that to get a lot of people interested in the Christian faith, one of the best things she could do would be to continue to show a real, genuine interest in every aspect of their culture.

Caring for cattle was the way to the Fulani heart.

Gathering new believers into viable fellowships is proving to be a tremendous challenge. It is hard enough for some Fulani youth to settle down for Bible school. A permanent location for a tribe would unravel nomadic life. But Ann feels that perhaps now is the time for the Fulani people as they move towards a future that is economically, politically, and socially uncertain. She will be there with them, loving and caring for them, believing that God will transform them into a people "gathered... accepted... to the honor of the Lord your God" (Isa. 60:7).

19. Why was Ann Croft's "strategy" effective? Would it be effective in other situations? Why or why not?

_____

_____

_____

_____

Summary

How do we go about reaching an unreached people group? There are several factors which affect the development of our strategy. First, we must fully understand the goal. Secondly, we must keep clear the vision of harvest, pruning, and reaping. Thirdly, we must develop the right methods to reach the people. Last but not least, we must make sure we understand the qualifications required of those who are sent to perform the task.

Although we may have in mind the immediate goal of making disciples, consideration of the long-term goal of evangelization will greatly affect the methods we use. "One by one" methodology is sometimes appropriate where the church is an accepted part of the culture, but where the church is still considered a foreign entity, a "people movement" approach is most desirable. Such an approach will require that new strategies be developed for each people because many traditionally applied methods will not be effective.

We must evaluate each people on the basis of their needs in order to discover how to evangelize them. This approach will lead us to an in-depth understanding of the people and their culture. The use of newly developed tools such as the Engel scale and the resistance/receptivity scale can also help us assess a people's spiritual condition and determine how the gospel should be presented in order to meet felt needs. By asking basic questions such as what people God wants us to reach, what these people are like, who should reach them, how we should reach them, and what the results of reaching them will be, we can fine tune the process of targeting an unreached people with the gospel. However, this planning must be balanced with the recognition that the Lord often works in mysterious ways to bring about His purposes. We must remain flexible in our planning and must give God the freedom to work as He sees fit in each situation.

Integrative Assignment

The following is the second worksheet of your unreached peoples assignment. Once you have determined what people you are targeting, you will want to answer the question: *What are the people like?*

WORKSHEET #2: PEOPLE GROUP DESCRIPTION

A. General Physical Description

1. What is the name or descriptive title of this people group?

_____

2. What is the approximate size of this people group?

_____

3. Of what race, class, caste, nationality, etc. are the people members?

_____

4. What is their first language? What other languages do they speak?

_____

_____

5. Where do these people live? What is their environment like?

_____

_____

6. What is the economic situation of this people group? Is there a specific profession which characterizes them?

_____

_____

7. What other physical distinctives are part of these people's cultural boundaries?

_____

_____

_____

B. Religious Background

8. Describe the religion or religions to which these people adhere.

_____

_____

_____

9. What percentage adhere to each religion? How many people are nominal in their faith, and how many are sincere practitioners of their religion?

_____

_____

10. Do the people seem satisfied with their religion and its practices? How does their religion cope with issues of illness and death?

_____

_____

_____

11. In light of the people's religious practices, what is the greatest spiritual need which the gospel can address?

_____

_____

C. External Influences on Evangelization

12. Are there government-imposed restrictions on evangelizing these people? If so, what are they?

_____

_____

_____

13. Are there sociological or economic factors inhibiting the evangelization of these people? If so, what are they?

_____

_____

_____

14. Describe any sociological, economic, or political factors that can be used to advantage in the evangelization of these people.

_____

_____

_____

15. Using the Engel scale, determine where these people are in their Christward movement.

_____

_____

WRITTEN REPORT

Write a short descriptive paper of your people. Also address the questions regarding the factors that may influence their conversion to Christ. You will be building your strategy on this information, so try to be as thorough as possible.

Questions for Reflection

As you begin researching a people group, adopt them for prayer. Commit yourself to this task daily. List specific ways you desire God to work among them. If you do this faithfully, the Lord will begin to etch His heart for them into you. Record this aspect of your journey to the nations below.

_____

_____

_____

_____

_____

_____

_____

_____

_____

_____

_____

CHAPTER 9

Entry Strategies, Evangelism, and Church Planting

Now that we have targeted a people and found out as much as possible about them, we must face the question of how to go about reaching them. There are three strategic aspects to this question. The first is to determine an *entry strategy*, that is, the best way of penetrating the area where the people live with the forces for evangelization. The second aspect is the specific *evangelistic tactics* which will be used in approaching the people with the gospel. The final aspect deals with *church planting strategies* which will allow for a cluster of culturally relevant churches to grow spontaneously throughout the people group.

In the first section of this chapter, we will consider two approaches to meeting the challenge of the apparent inaccessibility of some people groups. Next, we will look at different methods of evangelism and examples of effective and not-so-effective strategies. In the final section, a system for the spontaneous multiplication of churches will be examined. As you read, keep in mind the people group you have selected for your unreached peoples research paper. You will want to apply the principles presented to develop a strategy for reaching your "adopted" people.

I. Entry Strategies

Certain dynamics in the current world situation complicate the pioneer missionary's task. Four interrelated and opposing forces stand out.

1. The *resurgence of the traditional religions* of Hinduism, Buddhism, and Islam is being fomented internally by segments of each group. These groups are also attempting to extend their religions to other geographic areas. Increasingly, the missionary is being faced with people who have an awakened sense of their traditional religion.

2. The *rising tide of nationalism* has tended to bias populations against Christianity because Christianity is perceived to be a form of cultural imperialism.

3. The *revolutionary contexts* in which many unreached peoples exist creates some extremely sensitive situations for missionaries, who are often pressured to express allegiance to one faction or another. Compliance or non-compliance to these requests brings real physical dangers.

4. Due to the first three of these obstacles, *government restrictions to traditional missionary work* are now the norm, not the exception.

Creative Access Countries

Most of the unreached peoples of the world live in countries which have severe government restrictions on missionary activity. These countries do not grant visas to missionaries whose primary activities are evangelism and church planting. In some cases, visas may be granted for medical missionaries or others involved in relief and development. In these instances, the document may be granted on the strict condition that the missionaries confine their activities to their professional obligations and not be involved in "proselytizing."

Under these conditions, missions strategists have increasingly recognized the importance of using alternate strategies for entering the country or area where the target group lives. These *creative access strategies* often employ *tentmakers*, missionaries with secular occupations which they use to enter and remain in the target area.

In the following article, Ruth Siemens explains who tentmakers are and the practical reasons for employing this strategy.

❑ *Tentmakers Needed for World Evangelization* *

Ruth E. Siemens *

Recent events that have radically altered the world's landscape of nations have multiplied the opportunities and the need for tentmakers!

A vast new global job market began to emerge even before the Soviet Union (last of the European colonial empires) began crumbling into independent republics. Its nearby satellite nations and its client states on every continent, bereft of Soviet subsidies, and with no superpowers to play against each other, were already struggling to meet the tough new demands for international aid: market economics, multiparty politics, and improved human rights. The worldwide trend toward disassociation, the crosscurrents of association (the new European Community, the united Germanys, Yemens, Chinas, and Koreas, a Western Hemisphere bloc, Pacific Rim bloc, etc.), and a new vitality in Arab countries—are reshaping the international job market to provide more openings in more locations than ever before.

* Siemens, R. E. (1992). Tentmakers needed for world evangelization. In R. D. Winter & S. C. Hawthorne (Eds.), *Perspectives on the world Christian movement: A reader* (rev. ed.) (pp. D246-D248, D252-D253). Pasadena: William Carey Library.

** Ruth E. Siemens served for 21 years in Peru, Brazil, Spain, and Portugal for the International Fellowship of Evangelical Students (IFES). During six of those years she funded her ministry with tentmaking efforts in education. She is Founder and Director of Global Opportunities, an agency which helps to counsel and link Christian witnesses and international employment opportunities. She also lectures and writes extensively on the subject of tentmaking.

What are tentmakers
and how do they serve?

Historically, tentmakers are missions-committed Christians who, like Paul, support themselves in secular work, as they engage in cross-cultural ministry on the job and in their free time.

At the other end of the scale are regular missionaries, who receive church or individual donor support, and are usually perceived as religious workers (even if they do nursing or teaching in a mission institution). In between, is a continuum of combinations of the two options—all valid and biblical. A tentmaker may supplement salary with donor gifts, and a missionary may take a part-time job to augment donor support, or for more contact with non-believers. God leads people to alternate between the modes at different stages of life.

It is important to note that most evangelical expatriates are not tentmakers, because they have little or no commitment to missions or to ministry, unless to their own compatriots. Maybe one percent evangelize citizens of their host country and qualify as tentmakers.

It is important to note that tentmakers are in full-time spiritual ministry, even when they have full-time employment. The secular job is not an inconvenience, but the God-given context in which tentmakers live out the gospel in a winsome, wholesome, nonjudgmental way, demonstrating personal integrity, doing quality work, and developing caring relationships. Because they are under the daily scrutiny of non-believers, they deal with their failures in an open, godly way.

Verbal witness is essential because without words, their exemplary lives merely confuse. Tentmakers do low-key, "fishing" evangelism. Their appropriate comments about God, inserted casually into secular conversations, are "bait" that draw nibbles. They "fish out" the seekers—those "with ears to hear"—without attracting the attention of spiritually hostile listeners around them. The seekers' questions help pace the conversations, as they are ready for more, and show the Christian what to say—the truth they lack, their misconceptions, felt needs, hurts, hang-ups, and obstacles to faith.

This approach reduces evangelism largely to answering questions (Col. 4:5, 6 and 1 Pet. 3:14-16), which is easier and more effective than more confrontational approaches. Even veteran Christians can say, "I'm still learning about my faith, but would you like to see what Jesus said?" and take out a pocket Testament for a one-on-one lunch break Bible study. It grows into a weekly home study group, and then into a house church! Natural contact with colleagues, students, patients, clients, neighbors, and other social acquaintances make tentmaking ideal for church planting.

Tentmakers are in full-time spiritual ministry, even when they have full-time employment.

Tentmakers' free-time ministries vary widely. While I worked and evangelized in secular schools, God helped me also to pioneer IVCF-IFES university student movements in Peru and Brazil. A tentmaker couple translated the New Testament for five million Muslims while he did university teaching and she tutored English! A science teacher evangelized his students in rural Kenya and preached every third Sunday in the local church. A symphony violinist in Singapore had Bible studies with fellow musicians. A faculty person and an engineer set up a Christian bookstore in the Arab Gulf region. A theologically trained graduate student did campus evangelism and taught part-time in an Asian seminary. Some start needed ministries for men, women, children, professional people, prisoners or slum dwellers, literacy or publishing work—or whatever is needed. But evangelism on the job continues to be of major concern.

It is important to note that many tentmakers have theological and missiological training, even though God leads them to work as tentmakers—as lay people rather than as formal missionaries. But in this spiritual struggle for control of the world, not everyone needs officer's training. Foot soldiers must know how to do spiritual battle through prayer and how to use the "sword of the Spirit"—God's Word.

They need good personal and small group Bible study skills—for evangelism, discipling, training, and worship. All need a brief course on missions and cultural orientation for their target country.

It is important to note that tentmakers work together in fellowship and accountability groups. At home their churches and friends pray for them, and over-seas they work in tentmaker teams, or with a local national church, or as members of a tentmaker sending agency, or as field partners or full members of a regular mission agency, some of which now have tentmaker programs. An English language expatriate church overseas can be helpful, if it does not distract the tentmaker from concentrating on local citizens.

1. *Is a tentmaker really a missionary? Why or why not?*

_____

_____

_____

2. *What is the major ministry concern of the tentmaker? What does this involve primarily?*

_____

_____

_____

The term *tentmaking* as a missionary strategy is derived from the Apostle Paul's allusions to his secular trade. In Corinth, he joined himself to Aquila and Priscilla, who were of his same occupation—tentmaking (Acts 18:1-3). Several times throughout the epistles, Paul makes reference to the fact that he supported himself through his labors. Why did he do this when he probably could have received support from the churches and dedicated himself fully to ministry? Ruth Siemens elaborates on several of Paul's reasons.

Paul's reasons for tentmaking

Credibility

Paul says twice (1 Cor. 9:12; 2 Cor. 6:3ff) that he works in order not to put an "obstacle" in the way of the gospel in the Gentile world. He makes sure his message and motivation will not be suspect. He is not a "peddler of God's Word," not a "people pleaser" preaching to gain fatter profits. He does not want to be confused with the unscrupulous orators who roamed the empire, exploiting audiences. He is "free from all men"—owes no favors.

Identification

Paul adapts culturally to people, in order to win them—to the Jews as a Jew, to the Greeks as a Greek (an educated Gentile), and to the "weak" (the lower classes) as an artisan (1 Cor. 9:19ff). As a highly educated upper class person, Paul had no trouble making friends with the Asiarchs in Ephesus. But manual labor helps him identify with the lower classes, because most of the people in the empire were at the bottom of the economic scale. His identification with them is not phony—he earns his living (1 Cor. 4:11-12). This costly, incarnational service is not original with Paul. He imitates Jesus, whose identification with us cost Him everything (1 Cor. 11:1; Phil. 2:5-11).

Modeling

Paul shows how to live out the gospel in this idolatrous culture, because no seeker or convert had ever seen it before. He also models a Christian work ethic. In 1 Thessalonians 3:8 he says, "With toil and labor, we worked night and day that we might not burden any of you, and to give you an example to follow." Work is not optional for Christians. He transforms newly converted thieves, idlers, and drunkards into good providers for their families and generous givers to the needy (1 Cor. 6:10-11; Eph. 4:28; 1 Tim. 5:8). Imagine how these transformed bums affected observers! Paul gives much space in his brief letters to work, because without a strong work ethic, there cannot be godly converts, healthy families, independent churches nor productive societies.

More important, he establishes a pattern for lay ministry. Every convert is to be a full-time, unpaid evangelist—from the moment of conversion. They were to answer the questions of all who asked about their changed lives and new hope. Each convert represented a new beachhead into enemy territory, so they shouldn't usually move or change employment (1 Cor. 7:17-24). Nothing matures new believers like evangelism. Hundreds of homes and workplaces could be reached in a few days.

From the start, Paul's churches were self-reproducing—everyone evangelized. They were self-governing, not dependent on foreign leadership. They were self-supporting, not dependent on foreign funds (he taught Christians to give, but to the poor in their neighborhoods and in Jerusalem). Paul's church planting was only a means to his goal of producing a great worldwide missionary lay movement!

Self-support is a planned part of Paul's pioneering strategy, as a "skilled master builder," who warned others to heed how they built upon his foundation (1 Cor. 3:1ff). Local house church leaders who were appointed almost immediately were to keep their secular jobs. By the time growing congregations needed stronger leadership, it was clear which leaders had the respect of local Christians and non-believers, local funds were available for their support, and the pattern of unpaid evangelists was well established. Paid ministry was the exception. Paul never allowed his churches to become dependent on foreign funds or leadership.

How did Paul's strategy work out? Although Paul's evangelists were from unsavory, uneducated, pagan backgrounds, with neither anthropological nor missiological training, most had received the Lord at enormous risk, and they risked their lives to take it to others.

Paul establishes a pattern for lay ministry. Every convert is to be a full-time, unpaid evangelist—from the moment of conversion.

In 10 years (the three journeys took a decade), Paul and his friends (one small team), without support (no donor funds), evangelized six whole provinces, in a hostile environment. They did it by winning and mobilizing the largely uneducated, unpaid converts. In just over 20 years, Paul could say, "From Jerusalem to Illyricum I have fully preached the gospel of Christ.... I no longer have any room for work in these regions" (Rom. 15:19-24). He had evangelized the Greek-speaking half of the Roman Empire and now turned to the more Latin half—including Rome and Spain.

But how can he claim to be through with the Greek half, when neither he nor his team seem to have left the main cities? Paul said he was debtor to all classes, including the barbarians—those who were not native Greek speakers (Rom. 1:14-16). The Empire was never more than a chain of city colonies and military outposts, each with its own customs, local laws, and deities, respected by Roman authorities. Neither the Greeks nor the Romans had ever tried to integrate or to educate the hinterlands. Many languages were used, even in the cities—by the lower class laborers. (Remember Lystra in Acts 14?)

By turning these multi-lingual, lower class converts into unpaid evangelists, Paul virtually guaranteed the evangelization of the hinterlands, as converts ran to share the gospel in their home towns, and village people located their friends in the city. Converts took the gospel home, clothed in their own language and culture. After a few months in Philippi, Paul speaks of Macedonian churches. Paul's first follow-up letter to the Thessalonians says the gospel has already sounded out from them through the whole region! Corinth spreads the gospel through Achaia. Paul stays in Ephesus three years, but Luke writes that after two, "all Asia had already heard"—the whole province! It was indigenous, exponential growth!

Speed matters in hostile cultures. The gospel spread so quickly that by the time the opposition had geared up, it was too late to put out the fire.

We need to give much more attention to the different aspects of Paul's pioneering strategy and see how to apply it today—for example, by sending both models together. Donald McGavran said that church growth requires a large group of unpaid evangelists. But it is not easy to produce them, if the only models are missionaries on full donor support.

3. Why was tentmaking so important to establishing a dynamic, evangelizing first century church?

_____

_____

_____

Nonresidential Missionaries

A second strategic approach which is being given increasing importance today is the *nonresidential missionary*, that is, a person who resides outside the primary geographic region of the target group but carries out a number of focused activities to reach the group. The following information on this new approach is excerpted from an article by V. David Garrison.

❑ An Unexpected New Strategy: Using Nonresidential Missions to Finish the Task *

V. David Garrison **

Herein lies the great promise of nonresidential missions. By definition it utilizes every evangelization resource and method in existence and concentrates them directly on an unevangelized population target.

The resources already exist for evangelizing the world. The nonresidential missionary's arsenal, so to speak, is well-stocked. His is merely the task of redeploying these resources to their greatest strategic advantage. It is for this reason that the nonresi-

---

* Garrison, V. D. (1990). An unexpected new strategy: Using nonresidential missions to finish the task. *International Journal of Frontier Missions, 7*(4), 107-115.

** V. David Garrison has served as a foreign missionary in Hong Kong. He is currently Director of Nonresidential Missions for the Southern Baptist Foreign Mission Board and is the author of *Missions Beyond Boundaries*.

dential missionary is never in competition with any other missionary approach; his approach both includes and presupposes these other ministries as the key resources for accomplishing his own objectives.

Thus, the healthier and more diverse the world of Christian missionary resources becomes, the more vital the nonresidential missionary approach will be.

4. *What important underlying assumption does the author build on in suggesting a nonresidential mission strategy? Are there others he doesn't mention?*

_____

_____

_____

Essential characteristics

Nonresidence

The nonresidential missionary operates fundamentally from a nonresidential base. This means the missionary docs not reside among the unevangelized segment he intends to evangelize. While it may be possible and even beneficial for the nonresidential missionary to locate among or near his population target for purposes of language acquisition and investigation, the real work begins after the nonresidential missionary withdraws to an unrestricted setting in a world-class or crossroads urban center. The primary reason for nonresidence is due to restrictions that would be placed on a missionary living and working residentially among the people.

5. *Why is it preferable for a nonresidential missionary to live outside the main target area?*

_____

_____

_____

Networking

Unlike an itinerant missionary or a gospel smuggler, the nonresidential missionary is not necessarily committed to living as close as possible to the borders of his target population. Instead, he is looking for a place of residence which will allow maximum networking capabilities with other Great Commission Christians. Some important factors to consider in this regard are: (1) free flow of information (computers, telephone, postal, etc.), (2) locations where a diaspora population of the target segment reside (refugees, migrant workers, etc.), (3) location along a key travel route in and out of the region (for airplanes, trains, etc.).

It is inconceivable for a nonresidential missionary to attempt either a "lone ranger" approach to evangelizing his population target or even a "monodenominational" approach. By utilizing every possible Great Commission Christian contact, rather than a single, limited evangelistic contact, the nonresidential missionary is able to catalyze hundreds and thousands of evangelizing agents in a concerted effort at reaching his target assignment.

6. What is essential to effective networking?

_____

_____

Specific targeting

By limiting the nonresidential missionary to a single unevangelized population segment, the task is kept both manageable and strategic. Unevangelized population segments are those which have yet to receive an opportunity to hear and respond to the gospel of Jesus Christ. This should not be confused with a closed country, which may or may not be evangelized. Nor should it be equated with a population segment which, though non-Christian, has numerous options for receiving the gospel within its own context.

7. Why is a specific target necessary to this approach?

_____

_____

Four functions

Researching

Research is the first stage. It prepares the way for all subsequent nonresidential mission work. There are two worlds which the nonresidential missionary must master: (1) the world of his targeted population segment, and (2) the world of evangelization resources. The ultimate goal is to bring these two worlds together in a dynamic interaction which will lead to the evangelization of the population target in a manner that will result in a healthy, multiplying church.

Strategizing

After investigating the two worlds, the nonresidential missionary begins developing a comprehensive strategy for the segment's evangelization. As much as possible, this strategy should utilize the entire spectrum of evangelization options. Four fundamental categories of evangelization strategy have been identified: (1) prayer, (2) Scriptures, (3) media ministries, and (4) Christian presence.

Prayer. The least evangelized countries, cities, and peoples on earth have long been under the spiritual domination of Satan. Only prayer can break this oppressive control.

Scriptures. There is no limit to the effectiveness of God's Word once it is available to an unevangelized people. A crucial part of the nonresidential missionary's initial research is to determine the status of Scripture translation or accessibility and devise plans for making it available to the people. In many

> *There is no limit to the effectiveness of God's Word once it is available to an unevangelized people.*

cases, the population target may not even have a literate language. There are today numerous ways to present the Bible to the people apart from the written page. Radio broadcasts, audio cassette ministries, and even video formats such as the "Jesus" film are all capable of delivering God's Word to a people who can understand the spoken though not the written message.

Media ministries. Few societies today are without radio receivers, and virtually all nonresidential missionaries depend on radio broadcasts to transmit the gospel into unevangelized hinterlands. Other means of media communication include correspondence evangelism, utilizing both personal correspondence and mass mailings into restricted settings. In addition, the remarkably effective "Jesus" film can now be delivered into highly restricted countries.

Christian presence. Every nonresidential ministry, if it is to be effective, must identify opportunities for a witnessing Christian presence among the population target. Since traditional missionary presence is not formally allowed, the nonresidential mission strategist must rely on other avenues of Christian presence. Figure 9-1 shows the types of Christian presence and their lengths of service that a typical nonresidential missionary would seek to place in his targeted area.

Implementation

Implementation of this strategy requires careful coordination of goals and action plans with dozens of other Christian agencies and individuals. The nonresidential missionary has only the power of persuasion at this crucial juncture in his ministry. But he also has at his disposal literally hundreds of agencies and thousands of individuals from which to recruit.

Evaluating

The work of the nonresidential missionary is not complete without careful monitoring and evaluation of the segment to determine to what extent the various methods are proving effective. Evangelistic effectiveness, i.e., the production of viable self-sustaining and reproducing churches, of course, is the ultimate goal. To monitor effectiveness, the nonresidential missionary is expected to continually examine the conditions of the target segment using a range of indicators to measure evangelization.

CHRISTIAN WITNESSING PRESENCE			
TYPE	SHORT-TERM	MEDIUM-LENGTH	LONG-TERM
Mission related	English teachers	Exchange students	Tentmakers
Relief and development	Crisis surveys	Two-year relief workers	Agricultural development, health care, holistic community development
Third World missionaries	Tourist evangelists	Itinerant evangelists	Immigrants
Indigenous	Lay volunteers	Church planters	Pastors
Total Number	100 Short-Term	40 Medium-Length	10 Long-Term

Figure 9-1

8. How important is each of the four functions to reaching a people successfully?

_____

_____

_____

_____

9. What qualities and characteristics should a person have in order to be a nonresidential missionary?

_____

_____

_____

10. Could a local church serve as a nonresidential mission's "nerve center"? Why, why not, or under what conditions?

_____

_____

_____

II. Evangelism

The resurgence of traditional religions and heightened nationalism make it difficult at best for a pioneer missionary to communicate effectively a gospel which is culturally appropriate. Under these pressures, it may seem best to exercise a benign presence rather than pursue aggressive evangelization of a people. In the following excerpt, Herbert Kane helps clarify some of the issues surrounding the evangelization of the unreached.

❑ *The Work of Evangelism* *

J. Herbert Kane **

Purpose of evangelism

Evangelism has a twofold purpose, one immediate and the other remote. The immediate purpose is the conversion of the individual and his incorporation into the Christian church. The remote purpose is the proclamation of the Lordship of Christ over all creation and the extension of the kingdom of God throughout the earth. The first is emphasized in Mark's account of the Great Commission. "Go ye into all the world, and preach the gospel to every creature. He that believeth and is baptized shall be saved, but he that believeth not shall be damned" (Mark 16:1-16, KJV). The second is found in Matthew's version of the Great Commission. "All power is given unto me in heaven and in earth. Go ye therefore, and teach [*make disciples of*] all nations, baptizing them in the name of the Father, and of the Son, and of the Holy Ghost" (Matt. 28:18-19, KJV).

---

* Kane, J. H. (1980). *Life and work on the mission field* (pp. 246-250). Grand Rapids: Baker Book House.

** Drawing on 15 years of missionary experience in central China with the China Inland Mission, J. Herbert Kane taught for many years in the School of World Mission and Evangelism at Trinity Evangelical Divinity School, and was Professor Emeritus until his death in 1990. Kane has authored a number of missions textbooks, among them *Christian Missions in Biblical Perspective* and *A Global View of Christian Missions*.

It is quite impossible to exaggerate the importance of conversion. One of the strongest statements on the subject comes from Stanley Jones, who gave 60 years to the evangelization of India.

> We divide humanity into many classes—white and colored, rich and poor, educated and uneducated, Americans and non-Americans, East and West…. But Jesus drew a line down through all these distinctions and divided humanity into just two classes—the unconverted and the converted, the once-born and the twice-born. All men live on one side or the other of that line. No other division matters—this is a division that divides, it is a division that runs through time and eternity.*

Unfortunately, "conversion" is a dirty word in some circles. It is anathema among the Hindus of India. Gandhi inveighed against the missionaries for attempting to convert Hindus to the Christian faith. "If you come to India to make us better Hindus, fine; but don't try to convert us to Christianity." During the 1960s, two states in India passed anti-conversion laws; they were later repealed by the Supreme Court. Others in the Third World regard conversion as an act of cultural imperialism—all right for the 19th century but completely out of keeping with the more sophisticated mood of the 20th century.

Even in the West we find an aversion to the idea of conversion. Some theologians are embarrassed by the term and would like to get rid of it. J. G. Davies says: "I would be glad if the term conversion could be dropped from the Christian vocabulary."** Those who believe in baptismal regeneration obviously have no need of conversion; baptism has already made them a "child of God, a member of Christ, and an inheritor of the kingdom of God." Others regard conversion as a spiritual experience appropriate to skid row but hardly acceptable in more refined circles.

Some equate conversion with proselytism, which has always been in disrepute in respectable circles. Missionaries in India, Uganda, and other places have been accused of "buying" converts by giving them money, famine relief, educational advantages, and medical services, or by according them other kinds of preferential treatment. Because of the humanitarian character of their work, these charges seem to be substantiated. If a government wanted to press charges, it could easily produce the required "evidence." Some governments have forbidden young people under the age of 18 to accept Christian baptism.

The Christian missionary has no choice. His aim is to make converts. At the same time, he would vigorously deny that he engages in proselytizing.

In spite of the difficulties and dangers involved, however, the Christian missionary has no choice. His aim is to make converts, and if pressed to do so, he would have to acknowledge that such is the case, even in Muslim countries. At the same time, he would vigorously deny that he engages in proselytizing. Such reprehensible conduct is beneath the dignity of the Christian missionary. He will not use force, nor will he offer inducements. He will present the claims of Christ and hope that the listener will voluntarily acknowledge Jesus Christ as his Savior. Beyond that he will not go; to do so would be to violate the freedom and integrity of the individual.

Conversion, to be genuine, must involve a complete change of heart and life. The root meaning of the word is "to turn." It was said of the Thessalonian believers that they "turned to God from idols" (1 Thess. 1:9, KJV). It is therefore a threefold turning: from sin to righteousness, from death to life, from idols to God. It is morally impossible to embrace sin and righteousness at the same time. Paul asks: "What fellowship hath righteousness with unrighteousness? And what communion hath light with darkness? And what concord hath Christ with Belial?" (2 Cor. 6:14-15, KJV). By conversion the person becomes a "new creature, old things are

---

* Jones, E. S. (1959). *Conversion* (p. 5). New York: Abingdon Press.

** Davies, J. G. (1967). *Dialogue with the world* (p. 54). London: SCM Press.

passed away; all things are become new" (2 Cor. 5:17, KJV). The convert is then a "new man," with a new center of gravity, a new system of values, a new standard of morality, a new frame of reference, and a new purpose in life. The outstanding example of conversion in the New Testament is Zacchaeus in Luke 19. When this dishonest tax collector had a personal encounter with Jesus Christ, he was immediately and completely turned around. His confession is noteworthy. "Behold, Lord, the half of my goods I give to the poor; and if I have taken anything from any man by false accusation, I restore him fourfold." That is genuine conversion.

Following conversion, the convert does not remain in isolation. He becomes a member of the universal church, the Body of Christ, by the baptism of the Holy Spirit. By an act of his own he joins a local congregation and becomes part of its fellowship, work, and witness.

The second purpose of evangelism is the proclamation of the Lordship of Jesus Christ over all creation and the extension of the kingdom into all parts of the world. The church's earliest creed was, "Jesus Christ is Lord" (Phil. 2:11, KJV). There is a direct connection between the Lordship of Christ and the world mission of the church. This comes out clearly in Matthew's account of the Great Commission. It is precisely because all authority in heaven and on earth has been given by God the Father to God the Son that the church has the responsibility to make disciples of all nations. The kingdom of God becomes a reality only as the peoples of the world respond to the gospel and become part of the kingdom (Acts 26:18; Col. 1:13).

11. What is the true biblical meaning of conversion?

_____

_____

_____

12. Why is the term "conversion" important to Christian vocabulary?

_____

_____

_____

Varieties of evangelism

There are three kinds of evangelism: presence evangelism, proclamation evangelism, and persuasion evangelism. The first is the kind most strongly advocated in ecumenical circles. The second is most widely practiced by evangelicals. The third has supporters and detractors in both camps.

Presence evangelism

In spite of widespread aversion to this kind of evangelism on the part of evangelicals, it is a valid, even a necessary, kind to use. We dare not preach a gospel that we are not prepared to live by. Bishop Azariah of Dornakal attributed the mass movement in the Telugu country to the quality of life manifested by the Christians.

> It is universally admitted by all missions and churches that the reason most often given by the converts for accepting the Christian way of life is the impression produced upon them

by the changed lives of the Christian community.*

Not all Christians have this kind of testimony. Dr. Ambedkar was for many years the leader of the Untouchables in India. Realizing that Hinduism had nothing to offer his followers, Ambedkar decided to study the other religions with a view to joining one of them. After examining the claims of Christianity with Bishop Pickett, he remarked: "When I study the life of Christ in the Gospels, I think that I and my people should become Christians; but when I see the lives of the Christians here in Bombay, I say to myself, 'No, Christianity is not for us.'" Some time later, at an open-air service in Nagpur, Dr. Ambedkar and 70,000 of his followers renounced Hinduism and became Buddhists.

Let no one say that presence evangelism is not important. We have the same problem here in the West. It was the German philosopher Nietzsche who said: "I could more readily believe in your Savior if I could find more people who had been saved by Him."

If we insist on talking about the transforming power of the gospel, we had better be sure that we and our converts have really been transformed. Otherwise our words will have a hollow ring.

Proclamation evangelism

In spite of its importance, presence evangelism is not enough to lead a person to saving faith in Christ. At best it can only create within him a desire to know more. To be really effective, it must be accompanied by proclamation evangelism.

This is the form most frequently referred to in the New Testament. John the Baptist came "preaching," Jesus came "preaching." The apostles in the book of Acts preached; Paul said: "Jesus Christ sent me not to baptize but to preach" (1 Cor. 1:17, KJV). Certain things belong together. You ride a horse, you play a game. You preach the gospel. God has ordained that men should be saved through preaching (1 Cor. 1:21).

The gospel contains certain propositional truths that must be understood before saving faith can be exercised. These include the truths concerning God, man, sin, and salvation, and the facts concerning the life, death, and resurrection of Christ. These truths must be preached with all the clarity we can muster.

It is rather strange that proclamation evangelism, which occupied such a large place in the preaching and teaching of the early church, should have fallen into disrepute. The Billy Graham type of evangelism, which is based on "the Bible says" and directed to the salvation of the individual, is totally unacceptable in certain quarters today. When Billy spoke to the National Council of Churches in Miami several years ago, he was chided for his simplistic approach to the complex problems of present-day society. They said, "Billy, you'll have to give up this kind of preaching. You're taking us back to the 19th century." To which Billy replied, "I thought I was taking you back to the first century."

Presence evangelism is not enough to lead a person to saving faith in Christ. To be really effective, it must be accompanied by proclamation evangelism.

Alan Walker, a well known Australian evangelist, does not share their point of view. He said: "I confess I cannot understand the current depreciation of the preaching ministry. Some protest against an over-verbalizing of the gospel is justified, but the effectiveness of a man, a woman standing up to preach with conviction is undoubted."**

Persuasion evangelism

Persuasion goes one step beyond proclamation and tries to induce the hearer to believe the message for himself. There are those who repudiate this method, declaring that the evangelist is not responsible for results. He should be content to preach the gospel and leave the results with the Lord.

---

* Padilla, C. R. (Ed.) (1976). *The new face of evangelism* (p. 80). Downers Grove, IL: InterVarsity Press.

** Evangelism. (1939). *The Madras Series*, 3:42. New York: International Missionary Council.

There is something to be said for both sides. It is possible to overstep the bounds of propriety and bring undue pressure to bear until the person accepts the gospel under duress. It should be categorically stated that this approach is both wrong and harmful. The results of such a method can be disastrous. It has no sanction in Scripture and should be studiously avoided.

On the other hand, the word "persuasion" is not foreign to the New Testament; Paul said, "Knowing therefore the terror of the Lord, we persuade men" (2 Cor. 5:11, KJV). The New English Bible refers to Paul as "trying to convince Jews and Greeks" (Acts 18:4, NEB). In Ephesus, before moving over to the school of Tyrannus, Paul spent three months in the synagogue, "using argument and persuasion in his presentation of the gospel" (Acts 19:8, NEB). Preaching the gospel is serious business, fraught with eternal consequences for good or evil (2 Cor. 2:16). Paul was never guilty of presenting the gospel on a take-it-or-leave-it basis. He pled with men to be reconciled to God (2 Cor. 5:20). The apostles did not use force to win converts, but they did call for a response. Moreover, they expected results and when they did not get them they turned to other people more willing to receive the message (Acts 13:46).

13. *Some claim that evangelism is a matter of style and personality of the presenter. That is, some people prefer presence evangelism, others are "preachers," and still others are aggressive persuaders. To what extent is this claim true?*

_____

_____

_____

_____

14. *Is there any relationship between our expectations and the actual results of our evangelism? What implications do results have for mission strategy?*

_____

_____

_____

_____

_____

If indeed we must evangelize, the way we go about proclaiming the gospel has a significant effect on the response to the message. Instead of "good news," the gospel may be interpreted as "bad news." What the messenger does and how he lives are often more important than what he says. The following article demonstrates the importance of using methods of evangelism which truly present the gospel as "good news."

❏ *Evangelization of Whole Families* *

Chua Wee Hian **

Year: 1930
Locality: Northwest China

Case studies:

1. The approach and strategy of two single European lady missionaries.

2. The approach and strategy of the Little Flock Assembly of Chefoo, Shantung.

Objectives: Identical—to plant local churches and to engage in extensive village evangelism.

Case study 1

Two gifted and dedicated lady missionaries were sent by their missionary society to Northwest China. Their mandate was to evangelize and plant congregations in a cluster of villages. They spoke fluent Chinese; they labored faithfully and fervently. After a decade, a small congregation emerged. However, most of its members were women. Their children attended the Sunday School regularly. The visitor to this small congregation would easily detect the absence of men.

In their reports and newsletters, both missionaries referred to the "hardness of hearts" that was prevalent among the men. References were made also to promising teenagers who were opposed by their parents when they sought permission for baptism.

Case study 2

In 1930 a spiritual awakening swept through the Little Flock Assembly in Shantung. Many members sold their entire possessions in order to send 70 *families* to the Northwest as "instant congregations." Another 30 *families* migrated to the Northeast. By 1944, 40 new assemblies had been established, and all these were vitally involved in evangelism.

Contrasts between approaches

Now, in terms of dedication and doctrinal orthodoxy, both the Europeans and the Little Flock Assembly shared the same commitment and faith. But why the striking contrasts in results and in their strategies of church planting?

Consider the case of the two single lady missionaries. Day by day, the Chinese villagers saw them establishing contacts and building the bridges of friendships with women, usually when their husbands or fathers were out working in the fields or trading in nearby towns. Their foreignness (dubbed "red hair devils") was enough to incite cultural and racial prejudices in the minds of the villagers. But their single status was something that was socially questionable. It was a well-known fact in all Chinese society that the families constitute basic social units. These units insure security. In Confucian teaching, three of the five basic relationships have to do with family ties—father and son, older brother and younger brothers, husband and wife. The fact that these ladies were making contacts with individual women and not having dialogues with the elders would make them appear to be foreign agents seeking to destroy the fabric of the village community. A question that would constantly crop up in the gossip and discussion of the villagers would be the fact of the missionaries' single state. Why aren't they married? Why aren't they visibly related to their parents, brothers and sisters, uncles and aunts, and other relatives? So when they persuaded the women or the youth to leave the religion of their forefathers, they were regarded as "family breakers."

---

* Hian, Chua Wee. (1975). Evangelization of whole families. In J. D. Douglas (Ed.), *Let the earth hear his voice* (pp. 968-971). Minneapolis: World Wide Publications.

** Chua Wee Hian is General Secretary Emeritus of the International Fellowship of Evangelical Students (IFES). An Asian from Singapore, he has served as an associate secretary for IFES in East Asia and as editor of *The Way*, a quarterly magazine for Asian students.

By contrast, the Little Flock Assembly in sending out Chinese Christian families sent out agents that were recognizable socio-cultural entities. Thus the 70 families became an effective missionary task force. It is not difficult to imagine the heads of these families sharing their faith with the elders of the villagers. The grandmothers could informally transmit the joy of following Christ and of their deliverance from demonic powers to the older women in pagan villages. The housewives in the markets could invite their counterparts to attend the services that were held each Sunday by the "instant congregations." No wonder 40 new assemblies were established as a result of this approach to church planting and evangelism.

15. Why were the two women missionaries perceived as a threat to Chinese social structure?

_____

_____

16. What built-in success factors did the missionaries from the Little Flock Assembly have?

_____

_____

Evangelizing families in other cultures

The strategy of evangelizing whole families is applicable not only in Chinese communities. It is also effective in other Asian communities, African villages and tribes, and Latin American *barrios* and societies. Writing on the rapid spread of the Christian faith in Korea, Roy Shearer observed:

> One most important factor governing how the church grew is the structure of Korean society. In Korea, we are dealing with a society based on the family, not the tribe. The family is strong even today. The soundest way for a man to come to Christ is in the setting of his own family.*

He went on to relate repeated situations when heads of families returned to their clan villages and were successful in persuading their relatives and kinsmen to "turn from idols to serve the living God." He concluded:

> The gospel flowed along the web of family relationships. This web is the transmission line for the current of the Holy Spirit that brought men and women into the church.**

In her book *New Patterns for Discipling Hindus*, Miss B. V. Subbamma categorically asserted that the Hindu family might be the only social institution through which the gospel could be transmitted and received. Not all would agree with this assertion, because there are evidences of university students who have professed faith in Christ in the great university centers of India. Some could take this step of faith because they were free from parental pressures. However, as a general rule, Miss Subbamma's observation and deduction are correct.

Evangelizing whole families is the pattern of current missionary outreach in parts of Latin America. There in the Roman Catholic culture of web rela-

---

* Shearer, R. E. (1966). *Wildfire: Church growth in Korea* (p. 146). Grand Rapids: Eerdmans.

** Shearer (p. 150).

tionships, family structures are strong. Exploiting this social pattern, the Chilean Pentecostals, like the Little Flock Assembly in Shantung 40 years ago, dispatch families from among their faithful to be agents and ambassadors of church expansion. Through these evangelizing families, many assemblies and congregations have been planted in different parts of that continent. The phenomenal growth of the Pentecostal movement in Latin America reflects the effectiveness of using families to evangelize families.

At times it is difficult for individualistic Westerners to realize that in many "face to face" societies religious decisions are made corporately. The individual in that particular type of society would be branded as a "traitor" and treated as an outcast if he were to embrace a new religious belief. After the Renaissance, in most Western countries, identity is expressed by the Cartesian dictum, *Cogito ergo sum*: I think, therefore I am. Man as a rational individual could think out religious options for himself and is free to choose the faith that he would like to follow. This dictum does not apply in many African tribal communities. For the Africans (and for many others) the unchanging dictum is, *I participate, therefore I am*. Conformity to and participation in traditional religious rites and customs give such people their identity. So if there is to be a radical change in religious allegiance, there must be a corporate or multi-individual decision.

This is particularly true of Muslim families and communities. The one-by-one method of individual evangelism will not work in such a society. A lecturer friend of mine who teaches in the multi-racial University of Singapore once made this significant remark, "I've discovered that for most Malay students (who are nearly all Muslims) Islam consists not of belief in Allah the supreme God—it is *community*." Ambassadors for Christ in Islamic lands should cope not only with theological arguments concerning the unity and nature of God; they should consider the social and cultural associations of Muslims. Where sizable groups of Muslims had been converted, their decisions were multi-individual. An excellent illustration would be that of Indonesia. During the past 15 years, wise missionaries and

---

Conformity to and participation in traditional religious rites and customs give many people their identity. So if there is to be a radical change in religious allegiance, there must be a corporate or multi-individual decision.

---

national pastors had been engaging in dialogues and discussions with the elders and leaders of local Muslim communities. When these decision-makers were convinced that Christ is the only way to God and that He alone is the Savior of the world, they returned to their villages and towns and urged all members to turn to Christ. So it was not surprising to witness whole communities being catechized and baptized together.

Such movements are termed as "people movements," and many years before the Indonesian happening, Ko Tha Byu, a remarkable Burmese evangelist, was instrumental in discipling whole Karen communities and villages to Jesus Christ. Today the Karen church is one of the strongest Christian communities in Southeast Asia.

---

17. *What is the basic difference between Eastern and Western perceptions of the relationship between an individual and the group?*

_____

_____

_____

18. *What strategy for evangelism is needed to penetrate cultures which highly value "family" and "community"? Why?*

_____

_____

_____

The biblical data

When we turn to the biblical records, we shall discover that families feature prominently, both as the recipients as well as the agents of salvation blessing.

To begin with, the family is regarded as divinely instituted by God (Eph. 3:15). In fact, all families owe their descent and composition to their Creator. By redemption, the church—God's own people—is described as "the household of God" (Eph. 2:19) and the "household of faith" (Gal. 6:10).

In the Pentateuch, great stress is laid on the sanctity of marriage, the relation between children and parents, masters and slaves. This emphasis is underscored in the New Testament (see Col. 3:18–4:1; Eph. 5:22–6:9; 1 Pet. 2:18–3:7).

It is the family or the household that pledges its allegiance to Yahweh. Joshua as head of his own household could declare, "As for me and my house, we will serve the Lord" (Josh. 24:15). Through Joshua's predecessor Moses, Yahweh had taught His people to celebrate His mighty acts by sacred meals and festivals. It is interesting to observe that the Feast of the Passover (Ex. 12:3-4) was a family meal. The head of the family was to recite and reenact the great drama of Israel's deliverance at this family gathering. Through Israel's history, even until New Testament days, family feasts, prayer, and worship were regularly held. Thus the Jewish family became both the object of God's grace and the visual agent of His redemptive actions. Their monotheistic faith expressed in terms of their family solidarity and religion must have created a tremendous impression on the Gentile communities. One of the results was that large numbers of Gentiles became proselytes, "associate members" of the Jewish synagogues. Jewish families made a sizable contribution to the "missionary" outreach.

The apostolic pattern for teaching was in and through family units (Acts 20:20). The first accession of a Gentile grouping to the Christian church was the family of the Roman centurion Cornelius in Caesarea (Acts 10:7, 24). At Philippi, Paul led the families of Lydia and the jailer to faith in Christ and incorporation into His church (Acts 16:15, 31-34). The "first fruits" of the great missionary apostle in Achaia were the families of Stephanas (1 Cor. 16:15), Crispus, and Gaius (Acts 18:8; 1 Cor. 1:16; Rom. 16:23). So it was clear that the early church discipled both Jewish and Gentile communities in families.

It was equally clear that households were used as outposts of evangelism. Aquila and Priscilla used their home in Ephesus and Rome as a center for the proclamation of the gospel (1 Cor. 16:19; Rom. 16:5). Congregations met in the homes of Onesiphorus (2 Tim. 1:16; 4:19) and Nymphas (Col. 4:15).

As the above article demonstrates, the Bible strongly supports the concept of family. Where family and community are highly valued, the gospel does not need to be perceived as a threat to the social structure. In fact, it can actually be presented in such a way that it strengthens this structure. Due respect for the head of the household or the elders of the community should be shown by communicating and discussing the gospel first with them. If a household accepts the gospel, then worship and religious ceremony should incorporate the family unit.

19. *What tactical changes might the two women missionaries discussed in the preceding article have made, had they better understood the importance of the family to the Chinese?*

The above case studies could lead one to the conclusion that unmarried women should not have been sent into the situation described. The only practical tactical change might seem to be for the women to have gotten married or to have returned to their homeland. The women in question, however, might have found the situation beyond their control or perhaps had chosen singleness as a preferred state for godly service, as Scripture advises (1 Cor. 7:32-35).

The dilemma of the missionaries' "inexplicable" singleness might have been solved, had these women realized the problem it caused in the minds of the Chinese. It is probable, however, that their Western orientation prevented them from recognizing the problem, since being single in the West is acceptable, particularly for those devoted to religious work. Perhaps the first failure of the women, then, was not understanding that they, as messengers, would be perceived in such a way that their message would be discredited. Later, when young people became Christians and were baptized against their parents' wishes, the missionaries transitioned from being a cultural enigma to an absolute threat!

Understanding this problem would perhaps have led the women to seek a creative solution. One such solution would have been "adoption" into a Chinese family. When confronted with similar situations, other single missionaries have occasionally placed themselves under the authority and protection of the head of a family. By doing this, they have eliminated some of the mystery surrounding their presence, and an acceptable niche has been found for them within the existing society. Still other missionary women have faced the problem by seeking respectable roles in teaching, tutoring, or some other profession. By providing a needed service, they have done much to gain acceptance in the life of the society.

The main point is that whatever the social structure, it is of utmost importance to present the gospel in such a way that it is not perceived unnecessarily as a threat to that society. When the messenger cannot be understood, it is likely that the message will not be understood either.

A comprehensive mission strategy should consider who is best able to reach a given people group. If the national church in that country, at E-1 or E-2 distance, is able to reach them, then every effort should be made to encourage them to do so before an E-3 effort is initiated from the outside. Unfortunately, missions are often launched without a real attempt to understand who is in the best position to reach a particular people. The national church may be considered too weak or unmotivated to do mission work, so the foreign mission society takes it upon itself to enter the new field. Unfortunately, through this process the national church is often circumvented, reinforcing harmful patterns.

Every church planting agency is obligated, through obedience to Christ, to teach missions to its young constituency. The emerging churches in newly evangelized nations have suffered from a lack of vision for and understanding of the missionary task. Once enlightened by the Word of God and missions advocates, these churches have demonstrated themselves to be capable and creative in reaching the unreached.

Some missions are finally awakening to such problems and neglect and are starting to support the development of mission agencies among young churches. Expatriate mission personnel are being loaned to the young agencies in support roles. Training programs, sponsored by older missions, are being offered to national believers who are seeking to enter cross-cultural mission work. If we are to take the remaining task of world evangelization seriously, it is imperative that we see much more of this international and inter-agency cooperation.

20. In the above case studies, who was in the best position to reach the Chinese of the Northwest? In what ways could the two missions possibly have combined efforts?

_____

_____

_____

The initial strategy for evangelism needs to incorporate more than just "preaching." It also requires sensitivity to the target culture, some identification with the people, and an understanding of the best way to communicate the gospel within the cultural context, since the way the messenger is perceived determines to a large extent the effectiveness of the gospel penetration. A comprehensive strategy will also consider who is best suited to minister the gospel to a particular people. It will evaluate how the Spirit of God is leading individuals to commit themselves to the evangelization of a people, and it will reinforce that vision and leading.

III. Church Planting

Let us now project ourselves beyond the initial stages of evangelization. Let us assume that we have worked hard at understanding the people. We have learned their language and culture, gained their acceptance, understood their felt needs, applied our skills to communicate Christian love, and seen families come to Christ and organize into a church. How do we go about seeing these initial results multiplied throughout the people group?

In the following article, veteran church planter George Patterson outlines the principles behind the spontaneous multiplication of churches.

❑ *The Spontaneous Multiplication of Churches* *

George Patterson **

Our Lord Jesus Christ commands us to look on the fields that are ready for harvest (John 4:35). So— let's do it. How many men and women and children, persons with feelings like ours, still know nothing of Jesus' sacrificial death and life-giving resurrection? At least 2.2 billion persons! To shake their hands, at a rate of 60 a minute or 3,600 an hour, for 8 hours each day of the week, would take over 200 years! How painful to see so many unaware of God's pardon!

Our Lord sends us to disciple every "nation" (people group) by training them to obey all His com-

* Patterson, G. (1992). The spontaneous multiplication of churches. In R. D. Winter & S. C. Hawthorne (Eds.), *Perspectives on the world Christian movement: A reader* (rev. ed.) (pp. D76-D94). Pasadena: William Carey Library.

** In 1965 George Patterson began working in northern Honduras with the Conservative Baptist Home Mission Society. He adapted theological education-by-extension to "obedience oriented discipling." He trained Honduran pastoral students on the job as they raised up and pastored over 100 churches. Patterson continues to work with the CBHMS and now trains missionaries for church reproduction. He also directs a ministry called Cultural Adaptation Training (CAT).

mands—which include, of course, discipling *others* (Matt. 28:18-20). This means that we disciple a "nation" only when it is permeated by obedient disciples who also disciple other unevangelized peoples. So we don't simply go and start a church among a people. We, or those we send, must start the kind of church that grows and reproduces spontaneously as churches will, in daughter churches, granddaughter churches, great-granddaughter churches, and so on. *Spontaneous* reproduction of churches means the Holy Spirit moves a church (yours?) to reproduce daughter churches on its own, without outsiders pushing it (Acts 13:1-3).

Spontaneous reproduction of churches means the Holy Spirit moves a church to reproduce daughter churches on its own, without outsiders pushing it.

I began training pastors in Honduras in a traditional theological institution and had the traditional problems for the traditional reasons. I assumed the bright young men I trained were dedicated because they came to our resident Bible school. Our plan was for them to return to their home towns as pastors. But the graduates found the gold lettering on their diplomas did not go well with the white-washed adobe walls back home. It enabled them, however, to earn more in the office of the Dole Banana Co.

My raspy supervisor had the gall to blame us teachers; he told us, "Close the school; start discipling the people."

"No," I argued, "they're too hard."

"Excuses! They're poor, semi-literate, subsistence farmers, but you teach as though they were educated, middle class Americans."

I wrote my missionary buddies from language school, now spread all over Latin America, fishing for sympathy. They had the same problem!

"I'm a teacher without a classroom!" I complained.

"So," my supervisor rasped, "teach by extension."

"What's that?"

He handed me a smelly old saddle, explaining, "You're promoted. This is the Chair of Evangelism and Church Planting in your new extension Bible institute."

After a few weeks of blisters on my south side, I learned to communicate with the mission mule and announced, "Hey, I can do this TEE stuff. It's great."

My supervisor warned me, "Then your students had better raise up and pastor their own churches or we'll close down this Theological Education by Extension, too."

I took the pastoral studies to family men (biblical "elder" types) in the poverty-ridden villages, mountains, and cities. Unlike their single young sons, they had crops, jobs, or family responsibilities that kept them from going off to our resident Bible school. They also lacked the education to absorb its intensive teaching. But these older men, with roots in their villages and barrios, could begin pastoring with the respect of their people easier than the single young men could. By God's mercy I slowly learned to evangelize and disciple these *elders* in a way that enabled them to raise up and pastor their small village churches. As will be the case in many of today's remaining unreached fields, we began to see growth not through any one church growing big or fast, but through the slow, steady reproduction of many small churches.

I could have avoided years of sour stomach groping for principles of church reproduction had I looked first in the operator's manual. New Testament discipling principles, conscientiously applied, are enabling churches to reproduce in Honduras and many other fields. We must distinguish between these general *principles* and culture-specific *applications*. Some of the methods cited below, for example, will not fit in your golf bag if you work in Tokyo. But the biblical principles themselves, if applied with culturally relevant methods, should enable churches to reproduce wherever there is plenty of "good soil." Theologically speaking, good soil for the gospel seed to take root in and multiply is *bad people*, and lots of them (Rom. 5:20-21; Matt. 13:18-23; Eph. 2:1-10). Field testing of programs based on these principles gives consistently good results in Latin America and Asia, including hostile fields where evangelism is illegal.

The simplicity of the principles disappoints some educators. They expect something more sophisticated, at least new or expensive. Missionary or not, one can multiply disciples doing these four simple things:

1. Know and love the people you disciple (just as Jesus emptied Himself of His heavenly glory and power to become a man, take on Jewish culture, and draw near to the publicans and sinners).

2. Mobilize your disciples immediately to edify those they are discipling. (Don't just educate for some vague future.)

3. Teach and practice obedience to Jesus' basic commands in love, before and above all else.

4. Organize your church or program by building loving, edifying, accountability relationships between disciples and churches.

21. **Why can't the mission objective stop at the planting of a church or even the planting of several churches?**

_____

_____

_____

Know and love the people you disciple

We must know and love a people before we can disciple them. When Jesus told His disciples to "Look at the fields," they were finding it hard to love the Samaritans around them; they could not see them receiving God's grace.

Limit your area of responsibility to one people or community

We must focus on one people group, the one God has given us. Paul knew his area of responsibility before God (2 Cor. 10:12-16; Acts 16:6-10; Gal. 2:8). He knew what kind of churches to plant and where. For a *movement of church reproduction*, a church planting team needs a clear focus from God. My area was "the Spanish speaking people of the Aguan Valley and surrounding mountains." It helps to be exact.

At home or abroad every discipler needs to ask: "For whom am I responsible?" If a missionary fails to do this, the geographic and ethnic limits of his ministry remain blurred. He will jump from opportunity to opportunity. I asked one of these wandering gold prospectors in Central America what his area of responsibility was. "Oh," he said, "I am winning the country for Christ." He goes from city to city preaching in prisons and army camps; he bombs villages with tracts from his Cessna. It's fun and folks back home eagerly finance it. But he will never plant a reproductive church until he learns to hold the people of a community in his heart.

Choosing your people in a new field needs study and prayer. Confer with other missionaries, nationals, and God Himself for guidance. I found a map of my area made by Texaco (I don't know why; the average town only had two cars, one of which ran). But it showed where the villages were and kept me from getting lost so often. So, find the population centers, where you can buy safe milk, where others are not discipling, and—even before the milk—where folks want to know God and enjoy Him forever.

> *Knowing a people means touching the heart of individuals.*

Knowing a people means more than finding how many tons of figs they exported last year, that the average adult male has 7.4 children, or that their legislature has two chambers. It means touching the heart of individuals. Laughing with those who laugh. Weeping with those who weep. Playing marbles with two-year-old Chimbo and checkers with his grandpa (or whatever they play in the town square). It may help if you let him beat you. This applies to arguing religion, too. It's dangerous always to be "right" when you're the new kid on the block. Learn to appreciate the people and their ways, even the toothless old men. Listen and learn until you have discovered those things in their folk religion or culture that help communicate the gospel.

Once you know your area and people, discern which segment among them is most receptive to you and to Jesus Christ. To penetrate a restricted, resistant field, aim *first* at the working class or an oppressed minority. This contradicts some popular church growth theories. We are not dealing with second generation growth in Pasadena, California, however, but the *initial beachhead* where people get a curved blade in their ribs for witnessing. Jesus did not begin His public ministry among the influential middle class and natural leaders in the political nerve centers of Rome or Jerusalem, but with the working class upriver in Galilee where they spoke Hebrew with a backwoods accent—otherwise He would have been crucified prematurely.

22. *What is the most important reason for focusing on one specific target people?*

_____

_____

Let the church be of the people

Like most inexperienced church planters, I started "preaching points" at first instead of genuine New Testament churches. Someone went every week to a community where a group gathered to hear their pulpit oratory and sing (well, at least to sing). Converts were not baptized. Local leaders were not trained. The Lord's Supper was neglected. No one knew for sure who were Christians. Obedient, sacrificial discipling gave way to entertaining (a tradition brought by American missionaries). Preaching points develop a personality of their own; they stubbornly refuse to evolve into obedient, giving, reproductive churches. They become sponges soaking up the time and efforts of outside workers and producing nothing—except where God's sheer mercy overrides our routine.

Find what a church's people can do and plan that, before planning its structure, forms, and organization. I hope it takes you less time than it took me to learn that formal pulpit preaching is ineffective (often illegal) in many of today's remaining unreached fields. You can preach the Word with power in many other ways, if you know your people. We used dramatic Bible reading, songs with music and lyrics composed by nationals, poems, symbols, and story telling. They sang with more enthusiasm when they composed songs in the local style. Bach would have croaked (so would the average director of contemporary church music). But the music was *theirs*. I'd spend days preparing an evangelistic sermon for our first trip to a distant village. They'd listen politely. Then I learned to let them dramatize Bible stories in their own way (one rehearsal 15

> *Preaching points develop a personality of their own; they stubbornly refuse to evolve into obedient, giving, reproductive churches.*

minutes beforehand). They let local non-Christians play the fatted calf and other minor roles in the Prodigal Son, and the whole community complained for weeks. Not about the terrible acting but about the jerk who was too greedy to wait for his old man to die, to get his hands on his inheritance! Which all led to more conversions than a year of my sermons.

Let the new church's self-identity be evident. Know exactly what you are aiming at within the community: a well defined body of obedient disciples of Jesus Christ. Once I made the mistake of allowing more outside helpers to be present than members of the community during the first baptism and celebration of the Lord's Supper. The church died at birth. There must be a majority from the community itself, especially at the first baptism or worship meetings, or the church is not born as a distinct entity within the community. Our converts felt that they had simply been added to some organization of the outsiders. I robbed them of the thrill of looking at each other and saying, "We are now the church here!" They must see the new church being born as a part of their community.

---

23. List at least three lessons Patterson learned about letting the people be the church.

_____

_____

_____

List what you will do to reproduce disciples among a people

What you do first often determines the direction of your work, for good or bad, for years to come. Will it lead to reproductive churches? The right steps will vary for each field but will always include teaching the converts first to obey Jesus' basic commands (Matt. 28:18-20). Take the shortest route possible to start a real church: a group of believers in Christ dedicated to obey His commands. In a pioneer field let it start small, perhaps with only three or four members. It will grow if you disciple the people as Jesus said.

The first question you ask about an unreached people group is, "*Who* can best reach them?" The answer is often, "Church planters from a people that is culturally closer than we." You, or the missionaries you send, may need to train and mobilize church planting team members from another people group that is more similar to your target group in race, politics, economic level, educational level, lifestyle, and worldview.

Let's assume you research well all the factors: race, culture, logistics, urban versus rural backgrounds, language similarities, education and economic levels, etc. You learn the language. Then you go in a crowded bus to your new field, with a team of church planters as similar to the local people as possible in every aspect. Some or all of them may be from another developing country. You are happy because they do not have to make that long cultural leap that delays church planting by years (the less responsive the people are to missionaries, the more crucial this cultural fit). Now you finally arrive, unpack your toothbrush, take a deep breath, pray, step out the door, and find 50 thousand people living around you who think Jesus was John Wayne's cousin. Now what?

> *Churches dependent on charitable institutions are almost always dominated by the foreign missionary and seldom reproduce.*

Avoid institutions if possible at this beachhead stage (community development programs unrelated to church planting, schools, clinics, etc.); they will come later. In Honduras we developed community development work, but it grew out of the churches, not vice versa. We taught obedience to the great commandment of loving our neighbor in a practical way. A poverty program can aid church planting if the two are integrated by the Holy Spirit. But churches dependent on charitable institutions are almost always dominated by the foreign missionary and seldom reproduce. Your local missiologist may point to celebrated exceptions here and there, perhaps in a southern suburb of outer Myitkyina, or some place where a freak with 15 fingers was also born in 1967. But we don't build broad movements for Christ on exceptions.

To start a church that will multiply in the normal way in a *pioneer* field with no experienced pastors nor organized churches, take the following steps (change them where local circumstances require it):

1. Witness first to male heads of households. We often told them Bible stories they could pass on immediately, even before saved, to their own family and friends. We went with them to show them how. But why *male* heads of families? We worked in a *macho* culture (right where the word *macho* came from—where men carried sharpened machetes and used them readily). Female leadership, right or wrong, limited the outreach of brand new works. Later, when a church was established with male pastor and elders, women could take a higher profile. Be sensitive to your community's norms, especially in the first impressions you give of the church.

2. Baptize all repentant believers without delay (entire families when possible). At first, I acted as though a big buzzard were perched on my shoulder just waiting to pounce on our converts that fell away; I delayed baptism to make sure they were "safe." But I soon saw that the very reason many fell away was my distrust. That's the funny thing about God's grace; He wants us to let it slop over on the unworthy (Rom. 5:20-21).

3. Provide a style of worship that new elders-in-training can lead and teach to others. Don't invite the *public* until local leaders can lead the services. Celebrate the Lord's Supper weekly as the center of worship, especially until local men are mature enough to preach in an edifying, humble way.

4. Organize a provisional board of elders as soon as mature men are converted. Show them how to win and pastor their own people right away. Remember, this is for pioneer fields with no experienced pastors or well organized churches. We, like Paul, must use the best men God gives us as the churches multiply, or the new disciples have no leadership at all (Acts 14:23).

5. Enroll these new elders in pastoral training on the job. Don't remove them from their people for training. Meet with them every two or three weeks (more often if possible until they are mobilized).

6. Provide a list of activities planned for the congregation, starting with the commands of Christ and His apostles. Let everyone know where he is going and what he needs to learn for each activity. Use this as a checklist to monitor the progress of the elders you train, in both their studies and pastoral work, as they mobilize their own people in ministry.

24. Why does Patterson give the advice he does regarding starting up a reproducible church?

_____

_____

_____

Decide how you can best use your ministry gifts with the people

Define your own ministry. What spiritual gifts has the Holy Spirit given you? Before I turned over leadership to the Honduran nationals, my own job was: *To help the Honduran churches train their own leaders.* I could say it in one sentence. My ministry now is: "To train missionaries to reproduce churches in pioneer fields." What is your ministry?

Be concise. If you don't know, ask for help. You may work in a field for a year or two before you can pin it down. If you have been working hard in the same church for several years and still cannot briefly define your ministry, you probably have taken on too much. Trim your job down so that you can't help but do it well; then God may open new doors.

Since my preparation came primarily from books and classrooms, I failed to use my gift of teaching in proper harmony with other spiritual gifts. Like most recent seminary graduates, I used my superior knowledge of God's Word to "pull rank" on those who knew less. My teaching stifled their use of the gifts of servant leadership, evangelism, and other gift-based ministries. I had to do some painful repenting before I could work in harmony with a ministry team in which the Holy Spirit harmonized the use of several spiritual gifts.

25. According to Patterson, what steps must be taken in defining church planting tactics?

_____

_____

_____

Mobilize your disciples immediately to edify those they are discipling

To build up the church as a living, reproducing body, Paul instructs pastors and teachers to train the members of the church for the ministry, to edify the Body of Christ (Eph. 4:11-12).

Build edifying relationships with the leaders you disciple

Like most new missionaries, I took myself too seriously. I worried about what my disciples were up to. It took me years to learn to sit back with my coconut milk, laugh at my own goofs, and trust the Holy Spirit to do His work in my students. How can we enable the leaders we train to edify each other and their people through personal, loving relationships?

Paul left his pastoral disciple Timothy behind to work with the elders in newly planted churches with these instructions: "The things you have heard from me… these entrust to faithful men who will be able to teach others also" (2 Tim. 2:2). How dynamic and reproductive this loving "Paul-Timothy" relationship between teacher and student! If you have not yet tried to teach the way Jesus and His apostles did, you are in for a blessing. If it frightens you, start with just one or two potential leaders. Train them on the job; take responsibility for their effective ministry. Personal discipling does not mean "one on one" (Jesus taught twelve), nor is it just to deal with personal needs (Jesus spent most of His time personally discipling the top level leaders of the church, the very apostles).

In Honduras I usually taught from one to three students, in a way they could imitate and pass on to others immediately. I helped each one have an effective ministry. I taught and modeled what he would pass on to his own people and his own pastoral trainees in the daughter or granddaughter churches. These taught other elders who taught still others as Paul instructed Timothy. The chain grew to over a hundred pastors in training, all elders of churches. As soon as a new church was born, the

> *Personal discipling does not mean "one on one," nor is it just to deal with personal needs.*

outside worker enrolled a local leader, normally an elder highly respected by his people, and began passing on to him the same doctrine and materials as he was receiving himself. This new "Timothy" taught the rest of the new elders in his young church. It kept multiplying as long as each discipler did *everything* in a way his students could imitate immediately. I stopped teaching and preaching in the professional way in which I was used to (they admired it, but could not imitate it). I stopped using electronic equipment including movies, and anything else that was not available to all our workers. That's hard on a gadget-oriented Westerner used to gadgets, conditioned to using the very latest technology for the glory of Christ.

Once we developed loving, Paul-Timothy discipling relationships, we seldom had to discuss church planting. The Holy Spirit channeled the Word of God through these relationships to mobilize the Timothies, and church reproduction took care of itself. At first, I failed to trust the Holy Spirit and pushed the men myself. I dictated rules and prerequisites to keep the doctrine and the church pure and to make sure the men did their job. It stifled the work; one bitter failure followed another. I prayed, "Lord, I don't want a big ministry of my own; just let me help the Hondurans have a good ministry." God answered this prayer. I also learned through disappointments to let the people themselves decide on their own leaders, using 1 Timothy 3:1-7.

We learned not to plant the churches first, then train the leaders for them; nor did we train the leaders first, then tell them to raise up their churches. We married the two efforts in one ministry. My American culture pushed me at first to compartmentalize our organization, isolating its ministries. But I learned to let the Holy Spirit integrate diverse ministries and gifts in the united body (1 Cor. 12:4-26).

I also began with education objectives that focused on educating the man. But according to Ephesians 4:11-16, our education should seek only to edify the *church* in love. I had to discipline myself to keep my student's people in view as I taught, and not focus only on my student and the teaching content.

Before I learned to imitate the way Christ and His apostles discipled, I was satisfied if my student answered test questions correctly and preached good sermons in the classroom. I neither saw nor cared what he did in his church with what he was

TEACHER   PASSIVE STUDENT

Figure 9-2. The Traditional Teacher

TEACHER   STUDENT-WORKER

Figure 9-3. The Obedient Teacher

learning. I slowly learned to see beyond my student to his ministry with his people. I responded to the needs of his church by listening at the beginning of each session to the reports of my students. Then I often set aside what I had prepared and taught rather what each student's people needed at that time.

It was hard at first to let the developing churches' needs and opportunities dictate the order of a functional curriculum. In time, much of my discipling, like the teaching of the Epistles, became *problem solving*. Yes, if we start reproductive churches we will have problems. The apostles did, too. To avoid problems, don't have children and don't have churches.

26. *Why is Patterson so insistent about the urgency of on-the-job training that focuses on practical obedience?*

_____

_____

_____

Build edifying teaching relationships between elders and disciples

The pastor or leading elder sets the example for all the leaders. They in turn enable all the members of an infant congregation to minister to each other in love. A weak pastor dominates his congregation. He tries to do everything, or delegates it in a demanding way. He herds rather than leads (both Jesus and Peter prohibit herding in a demanding way: Matt. 20:25-28; 1 Pet. 5:1-4). Where do you suppose pastors on the mission field pick up the bad practice of herding others? It's not all cultural; they learned it from us missionaries. I furnished the only model the new pastors had in our pioneer field. Because of my superior education and resources, I made the decisions for my less educated colleagues. At the same time, like most new missionaries, I felt insecure and overprotected the first churches. A strong missionary, like a strong pastor, does not fear to give authority and responsibility to others. He does not force gifted, willing workers into existing slots in his organization, but rather builds ministries around them.

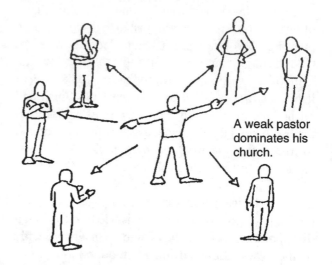

A weak pastor dominates his church.

Figure 9-4. A Passive, Pastor-Centered Church

A strong pastor promotes ties between all members.

New nuclei of leadership readily form both within the mother church and in daughter churches.

Figure 9-5. Interaction in a Dynamic Church
Teach your converts from the beginning to edify one another in love. Building a network of strong relationships provides for the large number of ministries required in the local church in order for it to grow and reproduce daughter churches.

27. *Why is the development of church-to-church relationships and the continuous development of leadership essential to sustaining an ongoing church planting movement? How might a missionary keep these things from happening?*

_____

_____

_____

Teach and practice obedience to Jesus' commands in love, above and before all else

Jesus, after affirming His deity and total authority on earth, commissioned His church to make disciples who obey all His commands (Matt. 28:18-20). So His commands take priority over all other institutional rules (even that hallowed *Church Constitution and Bylaws*). This obedience is always in love. If we obey God for any other reason, it becomes sheer legalism; God hates that.

Start right out with loving obedience to Jesus' basic commands

To plant churches in a pioneer field, aim for each community to have a *group of believers in Christ committed to obey His commands*. This definition of a church might get a D minus where you studied theology; but *the more you add to it, the harder it will be for the churches you start to reproduce*. We asked our converts to memorize the following list of Christ's basic commands:

1. Repent and believe: Mark 1:15.

2. Be baptized (and continue in the new life it initiates): Matt. 28:18-20; Acts 2:38; Rom. 6:1-11.

3. Love God and neighbor in a practical way: Matt. 22:37-40.

4. Celebrate the Lord's Supper: Luke 22:17-20.

5. Pray: Matt. 6:5-15.

6. Give: Matt. 6:19-21; Luke 6:38.

7. Disciple others: Matt. 28:18-20.

Memorize them; you can neither be nor make obedient disciples, unless they are basic to your Christian experience. They are the ABC's of both discipling and church planting.

Define evangelism objectives in terms of obedience

Do not simply preach for "decisions"; make obedient disciples. Only disciples produce a church that multiplies itself spontaneously within a culture. Consider the two commands: "Repent and believe" and "Be baptized." In Western culture a man stands alone before his God and "decides" for Christ. But in other cultures sincere conversion needs interaction with family and friends. Faith, repentance, and immediate baptism of the entire family or group—no invitation to make a decision—is the norm (Acts 2:36-41; 8:11; 10:44-48; 16:13-15, 29-34; 18:8). Repentance goes deeper than a decision; it is a permanent change wrought by God's Spirit. We are born all over again. Few purely intellectual decisions in any culture lead to permanent, obedient discipleship.

Do not simply preach for "decisions"; make obedient disciples.

We found that when we baptized repentant believers reasonably soon, without requiring a long doctrinal course first, the great majority then responded to our training in obedient discipleship. The detailed doctrine came later. Teaching heavy theology *before* one learns loving, childlike obedience is dangerous. It leaves him assuming that Christianity is having scripturally correct doctrine, and he leaves it at that.

He becomes a passive learner of the Word rather than an active disciple. Balanced discipling activates mind, heart, and hands. It integrates word, care, task. It learns, loves, serves. Emphasizing one of the three at the expense of the others yields spiritually unbalanced believers, not disciples.

The new members of the first New Testament church in Jerusalem obeyed all of the basic commands of Christ from the very beginning. After repentance and baptism they learned the apostles' doctrine (word), broke bread, prayed, and fellowshipped (care), and gave and witnessed, adding new members every day (task) (Acts 2:41-47). We also must teach each new convert from the very beginning to obey all these commands in love (John 15:15). Don't wait to start obeying Christ! The first few weeks of their new life in Christ are the most impressionable; these weeks will determine more than any other time of teaching whether or not they are (and make) Bible centered, active, loving *disciples*.

Define theological education objectives in terms of obedience

God does not bless methods; He blesses obedience. How can we help a student to train his congregation to do the things Christ orders us to do? One way is to combine *Theological Education by Extension with biblical discipling, orienting it to loving obedience to Jesus' commands.* Many criticized our TEE in Honduras because it violated their institutional rules (not on biblical grounds).

God's Word commands the pastor to "do the work of an evangelist" (2 Tim. 4:5). A pastor does many other things, but evangelism is basic. Education and evangelism married to each other in one extension ministry became an effective church planting tool for us; one reinforced the other. Isolating pastoral training from the other ministries of the body violates Scripture. God teaches that all spiritual gifts (including teaching) *must edify the body in loving harmony with the exercise of the other gifts* (Rom. 12:3-11; Eph. 4:1-16; 1 Cor. 12-13).

Orient your teaching to loving obedience

We taught our pastors to orient all church activity to New Testament commands. As they taught the Word of God, they accustomed their people to dis-

cern three levels of authority for all that they did as a body of disciples:

1. **New Testament commands.** These carry all the authority of heaven. They include the commands of Jesus in the Epistles which apply only to baptized, more mature Christians who are already members of a church. We don't vote on them nor argue about doing them. They always take precedent over any human organization's rules.

2. **Apostolic practices (not commanded).** We cannot enforce these laws because Christ alone has authority to make laws for His own church, His body. Nor can we prohibit their practice because they have apostolic precedent. Examples include: holding possessions in common, laying hands on converts, celebrating the Lord's Supper frequently in homes using one cup, baptizing the same day of conversion, Sunday worship.

3. **Human customs.** Practices not mentioned in the New Testament have only the authority of a group's voluntary agreement. If it involves discipline, the agreement is recognized in heaven (but only for that congregation; we do not judge another congregation by the customs of our own: Matt. 18:15-20).

Nearly all church divisions and quarrels originate when a power hungry person seeking followers puts mere apostolic practices or human customs at the top level as law.

Nearly all church divisions and quarrels originate when a power hungry person seeking followers puts mere apostolic practices or human customs (levels 2 or 3 above) at the top level as law.

We developed a "Congregation Activities Register" listing 49 activities for churches, based on the seven general commands of Christ listed above, and other commands in the Epistles. Under each activity in this chart we listed related studies. It became our pastoral training curriculum guide. We brought all major areas of Bible, doctrine, and church history precisely where they best aided a church activity. Theological education paralleled church development. The activities, besides the basic commands of Jesus, include: counsel, mobilize youth for ministry, train elders in the daughter church, develop public worship, etc. Each activity includes reading in the relevant areas of Bible, doctrine, church history, and pastoral work (all the essential elements of a traditional pastoral training curriculum), as well as questions to verify that the practical work was done. (An example of materials using this functional discipling curriculum is SEAN's *Train and Multiply* program, Casilla 561, Viña del Mar, Chile.)

Extension teachers use this chart every two weeks or so when they meet with their pastoral student, to register his progress and decide which of the activities they should begin next. In each leadership discipling session we do the following (to remember it, think of LEAP—Listen, Evaluate, Assign, Pray):

L   Listen as each student reports his field work done and plans what to do next. Write down his plans with a carbon copy to review at the next session when he reports his work; always listen first to his report: he will have something good or bad to tell you (either way, he will not listen well to your teaching or counsel until he has mentioned it).

E   Evaluate what he has learned. Ask questions about the content of reading he has done, scan his written answers in workbooks, listen to a brief talk on the subject just studied (especially to help him prepare to give it to his church or group).

A   Assign reading related to his pastoral work plans. Assign chapters in the Bible or other books (use only books on the level of his people, even if you have to write summaries of the essentials of a subject). Do not assign so much reading that he lacks time for his pastoral work. Do not lecture on things that you expect him to learn from his reading (enable him to be an active learner and doer rather than a passive listener: James 1:22).

P   Pray. Each participant prays for the work of another.

Don't forget. LEAP!

28. What are the basis and objective of the obedience oriented curriculum?

_____

_____

_____

Organize your church or program by building loving, edifying, accountability relationships between individual disciples and churches

Healthy daughter churches need loving, edifying discipling relationships within themselves and with the mother church (Acts 11:19-30; 14:21-28; 15:12, 28-31). If your church, church planting, or training organization is already formed, add this personal discipling to it; don't insist on ruthless changes.

Help each new church to reproduce

Each church should send extension workers to reproduce daughter churches, as did the Antioch church (Acts 13:1-3). The longer you wait to mobilize a church for multiplication, the harder it is to reprogram its thinking. Teach your elders the joy of sacrificing to separate their strongest tithers and leaders, in the power of the Holy Spirit as in Antioch, to extend Christ's kingdom. After prayer, perhaps fasting, hold a formal separation service with laying on of hands, as they did. Remember, it is not the individuals that reproduce, but *congregations* that pray and are moved by the Holy Spirit. Let each new church be a link in the chain. The individual extension worker is only an arm of his church.

Ask the new church leaders to chart their own plans. They must take the initiative (don't push your plans on them; simply teach them what the Word says about their task and let them respond). For example, we asked our pastors to draw a large map, with arrows to the villages which they planned for their church to reach directly or through their daughter or granddaughter churches. Their church workers then signed their names by those towns or neighborhoods for which they would pray and plan.

Show each new believer how to witness to friends and relatives

The Holy Spirit flows readily through the bonds that exist between family members and close friends (Acts 10:24, 44). Keep new converts in a loving relationship with them (don't pull them out of their circle to put them in a safe Christian environment, or those very bonds which aid the spread of the gospel become barriers).

We prepared simple gospel studies (mostly Bible stories) that even illiterates could use at once to share their new faith. We accompanied them to show them how to do it, modeling it all in a way they could immediately imitate.

Build edifying inter-church discipling relationships

At first I applied church "body life" only to local congregations. Then I learned to build inter-church discipling relationships with accountability. Elders in one church sacrificially discipled less experienced pastors in the daughter or granddaughter churches.

Sometimes travel was difficult for an older elder, and the main worker from the daughter church rode his horse to the mother church every two weeks or so.

Where the churches were one or two days' walk apart, the teacher and student took turns slogging through the muddy trails.

Extension worker from the mother church holds classes in the daughter church.

Figure 9-6

Extension student worker from the daughter church studies in the mother church.

Figure 9-7

Beware of the bad strategy of a mother church sending workers to several daughter churches at once, as though she were the only church with God's reproductive power.

The "hub" strategy illustrated below wears out the workers and discourages the mother church. God's power, inherent in all churches in which His Spirit dwells, enables a mother church to start a daughter church and train its new elders to help it develop and reproduce in granddaughter churches. Just disciple the disciplers and watch it happen! The primary links in the chain of churches in Honduras were volunteer extension teachers from the mother church.

The chain was not a hierarchy to control; volunteer teachers with no organizational authority worked with volunteer students. It took sweat and guts to build these loving ties between churches, helping men to know, love, and train each other for immediate pastoral ministry. In the process men were shot, put to death by machete, weakened by disease, and almost drowned. It was worth it.

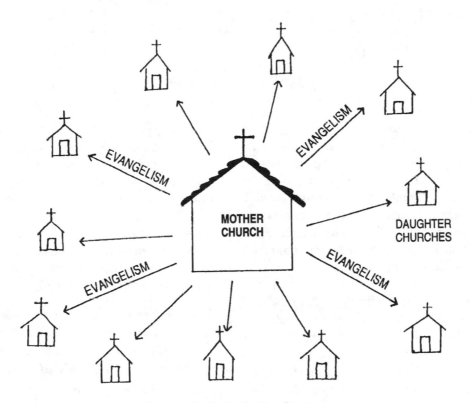

Figure 9-8. An Ineffective Strategy

29. *Why is the way a church is conceived and structured (organized) so crucial to its ultimate effectiveness?*

_____

_____

_____

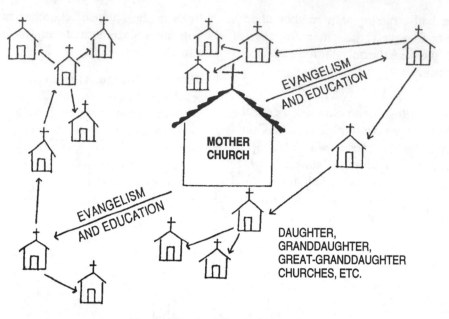

Figure 9-9. An Effective Strategy

The modern Western missionary's most common sin is controlling the national churches. I had to learn to keep out of the way and let the Spirit's power inherent in the churches produce the ministries by which the churches were edified and reproduced. I guided, encouraged, taught the Word, and counseled, but I no longer pushed. Then we saw the chain reaction; one of the extension networks produced five generations and over 20 churches.

We met occasionally to reaffirm our plans and decide which church would reach certain villages or communities. We divided our entire area of responsibility into nine regions and planned the steps to start a daughter church that would reproduce in each region. The pastoral students of the Honduras Extension Bible Institute have for many years been starting an average of five new churches a year, each of which has from one to three new pastors in training. After turning the leadership of this program to Hondurans, it has continued to reproduce in spite of other missionaries' pressure to revert to traditional pastoral training methods.

Pray for reproduction power

Christ's parables in Matthew 13, Mark 4, and John 15 compare the growth and reproduction of His churches to that of plants. Like all other living creatures God has created, the church has her own seed in herself to reproduce after her own kind. Every time we eat, we eat the fruit of God's tremendous reproduction power given to plants and animals. Look around out of doors; it's everywhere—grass, trees, birds, bees, babies, and flowers. All creation is shouting it! This is the way God works! Reproduction is His *style*. Pray for it! (God in His infinite wisdom acts a bit lazy when we don't ask Him to move; He limits His absolute power to our weak faith!) We ourselves don't make the

An obedient, Spirit-filled church has to reproduce at home or abroad. It's her very nature; she is the body of the risen, life-giving Son of God.

church grow or reproduce, any more than pulling on a stalk of corn would make it grow. Paul plants, Apollos waters, God gives the growth. We sow, water, weed, fertilize, and fence the crop, but rely on the church's own God-given potential to reproduce. An obedient, Spirit-filled church has to reproduce at home or abroad. It's her very nature; she is the body of the risen, life-giving Son of God.

Each new church in a chain, like a grain of wheat, has the same potential to start the reproduction all over again. When a chain gets too long for good communication, simply reorganize the teaching relationships. Don't assume that doctrine will get watered down the longer the chain. Each Spirit-filled teacher in the chain has the same love for the Word and will rejuvenate the flow. I discovered that the strongest churches were usually one or two links removed from me, the foreign missionary. The key to maintaining the chains is loving communication in both directions. Accurate student reports from each daughter church are essential for his teacher to respond applying the Word accurately to its life, needs, and opportunities.

An almost universal impediment to reproduction is missionary subsidies that stifle nationals' own giving and build a dependent spirit.

Pray for protection from traditions that hamper this spontaneous reproduction. We have mentioned teaching that neglects discipleship, and failure to mobilize newly repentant converts to obey beginning with baptism. Another almost universal impediment to reproduction is missionary subsidies that stifle nationals' own giving and build a dependent spirit. Don't rob poor believers of the blessing of sacrificial giving! God multiplies their mite by special celestial mathematics that will prosper them now and for eternity. Paying national pastors with outside funds nearly always stifles spontaneous reproduction and eventually leads to deep resentment when the source no longer equals the demand.

Most impediments come from rules that well meaning men make, who in weakness of faith fear the spontaneous and won't let the Holy Spirit surprise them:

"But our By-laws state clearly that our church must wait at least five years and have 100 members to start its daughter church."

"We need a strong home base before we can send missionaries."

"We can't do it until it's gone through the committee and budgeted."

"We can't baptize you even though you've met the Bible requirements of repentance and faith, until you take our six months' disciple's course; baptism is the graduation ceremony."

"You can't officiate Holy Communion; you're not duly ordained."

"What? Jesus commands it? Well, we'll vote on it and see."

"We can't allow everything the apostles did; times have changed."

"Discipling is for lay leaders; a real pastor needs seminary."

"You can't train other pastors until you finish the whole program."

"You must get your pastoral training in a formal seminary."

"We more experienced pastors will run our Association of churches."

"You can't obey Christ until you know the whole Word of God."

Sooner or later all such "can't do" laws without biblical basis replace simple obedience to Christ and stifle reproductive discipleship. They sound spiritual but contradict what the Spirit of God did in Scripture and does today where men do not limit Him. Our weak faith fears the spontaneous; we don't want God to surprise us.

---

30. *What procedure does Patterson suggest for planning field objectives?*

Planning a strategy leading to the spontaneous multiplication of churches requires much more than simply hoping that the Holy Spirit will do His work. Our plans must count on the Spirit's work and then allow it to happen. Using obedience to the commands of Christ and His apostles as a yardstick for measuring progress, we can combine evangelism and training to initiate and maintain church planting momentum. Under this strategy, new leadership is mobilized early. Training focuses on the developing church, not on the student. Paul-Timothy relationships are fostered between individuals and mother-daughter-granddaughter relationships between churches. Recognizing the principles of spontaneous growth, the wise missionary helps orchestrate the effort through encouragement, planning, and allowing the Holy Spirit to move as He wills to guide and control the work.

Summary

The complexity of our world and major forces opposing Christian witness are forcing mission strategists to look for creative ways of accessing unreached populations. Two such innovative approaches are the use of tentmakers and the use of nonresidential missionaries.

Once a people group is accessed, missionaries must use cultural sensitivity in order to evangelize the people so the gospel is really "good news" to them. Missionaries must pursue culturally appropriate evangelistic methods, while being careful not to fall into passive, non-persuasive activities. They must never forget that making disciples is the ultimate objective. They must also recognize that their effectiveness depends largely on how they are perceived. Before undertaking E-3 evangelism, missionaries should consider who can best reach an unreached group and should mobilize that person or group for the task.

Once the gospel has penetrated a culture and the initial group of believers has been gathered into a church, the missionaries should plan for ongoing spontaneous reproduction of churches among the people. By stressing obedience as the principal channel of discipleship, evangelism and training can be combined in raising up new leadership and congregations. Extension chains can be developed to sustain an ongoing church planting movement within the people group until the entire group is evangelized.

Integrative Assignment

As you complete this worksheet, you will be answering the following question: *Who should reach the targeted people group?*

WORKSHEET #3: THE FORCE FOR EVANGELIZATION

Who should reach them? In this worksheet, you will first evaluate the existing force for evangelization, including nearby churches, individuals from the group, and mission agencies. Try to determine *who* is in the best position to reach the targeted people group. If you don't have access to the information needed to answer this question accurately, assume that an E-3 effort is needed, which will be provided through the initiative of your church in partnership with an existing mission agency. If you think that existing converts from the group or a church at E-2 distance is best suited to reach this people, create your strategy based on how you might provide the initiative necessary to persuade and support this group in their effort to evangelize the targeted people.

A. Identify the Force for Evangelization

1. Is a viable church (comprised of any people group) present in the country or region where the targeted people live? If so, rate its potential as a primary evangelizing force.

_____

_____

_____

2. If there are individuals within the group who have become Christians, rate their potential as a force in evangelizing their people.

_____

_____

3. List any mission agencies which have targeted this group. If there are none, what agencies might be most interested in targeting this group for church planting?

_____

_____

4. Are there translated portions of Scripture, Christian medical work, schools, radio, or other aids to evangelism that are present among your targeted people due to other Christian efforts?

_____

_____

_____

5. What additional specialized agencies (Bible translation, radio, etc.) might be engaged to help in reaching these people?

_____

_____

_____

6. What is the potential contribution you and/or your church can make to reach this group?

_____

_____

_____

B. Mobilize the Force for Evangelization

7. Who will sponsor this mission effort? If it is your church, will it relate to a mission agency? Which one?

_____

_____

_____

8. How can each of the forces for evangelization be mobilized to its fullest potential? List possible obstacles and solutions. Would a strategic partnership be helpful?

_____

_____

_____

C. Personnel

9. What kinds of missionaries or *combinations* of missionaries will be involved in this effort (regular, tentmakers, nonresidential)? How and where will they be recruited?

_____

_____

_____

10. What skills and qualifications will the missionary team need? Will they receive training? What, where, and how?

_____

_____

_____

11. What leadership structure will exist on the field? How and where will this be developed?

_____

_____

_____

12. How will the missionaries be supported or support themselves?

_____

_____

_____

Questions for Reflection

It may seem presumptuous to predict how God might work in reaching a people group with the gospel. It is true that there is much we cannot know, but we must move forward by making plans based on what we do know, in accordance with God's will as revealed in Scripture. We can trust God to straighten our plans as we go along. Consider the wisdom found in Proverbs 16:9 and 16:3. What important principles related to strategy are contained in these verses? Write your thoughts below.

_____

_____

_____

_____

_____

_____

_____

_____

_____

CHAPTER 10

Evangelism and Social Action: Two Partners in Mission

Thus far in our study, we have learned basic principles which form the backbone of our approach to the remaining task of mission. We have attempted to see the world as God sees it, people by people. We know that there are thousands of people groups needing a specific cross-cultural strategy if they are to be reached.

The unreached peoples, for the most part, are also the world's poorest and most oppressed groups. Attempting to meet their needs is not only a good activity, but also an indispensable component of Christian mission. A starving man cannot hear the gospel clearly because his need for food overrides any other possible interest.

The Protestant church, until the early 20th century, tended to keep social action integrated with evangelistic outreach. Social action was seen as a natural overflow of gospel outreach. The first missionaries to follow William Carey overseas were actively engaged in a wide range of holistic ministries, including medical care, Bible translation which led into literacy and schooling, child care, printing, agricultural assistance and reform, animal husbandry, food production, orphanages, and campaigns against social evils such as widow burnings and child destruction.

Evangelicals retreated from Two Thirds World development ministries during the first half of this century. The "great divorce" between evangelism (as proclamation) and social action (as demonstration) came in reaction to a larger nationwide theological debate which arose in American Protestantism in the 1900-1930 period between the "liberals" and the "fundamentalists." In reaction to dangerous slippages in doctrine and as a backlash against liberalism, the evangelical church went into a period of retreat and separatism resulting in what has been called the "Great Reversal." All progressive social concern was nearly eliminated among evangelicals by 1930.

The social gospel (which was strongly identified with theological liberalism) emphasized Christian obligation to respond to physical need and oppression, the priority of social concern, and the task of establishing the kingdom of God on earth now through human efforts. The fundamentalists rejected these concerns and emphasized spiritual need, evangelism, and the future heavenly aspects of the kingdom of

God. Theological conservatives began to rigidly dichotomize and separate evangelism and social concern—word and deed.

The social discontent in America of the 1960s and '70s demanded evangelical involvement in social concern.* With the advent of "on the spot" television coverage and a whole series of natural disasters, worldwide attention has been drawn to the physical needs of our globe's poor. Drought, cyclones, earthquakes, floods, and the plight of refugees have received substantial coverage. This exposure has aided immeasurably the flow of funds to evangelical agencies which are involved in relief and development assistance. It has also resulted in dramatic increases in evangelical attention toward social concern and Two Thirds World needs. The Lausanne Covenant, a major evangelical missions document produced during the 1974 Lausanne Congress on World Evangelization in Lausanne, Switzerland, directly addressed the relationship of evangelism and social concern, bringing this issue squarely into current evangelical missions dialogue.

In this chapter, we will attempt to discover a balanced approach to social action and evangelism. In the second section, we will survey the state of human need, defining who the needy are and where they are found. The last section will be devoted to examining a holistic framework for evangelization through Christian community development.

I. Holistic Mission

The debate over evangelism vs. social action in mission has been a polarizing subject for Christians. It seems that the issues have been couched in terms that demand that believers choose one side or the other. This dilemma is poignantly brought out and dealt with in the following article.

❏ *Do We Have to Choose?* **

Bryant L. Myers ***

It was a beautiful evening in the Kalahari Desert of Botswana. The heat of the day was slipping away. The sounds of the bush surrounded us. The Han clan we were visiting had eaten, the evening fire was lit. In the sky there were more stars than I ever knew were there.

Anna, a German missionary from South Africa, was talking quietly in Afrikaans to a Tswana who then spoke in Tswana to another man who spoke the

Han's melodic language of soft clicks. He in turn spoke to the Han men, women, and children. In the Han culture, everyone has a voice around the fire.

The Han also are called Bushmen. They were the original inhabitants of Southern Africa. They were there before the black Africans invaded from the north and long before the first Europeans set foot in the Cape. They are the only hunter-gatherers left on our planet. Living in complete harmony with the

---

* One of the most significant of many evangelical books in the 1970s for Two Thirds World attention was Ron Sider's *Rich Christians in an Age of Hunger.*

** Myers, B. L. (1992, September). Do we have to choose? *MARC Newsletter, 92-3,* 3-4.

*** Bryant L. Myers is Vice President for Research and Development at World Vision International and the Executive Director of MARC (Missions Advanced Research and Communications Center). He serves on the board of Evangelicals for Social Action and chairs the Strategy Working Group of the Lausanne Committee for World Evangelization.

desert, for centuries they moved from water to water, living off desert plants and animals, always giving thanks to each animal they killed for giving them a meal.

The Han have always been despised by everybody. The warrior tribes of Tswana, Zulu, and Xhosa always despised the gentle Han. For centuries they killed the Han for "stealing" cattle, and when the whites came to Southern Africa it was more of the same. To the Han every animal was a gift of god for the purpose of food. The idea of someone owning a cow was something they could not understand.

Their oppression was complete. A Han woman's only value was as a slave, a nanny for young children, or a concubine for the men. Han men were good for nothing, often hunted for sport, until they became "domesticated" and were used as cheap farm hands, army scouts, and a market for alcohol.

Today the Han are almost gone. There's very little room left in the desert anymore. For the most part, they huddle in desert outposts, begging and drinking. Everywhere they are forced to be like someone else. Their culture is not valued. The Han are the poorest of the poor in Southern Africa. There is no room for them in the human inn.

A long time ago, I read several books by Laurens Van Der Post in which he told the Bushman story. He recounted the intense harmony their culture shared with the earth, their ability to share without owning anything. Van Der Post's message to anyone who would listen is that the Han story is an important part of our story for the simple reason that, as hunter-gatherers, theirs was the first chapter of the human story, one we no longer can remember. Since then, I've always been fascinated by the Han.

Years later, because of a good friend who had heard my stories about the Han people, I found myself in the Kalahari Desert sitting beside a Bushman fire. I was full of wonder and excitement. I watched in-

tently as Anna tried to share the gospel with the Han squatting around the fire. I couldn't understand much since the conversation was being translated from Afrikaans to Tswana to the Han language. But, I could understand its music. The conversation was quiet and gentle, everyone listening intently.

Suddenly, the only young woman at the fire burst into an angry series of clicks and gestures. I turned to my Afrikaans-speaking friend, "What was that all about?" "I'm not sure," he said, "the translation wasn't clear."

Later that night, sitting in Anna's simple house, I asked her the same question, "What did the young woman say when she became so upset?" Anna shook her head wearily. "It's always the same. I've heard it many times before. I have no answer," she sighed sadly. We knew from earlier conversations that, in her lifetime of missionary work in the Kalahari, only three Han had become Christians.

"What did she say?" I persisted.

"I had just finished explaining to them that Jesus Christ, the Son of God, had died and was raised from the dead so that our sins could be forgiven. The young woman didn't believe me. She said, 'I can believe the Son of God was willing to die for a white man. I might even be able to believe that the Son of God would die for a black man. But, I could never believe that the Son of God would die for a Bushman.'" We wept together in the silence that followed.

What does one do with such a story? How does one think about Christian mission to people for whom centuries of oppression, neglect, and systematic dehumanization are so deeply internalized and reinforced? What is the good news to those whose poverty and alienation are so deeply rooted? I have no answers. This experience has haunted me for many years.

1. *What was the fundamental barrier to belief for the Han woman?*

Understanding poverty

Recently, from another part of World Vision's world, some ideas have begun to emerge which helped me move forward a little. The following is based on the reflections of my Indian friend and colleague, Jayakumar Christian.

As a Christian organization committed to empowering the poor in the name of Jesus Christ, we spend a lot of time trying to deepen our understanding of the causes of people's poverty. This is not an academic exercise and it's not for our benefit. Helping poor people understand why they are poor is a critical element in their being able to work for their own development. Sadly, understanding the causes of poverty is a very complex and nuanced task.

Most poor people believe they are poor either because they understand themselves to be in some way responsible or because God or the gods mean for them to be poor.

We have to begin with the fact that most poor people believe they are poor either because they understand themselves to be in some way responsible or because God or the gods mean for them to be poor. This is a result of two different processes. The first is an internalization of their own powerlessness and poverty—the psychological process of blaming oneself. The second is a process of socialization whereby they are being taught, by the rich and powerful (and sadly, sometimes the church), that their poverty is part of the natural order of things.

Historically, evangelicals have seized on the first reason and have tended to overlook the second. The first lends itself to understanding mission as simple proclamation: "You are a sinner, but God has sent His Son for the forgiveness of sin. If you accept Jesus as your Lord and Savior, you will be saved. Jesus Himself promised life abundantly." This missiological point of departure leads to ministries like proclamation, personal discipleship, and inner healing. For the Han woman, this promise simply was not believable.

The problem with this is that ignoring the impact of society and the accompanying socialization means that chronically unjust contexts are never confronted. The society, whose systems of economics, politics, and law sustain poverty and marginalize people (doing what the Bible calls "grinding the faces of the poor"), continues to be unaware of its own sin and complicity. By ignoring this reality, the call to repentance is directed only at the poor. Those who sustain unjust relationships are overlooked.

Ecumenical folk tend to go at this problem the other way around. They often limit their mission focus to the socialization issue. "No, the God of the Bible did not and does not want you to be poor. You are poor because the rich and powerful have created systems of politics, economics, and laws which are designed to keep you poor and to protect their wealth and power. Jesus came to liberate the powerless and bring down the rich and powerful." This missiological point of departure leads to ministries of "conscientization," community organization, and working for justice.

The problem with an approach that challenges only the social reinforcement of poverty is that the end point of ministry becomes access to power and resources. While the poor desperately need access to power and resources in the social arena, they also need to hear the news about the possibility of being rightly related to God.

This approach is also inadequate from the perspective of the rich and powerful. While it exposes their sin, it does not deal with whatever it is the rich have internalized, which allows them to be unaware of or to rationalize their oppressive behavior. They are not told that God has good news for them as well. They are simply demonized. Yet, if the rich are not transformed, nothing changes for the poor.

2. In what two ways do most of the poor understand their poverty?

_____

_____

_____

3. Why does the author feel it is an error simply to focus on the poor in attempting to alleviate poverty?

_____

_____

_____

The question of identity

Thinking about the causes of poverty in this way gave me another perspective on the story of the young Han woman. I began to realize she is captive to her own processes of internalization and self-blame as well as to her socialization from the context in which she lives. The good news of Jesus Christ, presented solely in terms of sin management and restoring her relationship with God, could not get through to her, for the simple reason that her context so strongly reinforced her sense of unworthiness that the good news was not believable. While it is true that she needs to hear the good news Jesus brings for her inner self, it is also true that her profound sense of alienation cannot be relieved without also transforming the poverty-sustaining oppression of the world in which she lives. If the way white and black folk live with and value the Han isn't seen to change, it's hard to see how her view of herself and her people can change.

Once again we arrive at the conclusion that Christian mission must be holistic. It must include both the interior and the exterior, the forgiveness of sins and the fullness of life, evangelism and justice. The whole message of Jesus must be for both the life inside oneself and the world in which one lives and from which one learns. The reason for this is that there is a deeper, underlying issue which links both self-blame and oppression. This issue is identity, both individually and in relationship. The questions, "Who am I?" and "Who are we?" are answered both from within oneself and by one's context.

This of course is precisely the question the gospel of Jesus Christ is trying to answer. The gospel tells us who and whose we are. The good news is that, through Jesus Christ, we can be sons and daughters of God and heirs to His emerging kingdom on earth. We no longer have to live under bondage either to ourselves or our societies. This is good news for both the Han woman and for the white and black people who inhabit the structures which oppress her so profoundly.

> *Christian mission must be holistic. It must include both the interior and the exterior, the forgiveness of sins and the fullness of life, evangelism and justice.*

Understanding the question of identity as the heart of the matter is the key to enlarging our missiological playing field. Now one does not have to choose between what has been presented by some as two incompatible or mutually exclusive frameworks for understanding human need. In fact, choosing one over the other reduces the gospel either to proclamation or to the pursuit of just relationships. Those evangelicals or ecumenicals who insist on a choice are both wrong, but for different reasons.

4. How does the concept of holistic mission attempt to reconcile the debate over evangelism vs. social action in mission?

_____

_____

_____

Holistic mission demands that Christian mission minister both to man's spiritual needs *and* to his physical, emotional, and social needs. It must be a "both/and" approach, not "either/or." In principle, most contemporary evangelicals would not argue this point. The debate continues, however, in relation to what proportion of Christian mission each need should occupy. In the following excerpt, Peter Wagner defines the parameters of the current debate.

❑ On the Cutting Edge of Mission Strategy *

C. Peter Wagner

The mission—no options here!

The definition of mission has been a topic of constant debate for the past 100 years. It revolves chiefly around the relationship of what have been called the *cultural mandate* and the *evangelistic mandate*.

The *cultural mandate*, which some refer to as Christian social responsibility, goes as far back as the Garden of Eden. After God created Adam and Eve, He said to them: "Be fruitful and multiply; fill the earth and subdue it; have dominion over the fish of the sea, over the birds of the air, and over every living thing that moves on the earth" (Gen. 1:21). As human beings, made in the image of God, we are held accountable for the well-being of God's creation. In the New Testament we are told that we are to love our neighbors as ourselves (Matt. 22:39). The concept of neighbor, as the parable of the Good Samaritan teaches, includes not only those of our own race or culture or religious group, but all of humanity. Doing good to others, whether our efforts are directed toward individuals or to society as a whole, is a biblical duty, a God-given cultural mandate.

The *evangelistic mandate* is also first glimpsed in the Garden of Eden. For a period of time, whenever God went to the Garden, Adam and Eve were waiting for Him and they had fellowship. But sin entered into the picture. The very next time that God went to the Garden, Adam and Eve were nowhere to be found. Fellowship had been broken. Humans had been alienated from God. God's nature, in light of the events, was made clear by the first words which came out of His mouth, "Adam, where are you?" (Gen. 3:9). He immediately began seeking Adam. The evangelistic mandate involves seeking and finding lost men and women, alienated from God by sin. Romans 10 tells us that whoever calls on the name of the Lord will be saved. But they cannot call if they have not believed, and they cannot believe if they have not heard, and they cannot hear without a preacher. "How beautiful are the feet of those who preach the gospel of peace" (Rom. 10:15). Bearing the gospel which brings people from darkness to light is fulfilling the evangelistic mandate.

Both the cultural mandate and the evangelistic mandate are essential parts of biblical mission, in my

* Wagner, C. P. (1992). On the cutting edge of mission strategy. In R. D. Winter & S. C. Hawthorne (Eds.), *Perspectives on the world Christian movement: A reader* (rev. ed.) (pp. D45-D47). Pasadena: William Carey Library.

opinion. Neither is optional. There is a growing consensus on this point in evangelical circles.

This was not true as early as 22 years ago when the Berlin World Congress on Evangelism was held in 1966. Not only was virtually no mention made there of the cultural mandate (Paul Rees of World Vision was a minor exception), but such a prominent evangelical spokesman as John R. W. Stott defined mission as including only the evangelical mandate, and not the cultural mandate—although he did not use that precise terminology. One of the first evangelicals to stress the cultural mandate in a public forum was Horace Fenton of the Latin America Mission at the Wheaton Congress on the Church's Worldwide Mission, also held in 1966. Following that, the social consciousness generated by the social upheavals of the 1960s brought the cultural mandate to prominence, until it was given a relatively high profile on the platform of the International Congress on World Evangelization at Lausanne in 1974. By then John Stott himself had changed his views, recognizing that mission included both the cultural and the evangelistic mandates. The Lausanne Covenant makes a strong statement on the cultural mandate in Article 5, and on the evangelistic mandate in Article 6.

The current debate involves four positions: (1) those who would prioritize the cultural mandate over the evangelistic, (2) those who would give equal weight to both—even arguing that it is illegitimate to divide them by using such terminology, (3) those who would prioritize the evangelistic mandate, and (4) those who would hold the pre-Lausanne view that mission is the evangelistic mandate, period.

While we must not neglect our Christian social responsibility, it must never get in the way of soul-winning evangelism.

My personal view is that of the Lausanne Covenant. But I spend little time fussing with those who hold that mission should be understood as evangelism and that social ministry should be termed a Christian duty or an outcome of mission rather than part of mission itself. I see either of these positions as contributing more positively to the evangelization of the world than the other options. But I do not accept the prioritization of evangelism solely on pragmatic grounds. I believe it best reflects the New Testament doctrine of mission. Jesus came to seek and to save the lost (Luke 10:10), and we move out in Jesus' name to do the same. While we must not neglect our Christian social responsibility, in my opinion, it must never get in the way of soul-winning evangelism.

5. In your own words, define the cultural mandate.

_____

_____

_____

6. Which of the four positions mentioned by Wagner are the only viable ones in his thinking? Do you agree? Why or why not?

_____

_____

_____

_____

It seems that somehow, the church's mission must reconcile polarized positions on evangelism and social action. This implies a balanced viewpoint which is not dominated by one side or the other. The vision of this kind of ideal "partnership" between these two approaches to mission is clouded, however, by a pragmatic issue: which approach should act as the "leading partner"? In the following article, Samuel Moffett articulates his views on this matter of key strategic importance.

❏ Evangelism: The Leading Partner *

Samuel Moffett **

The New Testament uses the word *evangelize* in what seems to be a shockingly narrow sense. A whole cluster of verbs, actually, is used to describe evangelism: "preaching the word" (Acts 8:4), "heralding the kingdom" (Luke 9:2), "proclaiming the good news" (Luke 4:18; 8:1). But in essence, what all these words describe is simply the telling of the good news (the gospel) that Jesus the Messiah is the saving King. Evangelism was the announcement of Christ's kingdom. It was more than an announcement. It was also an invitation to enter that kingdom, by faith and with repentance.

What evangelism is not

Evangelism, therefore, is not the whole of the Christian mission. It is only a part of the mission. Jesus and the disciples did many other things besides announce the kingdom and invite response. Evangelism is not worship or sacraments. "Christ did not send me to baptize but to evangelize," said Paul (1 Cor. 1:17).

And it is not church growth or church planting. The planting and growth of the church are surely goals of evangelism and its hoped-for results. But evangelism does not always produce a church or more members for it. Neither is evangelism confined to apologetics. Paul says, "We try to persuade" (2 Cor. 5:11), but insists that he was sent to tell the good news "without using the language of human wisdom" (1 Cor. 1:17, 20).

Finally, evangelism in the New Testament was not confused with Christian service, or Christian action and protest against the world's injustices. A revealing and disturbing incident in the book of Acts tells how Greek speaking Jews among the early Christians rose as a minority group to complain of discrimination in the distribution of funds. The reply of the apostles seems almost callously narrow: "We cannot neglect the preaching of God's word to handle finances" (Acts 6:1-2, TEV). Of course, they did immediately proceed to do something about the injustice. But they did not call it evangelism.

In kingdom context

In the context of the kingdom, however, the evangelistic proclamation was never so narrow that it became isolated from the immediate pressing needs of the poor, the imprisoned, the blind, and the oppressed.

Here I am reminded of Korean evangelism. I asked a pastor in the Philadelphia area why his church was growing so fast. "When Koreans come in," he replied, "first I get them jobs; I teach them some English; I help them when they get in trouble with their supervisors. I invite them to church. And then I preach to them the gospel." That is putting evangelism into context.

But if there is anything worse than taking the text out of context, it is taking the context without the

---

* Moffett, S. (1992). Evangelism: The leading partner. In R. D. Winter & S. C. Hawthorne (Eds.), *Perspectives on the world Christian movement: A reader* (rev. ed.) (pp. D207-D209). Pasadena: William Carey Library.

** Dr. Samuel Moffett was born and raised by missionary parents in Korea. He returned as a missionary to serve first in China and then in Korea, where he served as Dean of the Graduate School of the Presbyterian Seminary in Seoul. He now serves as Henry Winters Luce Professor of Ecumenics and Mission Emeritus at Princeton Theological Seminary. He has written numerous articles in missions and theology.

text. Just as Christ's salvation is never to be isolated from the immediate, real needs of the people, neither is it to be identified with those present needs. When Jesus quoted the Old Testament about "good news to the poor" and "freedom for the oppressed," He did so on His own terms. His salvation is not Old Testament *shalom*, and His kingdom is not Israel.

There is nothing quite so crippling to both evangelism and social action as to confuse them in definition or to separate them in practice. Our evangelists sometimes seem to be calling us to accept the King without His kingdom; while our prophets, just as narrow in their own way, seem to be trying to build the kingdom without the saving King.

More than balance

There was a time when most Christians believed that evangelism was the only priority. They were wrong. Then the Church swung too far the other way. The only Christian priority for some has been social justice through reconstruction. That, too, is an important priority. But it is not the only one. And when they made it the only clear mission of the Church, the result was a disaster. In trying to speak to the world, they almost lost the Church.

Others tried to restore the balance by pointing out that "Christ mediates God's new covenant through both salvation and service.... Christians are called to engage in both evangelism and social action." But even that is not enough. What the Church needs for the future in mission is more than balance. It needs momentum. Not an uneasy truce between faith and works, but a partnership.

Now in most practical working partnerships, there must be a leading partner, a "first among equals," or nothing gets done. Which should be the leading partner in mission? Evangelism or social action?

I submit that what makes the Christian mission different from other commendable and sincere attempts to improve the human condition is this: in the Christian mission our vertical relationship to God comes first. Our horizontal relationship to our neighbor is "like unto it," and is just as indispensable, but it is still second. The leading partner is evangelism.

This is not to exalt the proclamation at the expense of Christian action. They belong together. But it does insist that, while without the accompanying deeds the good news is scarcely credible, without the Word the news is not even comprehensible! Besides, the real good news is not what we in our benevolence do for others, but what God has done for us all in Christ. Evangelism, as has been said, is one beggar telling another where to find bread.

The supreme task of the Church, then, now and for the future, is evangelism. It was the supreme task for the Church of the New Testament. It is also the supreme challenge facing the Church today.

Half the world unreached

The determining factor in developing evangelistic strategies, I believe, is that evangelism moves always in the direction of the unreached. It must focus on those without the gospel. More than one-half of the world's people are still without the simplest knowledge of the good news of God's saving love in Jesus Christ. There is no greater challenge to evangelism in mission than that.

Christians are rightly concerned about the grievous unbalances of wealth and food and freedom in the world. What about the most devastating unbalance of all: the unequal distribution of the light of the knowledge of God in Jesus Christ?

In this connection it may be useful to note that for general strategic evangelistic planning, some missiologists suggest as a rule of thumb that "a group of people are classified as unreached if less than 20 percent claim or are considered to be Christian." Christians are rightly concerned about the grievous unbalances of wealth and food and freedom in the world. What about the most devastating unbalance of all: the unequal distribution of the light of the knowledge of God in Jesus Christ?

I am not overly addicted to statistics. But what does it say about a "six-continent approach to evangelism," for example, to find that most of our church mission funds still go to ourselves on the sixth continent, which is between 70 percent and 80 percent at least nominally Christian? Africa, however, is perhaps 40 percent Christian by the same rough and imprecise standards. And Asia, which holds more than one-half of all the people in the world, is only three percent to four percent even nominally Christian.

In the next 10 years, the number of non-Christians which will be added to the population of Asia will be greater than the entire present population of the United States multiplied almost three times (650 million, compared to 220 million). Treating all six continents as equals for strategical purposes is a selfish distortion of the evangelistic realities of the world.

One last thought. There is an unexpected bonus to keeping the definition of evangelism simple. It means that anyone can get into the act. One of the happiest lessons I ever learned about evangelism came not from a professional evangelist, but from a watermelon vendor.

It was in a Korean village, and my wife came up to ask him how much a watermelon cost. He was so surprised at finding a long-nosed foreigner who spoke Korean that at first he was struck dumb. He even forgot to tell her the price. There was something more important he wanted to say. He asked, "Are you a Christian?" And when she replied, "Yes," he smiled all over. "Oh, I'm so glad," he said, "because if you weren't I was going to tell you how much you are missing."

If more of us were so happy about what we have found in the Lord Jesus Christ that we couldn't wait to tell those who have not found Him how much they are missing, we would need to worry no longer about the future of evangelism.

7. Why must evangelism be placed in the "context of the kingdom"?

_____

_____

8. What primary scriptural justification does the author make for recognizing evangelism as the "leading partner"?

_____

_____

_____

9. If evangelism is indeed the leading partner, how will this affect our overall mission strategy?

_____

_____

_____

There are both scriptural and pragmatic reasons for developing a holistic view of missions. A framework which includes both aspects of ministry is important to contemporary missions. Nevertheless, it is also apparent that one of the primary distinctives of evangelical mission is its recognition of evangelism as the leading partner in this alliance. With this in mind, we will now shift our thoughts to the current state of world needs.

II. The World's Needy

We live in a desperately hurting world. The horrors of wars, famines, and natural disasters are brought into our homes daily through mass media. Refugees stream across borders into precariously built camps, while AIDS ravages entire populations of some nations in Africa and Asia. Hundreds of thousands of abandoned children roam the streets in South America. Poverty is the norm in many parts of the globe, and starvation is a common occurrence. In more affluent sectors of society, drug abuse and a general breakdown of the family and its values have produced a sense of perpetual crisis. Everywhere we go, we are met with devastating physical, social, and spiritual need.

In attempting to evangelize a specific unreached group, we have learned that one of the key steps in planning an effective strategy is attempting to determine people's perceived needs. It is often these needs that give readiest access to the people and that allow us to demonstrate God's love in ways that are tangible and real. In essence, the major emphasis in our getting to know a people group and identifying with them is this understanding of their needs in order to minister to them effectively.

Who are the most needy? The following definition of the needy and where they are found is excerpted from the video script *Is There Good News for the Poor?*

❏ *Is There Good News for the Poor?* *

Tom Houston and Eric Miller

Tom Houston: In the Gospel of Luke, Jesus visits the synagogue in Nazareth immediately after He had resisted the temptations to use popularity, publicity, or power to accomplish His mission.

Standing, Jesus read from Isaiah 61:

> The Spirit of the Lord is upon me. He has anointed me to preach the Good News to the poor, He has sent me to proclaim liberty to the captives, and recovery of sight to the blind, to set free the oppressed, to announce the year when the Lord will save His people (Luke 4:18-19, TEV).

Later, when John the Baptist sent his disciples to ask about His credentials as the Messiah, Jesus healed many people of their sickness, diseases, evil spirits, and gave sight to many blind people. He answered John's messengers:

> Go back and tell John what you have seen and heard: the blind can see, the lame can walk, the lepers are made clean, the deaf can hear,

the dead are raised to life, and the Good News is preached to the poor (Luke 7:22, TEV).

Clearly for Luke, bringing or preaching Good News to the poor is central to Jesus' understanding of His mission. The poor are to be special beneficiaries of His Good News. As I studied Luke's Gospel, I was puzzled because Luke sees the poor as central to the mission of Jesus and then seems to say little about the poor as such. I felt I was missing something that was there.

As I looked more closely, I noticed something similar in both places where Luke talks about Good News for the poor. In Jesus' announcement of His mission in Luke 4:18-19 (TEV), He proclaimed:

> The Spirit of the Lord is upon me. He has anointed me to preach the Good News to the poor, He has sent me to proclaim liberty to the captives, and recovery of sight to the blind, to set free the oppressed, and to announce the year when the Lord will save His people.

---

* Miller, E. (Producer). *Is there good news for the poor?* [Videotape]. Madison: IVP Missions/2100 Productions.

Could it be that Jesus was including the captives, the blind, and the oppressed among those whom He calls poor?

Then I looked at Luke 7:22 (TEV), at the evidence Jesus gives that He is the Messiah:

> Go back and tell John what you have seen and heard: the blind can see, the lame can walk, the lepers are made clean, the deaf can hear, the dead are raised to life.

Perhaps the blind, the prisoners, the oppressed, the lame, the lepers, and the deaf are examples of the poor that Jesus is speaking of.

In other words, the Good News is preached to the poor. Perhaps the blind, the prisoners, the oppressed, the lame, the lepers, and the deaf are examples of the poor that Jesus is speaking of. Blind and lame people in the Gospels were often beggars. Prisoners were often in jail for debt or theft and did not come out until they had paid the last penny. Lepers were outcasts from society and were cut off from all means of making a living. If "the year when the Lord will save His people" was a reference to the Year of Jubilee, that year was intended to benefit debtors, slaves, and those dispossessed of their land.

The two words used for "the poor" in the New Testament are *penes* and *ptochos*. *Penes* refers to the person who is oppressed, underpaid, the working poor. *Ptochos* refers to the person who has no work to do and thus has to beg. It is sometimes translated "poor" and sometimes "beggar." The basic idea is dependence on others for the essentials of life, like food, clothes, shelter, and health.

With that in mind, when we read Luke and Acts with this linguistic clue, we discover many references to the poor:

1. The hungry and their children, that Mary says will be filled with good things (Luke 1:53);

2. The people, and their children, who are oppressed by tax collectors who take more than their due, and by soldiers and policemen who take their money or bring false charges against them (Luke 3:12-14);

3. The disabled blind, deaf, lame, paralyzed, lepers, and demon possessed, and their children, who cannot work for a living and are cut off from society (Luke 3-7);

4. The widows, like the one in Nain, whose only son died, leaving her with no breadwinner in her home (Luke 7:11-17);

5. The widows who cannot get justice from judges (Luke 18:2-5), whose houses are expropriated by hypocritical religious leaders (Luke 20:47);

6. The women with medical problems who have spent all their money on doctors (Luke 8:43);

7. The victims of famine in Judea, and their children, who were helped by the Christians in Antioch (Acts 11:27-30).

It is evident in Luke and Acts that the poor to whom Jesus and the early church brought Good News included the naked, the hungry, the disabled, the oppressed, the imprisoned, the sick, the bereaved widows, and orphans. But the question remains, *What kind of Good News was needed by all these people?*

What was the Good News?

It was the kind of Good News that brought a prostitute to wash Jesus' feet with her tears and wipe them with her hair, and then hear Jesus say, "Your sins are forgiven" (Luke 7:36-50, TEV).

It was the kind of Good News that brought the leper to kneel and say, "If you want to, you can make me clean," and feel Jesus' touch and hear Him say, "I do want to.... Be clean!" (Luke 5:12-15, TEV).

It was the kind of Good News that prompted a disabled man's friends to bring him to Jesus and have their faith rewarded by hearing Jesus say, "Your sins are forgiven you, my friend.... Get up, pick up your bed, and go home" (Luke 5:17-24, TEV).

It was the kind of Good News that challenged a prominent religious leader to think about inviting the poor, the crippled, the lame, and the blind, who could not repay him, to a banquet as the true way to blessing (Luke 14:1-14).

The Good News of the kingdom of God is that sin, disease, and oppression are never the last word. Where Jesus is King, He brings forgiveness, healing, and liberation.

Because evangelism and social concern were inseparable in the mind of Jesus, they must be inseparable in our minds and ministry.

Jesus expected—and it should be expected today—the preaching of the Good News to bring help and hope to the sinner, help and hope to the poor. Because evangelism and social concern were inseparable in the mind of Jesus, they must be inseparable in our minds and ministry.

As representatives of Jesus, we must ask, *Who are the poor today who are desperately calling for Good News?*

Who are the poor—today?

Young voices: We are the blind.

Narrator: Two hundred fifty thousand children will become permanently blinded this year for lack of a 10-cent vitamin A capsule or a daily handful of green vegetables.* And that is only one instance where people become blind because they are poor.

Young voices: We are the lame.

Narrator: Each year 230,000 children are struck by polio because they do not receive the immunization which has virtually eliminated polio in the West.

Female voices: We are the mothers who lose our children before they are five years old.

Narrator: Fourteen million children will die this year from common illnesses and malnutrition. Most could be saved by relatively simple, low-cost methods. Two and a half million of them die from dehydration due to diarrhea, yet a solution of eight parts sugar and one part salt in clean water could save their lives.

Male and young voices: We are the husbands who lose their wives, and the children who lose their mothers and become orphans from preventable deaths in childbirth.

Narrator: In the next 24 hours more than a thousand young women will die because of something going wrong at childbirth. As long as the nutrition of girls is placed second to that of boys, as long as women eat last and least and work hardest and longest, as long as half of the babies in the developing world are delivered with no trained person in attendance, child bearing will remain 150 times as dangerous as in the West.

Mixed voices: We are the people who cannot read.

Narrator: Many are poor because no one has taught them to read. They are cut off from much that could enrich their lives.

Young voices: We are the children who cannot go to school.

Narrator: In the last few years, governments of the 37 poorest nations have cut spending on health by 50 percent and on education by 25 percent, in order to pay the West the interest that they owe on their huge debts.

Mixed voices: We are the refugees who have lost our homes.

Narrator: Today 14 million displaced people have lost citizenship, homeland, relationships, and the opportunity to work, and much that gives life meaning.

Young voices: We are the orphans.

Narrator: Thousands of children are orphaned by war, civil strife, revolution, and terrorism. Millions more are being abandoned by their parents. There are 3 million of these in Brazil alone.

Women's voices: We are the prostitutes.

---

* *The state of the world's children 1989* (p. 40). London: Oxford University Press.

Narrator: To provide for their children, many women are forced to turn to prostitution. Many children in cities like Bangkok are sold by desperate parents as slave labor or for sexual exploitation.

Young voices: We are the children of the streets.

Narrator: One hundred million children living in the streets of our great cities are drawn inevitably into a life of crime and corruption.

Young voices: We are teenagers, losing our future.

Narrator: The future of many teenage boys and girls in our cities has been taken captive by drug pushers, violence, and promiscuity; they end up as unmarried mothers, victims of drug violence, or wasting away from AIDS.

Mixed voices: We are the prisoners.

Narrator: The world's prisons are overcrowded. Some are in prison for crimes, some for conscience, others are the victims of unjust legal systems. All their families suffer.

Mixed voices: We are the destitute.

Narrator: There are nearly one billion people who are defined as "the absolute poor," whose existence is characterized by malnutrition, illiteracy, and disease, and is beneath any reasonable definition of human decency.

10. How do the authors define the poor?

_____

_____

_____

11. What signifies "good news" to these poor? Is that the same "good news" we have to offer them?

_____

_____

_____

12. Why is Christian witness so closely linked to ministry to the poor?

_____

_____

_____

We don't have to travel far to come in contact with the poor and destitute. In a world full of need, how do we determine where to focus our attention? Even the cities of the affluent West are filled with homeless and indigent peoples, as well as working poor, drug abusers, and others with desperate needs. In the following article, Bryant Myers seeks to present some criteria for application to mission strategy.

❏ *Where Are the Poor and the Lost?* *

Bryant L. Myers

The issue is strategy. The place is the world. The primary problem is how to allocate the limited resources available for sharing the good news with those who have never heard the name of Jesus Christ. The second question is, What strategy might be most effective?

Who? Where? How? Hard questions, loaded questions. Even theological questions. What information might help us begin to struggle toward some answers?

When we use the phrases, "most needy peoples" and "poorest of the poor," we intend to include those who have both great physical need, as well as the need to hear the good news.

In recent times, the phrase "the poor and the lost" has been used to communicate our meaning more explicitly.

World Vision recently undertook a research effort to gather demographic and socio-economic information which covers both the spiritual and the material dimensions of need in the world.

Traditional sources of information on poverty do not include the spiritual dimension. Don Brandt, a research specialist in World Vision International, worked with staff from MARC (Missions Advanced Research and Communications Center) and developed four indices, made up of a number of indicators. The four indicators attempt to approximate the need for and the openness to the good news in a variety of ways. These indices must be used with a great deal of care. They do not stand up fully to the rigorous tests one normally associates with sociological research. They are rough measures designed to be applied loosely and with discretion by managers who are facing decisions about the allocation of resources.

There are four different ways in which we can view the world in answer to the question: Where are the poor and the lost in the world? We have combined one spiritual index with one index of physical need.

1. Which countries have the highest child mortality rates and the highest constraints to evangelism?

2. Which countries are the highest on the human suffering index and have the largest percentage of non-Christians in their population?

3. Which countries are highest human suffering and highest constraints to evangelism?

4. Which countries have the highest numbers of people living in absolute poverty and the largest non-Christian population?

When we screen the countries of the world through these evangelization indices and six socio-economic indices, 14 countries show up on all of them. We can consider them the most needy in terms of both poverty and the need for hearing the good news.

Eleven of these countries are primarily Muslim: Afghanistan, Algeria, Chad, Indonesia, Mali, Mauritania, Morocco, Niger, Somalia, Sudan, and Yemen. Two are Buddhist: Vietnam and Cambodia. Nepal is Hindu. Eight are in Africa, four in Asia, and one in the Middle East.

The most dominant impression one gains from looking at the world in this way is that the lost are often materially poor. Whether one approaches the data from a desire to learn where the good news needs to be heard, or a desire to find the poorest of the poor, the answer is the same.

The second dominant impression one gains from looking at the world this way is that those who are poorest and in greatest need of hearing the name of Jesus live in Muslim or Buddhist contexts. Both religions tend to be highly resistant to the good news of the gospel for different reasons. Islam understands Christians as being expressions of the ancient

* Myers, B. L. (1989). Where are the poor and the lost? In F. K. Jansen (Ed.), *Target earth* (pp. 94-95). Pasadena: University of the Nations/Global Mapping International.

enemy, Christendom—a source of secularism, Westernization, and a very suspect spirituality. Buddhism evades the truth encounter by offering to assimilate Jesus as just another god, while labeling Christianity as an unwanted foreign intrusion from the West. People, in both contexts, not only have not had an opportunity to hear the gospel, but they live in environments that are not open to having it proclaimed.

Both of these general conclusions lead up to some interesting thoughts about missions in the years ahead. If those with whom we desire to share are poor and closed to the good news, what kind of strategy would make the most sense?

It would seem that the place to begin is with the second of the two great commandments singled out by Jesus: Love your neighbor as yourself. A ministry of love, care, compassion, and ultimately of transformation seems the only right place to begin.

At the same time, one could hardly claim to love one's neighbor if one did not feel compelled to share one's valuable possession—the news about the person who saves and transforms. Furthermore, when one begins by sharing the worth of the gospel through signs and deeds of love and mercy, it is likely that the people will become increasingly willing to listen to words about the truth of the kingdom of God and its King.

> *If the lost are often poor, then a holistic ministry—one in which compassion, social transformation, and proclamation are inseparably related—would seem to be the strategy for this time in human history.*

What does this suggest? If the lost are often poor, then a holistic ministry—one in which compassion, social transformation, and proclamation are inseparably related—would seem to be the strategy for this time in human history. If incarnation is the model practiced by the One who ministered to such as these, then holistic practitioners, people whose lives are eloquent concerning the values and worth of the gospel, would seem to be the messengers of the hour.

13. *What two primary indexes are combined to determine strategic countries for world evangelization? Do you agree with this approach?*

_____

_____

14. *What religious affiliation do the most needy groups tend to hold? What is their general response to the gospel? Why?*

_____

_____

15. *Answer the author's question: "If those with whom we desire to share are poor and closed to the good news, what kind of strategy would make the most sense?"*

_____

_____

_____

If it is true that "the poor and the lost" are primarily found in countries that are severely restricted to Christian witness, how does God open the doors of opportunity? Many Christian relief and development organizations work among these peoples and offer opportunities for service.* While they focus primarily on alleviating human suffering and poverty rather than on church planting, they often support spiritual ministry to the extent they are able.

The poor, oppressed, and war ravaged have always sought to alleviate their condition by moving to locations where their lot could be improved. With little to lose in their traditional countries or areas of residence, they set out to escape their circumstances. While reaching people through their needs is a basic principle of successful evangelization, refugees are particularly open to spiritual influence. These people are often uprooted suddenly from their homes and cut off from the traditions and filial pressures that have kept them isolated and in spiritual darkness. They are ready to hear a new message, particularly if that message is ministered with practical love which addresses their displacement and also their felt need for a new identity.

The following excerpts from an article by Paul Filidis explain the dynamic opportunity these migrating populations represent for those who wish to reach the least reached.

❏ *Worldwide Migration: Phenomenon and Opportunity* **

Paul Filidis

Many mission fields have arrived at our doorsteps!

Millions of people worldwide are on the move. Their reasons for packing up are diverse; the effect on their new host societies considerable. Communication media are said to have made the world a global village, but immigration and emigration—both voluntary and involuntary, legal and illegal—all amalgamate and internationalize the world's community on a face-to-face level and scale never witnessed before.

The plight of war refugees is usually the most newsworthy and thus most evident. The United Nations reports that there are currently over 16 million refugees who have had to flee their country, while at least the same number of people are displaced within their own country's borders.

But migration is not only due to war. While many seek to escape disaster and starvation, or are forcibly relocated by their governments, huge numbers are drawn by the glitter of ever-expanding urban centers. According to U.N. estimates, nearly 500 million people will have moved to the city during the last decade of this millennium.

Great numbers of job seekers (mostly from the southern hemisphere) come to claim their share in the (often-flaunted) prosperity of the North. For many, their dreams either remain elusive or are achieved at a cost—the loss of home, family, and cultural identity.

---

* Some of the more prominent Christian organizations involved in relief and development include Church World Service, Compassion International, Food for the Hungry International, Inter-Church Aid, Lutheran World Federation, Mennonite Central Committee, Tear Fund, World Concern, World Relief, and World Vision.

** Filidis, P. (1991, August). Worldwide migration: Phenomenon and opportunity. *World Christian News, 4*(2), 1-3.

Foreign study opportunities also contribute tremendously to international relationships. Millions of foreign students are conveyors of their home culture as well as of the values assimilated abroad.

Are immigrants today's conquerors?

Some observers interpret these demographic developments in a more threatening light. They comment that today's conquerors, unlike the past, are less likely to come in the form of invading military armies. Instead, the "takeover" of a nation occurs more slowly from within as millions of immigrants alter the fabric of the host societies. Other observers paint a more positive image, majoring on the opportunities to share with the less well-off, to provide refuge, and to be enriched by other peoples' cultures.

As economic conditions worsen, attitudes toward foreigners deteriorate as well. They are then seen as a threat to the society, causing changes to the character of a nation, competing for jobs and social benefits.

During economic booms, immigrants are often welcomed, filling job areas deemed less desirable by the locals. As economic conditions worsen, however, attitudes toward foreigners deteriorate as well. They are then seen as a threat to the society, causing changes to the character of a nation, competing for jobs and social benefits. Here are just a few examples of diverse migration cases:

- The racial composition of the U.S. population changed more dramatically in the past decade that at any time in the 20th century. Largely due to immigration (about 700,000 immigrants are permitted into the U.S.A. annually), Asians increased by 107 percent, and Hispanics by 53 percent.

- Tens of thousands of Hong Kong Chinese, dreading the future prospect of Chinese rule, are buying their way into new home countries.

- Millions of Afghan refugees, suspicious of developments at home, are staying put; many have begun a new existence elsewhere.

- Until the recent Kuwait crisis, millions of South and East Asians had been employed in the Middle East.

- Millions of North Africans and Middle Easterners have made their home in Western Europe. Some analysts anticipate 25 million more during the next three decades.

- Khomeini's era has led 3 million Iranians to begin a new life in exile.

- The Chinese rural work force of 400 million is double what the country needs. Hundreds of thousands are migrating to the big cities. Guangzhou, a city of about 4 million, has had an estimated 30,000 migrants descend on it daily in recent weeks.

- Asylum requests for Europe and North America have increased from an annual average of 25,000 during the '70s to 70,000 in the '80s. In 1990 the number exploded to over 500,000, with the majority from the Two Thirds World.

- In the U.S.A. alone, an estimated 350,000 foreign students—future potential leaders in their home countries—study in any given year.

16. How many kinds of "migrations" does the author describe? List these.

---

17. *With what two perspectives can today's "invasions" be viewed?*

_____

_____

_____

A strategic development and opportunity

The internationalization and mingling of the world community has of course many ramifications. From a missions point of view, it constitutes a significant trend. Many peoples that were hitherto less approachable because of political, geographical, cultural, and linguistic barriers are now more accessible.

People who formerly may never have listened to the gospel message now consider it with interest—at least for a season. They do so, often, because they are in a vulnerable state, detached from the sway of their traditional socio-cultural context. Although the occasion may be tragic, as in the case of war refugees, similar dynamics apply to immigrants, guest workers, urban migrants, and to those who study abroad.

An estimated 1,000 largely non-Christian ethnolinguistic peoples from the Two Thirds World are now represented in sizable numbers in "Christianized" countries. About 200 of these peoples are from the "World A" (constituting the world's *least evangelized* population segments).

Besides the basic biblical injunction to show kindness to strangers, Christians in these host societies frequently have a unique opportunity to declare and demonstrate the gospel to those belonging to *unreached people groups*. Numerous stories of Christians extending helping hands in a context of hospitality and friendship evangelism have proven this strategic development to be a very rewarding opportunity.

18. *How does what we know about both forced and voluntary migrations contribute to our understanding of mission strategy?*

_____

_____

_____

Much of what has been discussed in this section supports strategies which use aid and relief to access unreached populations. There is, however, a proactive side of social action which focuses on helping others help themselves. In the following section, we will focus on community development as a strategic framework for mission strategy.

III. Community Development

Development is not a new concept. Since the middle of the 20th century, as a matter of policy, Western governments have attempted to aid poorer nations through various large-scale economic strategies. Based on theoretical models of economic development, massive infusions of dollars have been aimed at raising per capita income levels. Billions of dollars later, the general conclusion is that these large-scale development efforts have been ineffective in alleviating poverty, while contributing to serious problems such as the mass migration to cities.

Interestingly, development economists have come to similar conclusions about strategizing for development as missiologists have about reaching the unreached. There are no "standard" solutions to development. While economists don't speak of a "unique solution" strategy, they do admit that there is a need to incorporate institutional and cultural variables more fully into the equation. In the following article, Edward Dayton draws some further conclusions about development based on its history and points out why Christians are best prepared to implement successful strategies.

❏ *Evangelism as Development* *

Edward R. Dayton

Development is a many-meaning word. For some it has a sense of Western imperialism: the "developed" country is attempting to impose their own values and desires on "lesser developed" countries. "Developed to what?" they ask. For what? There is a built-in assumption that things are better when they are "developed."

Development has about it the ring of human progress. *Human* progress. It can find its roots in the Age of Enlightenment, when for the first time in history, a large segment of society began to believe that they really could control their destinies. The humanists of the 17th and 18th centuries were stimulated in their thinking by the great discoveries (for the West!) of the Americas and the African Continent. What we can now see were often coincidences of history worked together to convince them that by dint of hard work and high ideals man could triumph over his situation. The stories of Horatio Alger became the everyday coin of our belief. The Calvin-inspired Protestant ethic became an end in itself. "Progress" was measured by acquisition.

Once the West was won, those who were a part of the grand adventure naturally concluded that what

they had been able to accomplish should be a possibility for others. They looked with compassion, mixed with a good degree of superiority, at their neighbors in less "developed" countries and set about to help them develop. Failures outnumbered successes at every turn. The American State Department's Agency for International Development finally concluded that there was little hope for replicating the developed West through massive doses of Western technology. It was a somber, but wise, conclusion.

> **The assumption is that if we can deal with an entire community that is still intact in its community setting, that development is possible.**

We are now involved in a fall-back situation of operating on the principle that our mistake was one of scale. To attempt to develop an entire nation was beyond our scope, but there still remains the possibility of *community* development. The assumption is that if we can deal with an entire community that is still intact in its community setting, that develop-

---

* Dayton, E. R. (1979, March). Evangelism as development. *MARC Newsletter*, 4-5.

ment is possible. There are many who agree that this is the right approach. We do too.

Now, the goal of community development always was and still remains to bring a group to a place of self-reliance or self-sufficiency: they find within themselves all that is needed to maintain life at a desired level. The fly in the ointment is the underlying premise of those involved in micro-development, namely, given the right circumstances and resources, mankind is capable of creating for himself a *good* society. The premise is false.

The premise is wrong because man's values are flawed. The natural man is turned in on himself, concerned for himself and his own welfare. Given a choice between his own welfare and the welfare of his society, he will usually erroneously conclude that his own best ends are served by serving himself. This is particularly true if he follows the model of the West. For the model of the West is, "*You* can do it! Look at me. *I* did it!" Or, to put it in the title of a not-so-old popular tune, "I Did It *My* Way."

And so it is quite easy for us to become involved in valueless community development. We can look with Christian compassion on a group of people living on the edge of poverty and conclude that if they had a better water system, better farming methods, and basic preventive medicine, they would be all right. Community development is possible. But, along with those changes in material standards, there needs to be a change in spiritual standards. There needs to be the announcement of the gospel of the kingdom, the possibility of a radical change at the core of one's being.

Don't miss the point: It's not a question of material development that is accompanied by the gift of eternal life found in Christ. It's a question of the basic motivation to want to change, to want to find a new relationship with one's neighbor, to want to put spiritual values before material values. Evangelism is at the core of true development. It is the catalyst that makes the rest of the mix take form and endure.

Perhaps an extreme example will make the point. World Vision is currently involved in an area of the world which has recently been resettled by the government. Each family has been given a plot of ground, half of which is to be used for a cash crop controlled by the government and the other half of which can be used for personal use. People have come from many different settings to take advantage of this offer. They each have a means of livelihood. Their material needs are met, but there is a great deal of unrest, strife, and social upheaval. Our "development" solution is to support the establishment of a Christian community center that will bring a common value system to the community. The anticipation is that as people become one in Christ, they will relate to one another in a new way. Helping to plant a church that will provide the missing values turns out to be the key element of development.

Evangelism is at the core of true development. It is the catalyst that makes the rest of the mix take form and endure.

Christians have been uniquely equipped to do development. First, we come to the task with the right motivation. The love of Christ constrains us. The demands of righteousness and justice are upon us. It is not a question of can we, but first a question of *should* we.

Second, Christians come to the task with a balanced sense of the times in which we live and an ability to work out our lives in the midst of the tension that, while we believe we are called upon to work against the forces of evil we find in our world, at the same time we believe that only in Christ's return will that evil be permanently defeated.

But Western Christians live in the midst of what a recent writer has called the Culture of Narcissism, a culture in which the individual is turning in on himself to find a fulfillment or self-understanding or self-awareness or a host of other "in" words. We tell ourselves that the society is out of control. Our leaders are found incompetent or corrupt. Our technology threatens to overcome us rather than save us. History loses its meaning for us. What was right 70 years ago is no longer important. Today's problems, we reason, are so different that we will have to make up the rules as we go along. And without recognizing what is happening, we Christians easily follow the same path. We adjust our theology to fit the circumstances we can't change. And therefore it becomes easy for us to conclude that what one values, what one holds most important, probably varies for everyone. And who are we to tell someone else how to live? And that's about the way non-Christian development approaches the task.

The message of the gospel is a radical message. It not only says, "Change your mind about things," it also demands, "Let Christ change your life—think about your sister and your brother. What's important is not how much you acquire but how you live out your life." Salvation is not just eternity. Salvation begins now with a new mind in Christ.

Let's listen again to that message—daily. And if we really believe that Christ changed our life, let's believe that evangelism is a key part of development.

19. *What approach have experts concluded should be used for development? How does this differ from previous approaches?*

_____

_____

_____

20. *Why is secular community development bound to fail?*

_____

_____

_____

21. *What unique qualities do Christians possess that allow us to believe that we can succeed in community development?*

_____

_____

_____

Christians are in a unique position to implement community development. Indeed, it is a "natural" instinct which has drawn countless missionaries into innumerable "projects." Unfortunately, many of these projects have failed, not for lack of good intentions, but because of inadequate understanding and resources to carry out the plans. The following excerpt from "Helping Others Help Themselves" more fully explains the nature of community development and the team approach which can most adequately ensure the success of development projects.

❑ *Helping Others Help Themselves: Christian Community Development* *

Robert C. Pickett and Steven C. Hawthorne **

Many factors point to the need for "Community Development." In the Third World the poorest and those unreached by development are mostly (80 percent plus or minus) in remote rural areas which suffer from lack of transportation and communication. There is little hope for them to enter into the international trade and buy their basic needs—they must be shown how to produce and meet their own needs themselves in the context of Christian sharing. Development seldom continues well or far if the spiritual needs are not simultaneously being met.

Evangelism is the key to community development, when people are freed from their fears or indifference—or even hate—to truly help one another.

Many people in developing countries become defeatist or fatalistic and think of themselves as poor and incapable. They think their country or area is also poor and lacking in resources. The challenge for the Christian (who ideally is also a developer) is to help the local people see hope—for the abundant life here on earth as well as for the life eternal. After hope comes the need for the local people to become motivated to contribute to their own development. Then comes the adequate assessment of their own personal talents, abilities, and resources as well as the natural resources about them. This can bring release from the syndrome of, "We're a poor people in a poor country and cannot improve."

Another factor hindering development is the tendency of many people to look at factors limiting food production, for example, and then blame the lack of adequate programs or performance on the "flood, drought, pests, diseases, etc." The challenge is to adequately assess these problems, make plans to overcome them, and begin adequate production on a renewable basis. The tendency to "find a scapegoat" must be overcome if adequate development is to take place.

Christian community development is the key. Evangelism, in turn, is the key to community development, when people are freed from their fears or indifference—or even hate—to truly help one another. Community development begins where there are hearts of love and hope in a community.

22. What are the primary factors hindering development?

---

* Pickett, R. C., & Hawthorne, S. C. (1992). Helping others help themselves: Christian community development. In R. D. Winter & S. C. Hawthorne (Eds.), *Perspectives on the world Christian movement: A reader* (rev. ed.) (pp. D216-D219). Pasadena: William Carey Library.

** Robert C. Pickett is a professor in community development at William Carey International University in Pasadena, California, and was for 22 years a professor of agronomy at Purdue University. He has worked as a consultant for crop improvement and community development projects in over 100 countries.

Steven C. Hawthorne is part of Hope Chapel in Austin, Texas, and serves with the Antioch Network, helping churches with practical vision to plant new churches among the world's least evangelized peoples. He has led on-site research projects in Asia and the Middle East.

23. *What is the key to successful Christian community development?*

_____

_____

_____

Physical development factors

Christian community development efforts must address themselves to the whole need complex of a community. Care must be taken to work with the cultural "givens" of the community. Changes must be proven to be desirable. The survival patterns of many communities are so fragile that unforeseen side effects of improvements can prove disastrous. The risk of doing things differently often appears too great to those at or under a subsistence level of living. Any tools, foods, and new technology must be carefully studied to insure that they are appropriate culturally and are renewable and sustainable physically. But most community development is a simple matter of a partnership of strengths and common sense of different cultures. Several basic development factors should be coordinated for holistic development:

1. Water

Pure drinking water is a daily necessity, and water for at least garden irrigation is desirable. Nonpotable water is perhaps the greatest purveyor of human physical misery. Diseases and parasites from the water lead to lethargy. Pure water can often be provided by constructing protected wells. Communities can be instructed on how to boil, filter, or chemically treat their water.

2. Sanitation

The prevention of contamination of water and food by diseases and parasites is largely a matter of education. Simple instruction in proper washing of hands and food and the proper disposal and isolation of human and animal wastes can make a great difference.

3. Food

Both the amount of food, i.e., total calories, and the nutritional balance are important. Many people do not have enough to eat, but many more suffer from nutritional deficiencies of protein, vitamins, and minerals not present in the usual basic diet of cereals, or in roots and tubers which are high in carbohydrates and starch but deficient in the other necessities. Thus, improvements must be made both in amount of food and in a proper balance of protein, vitamins, and minerals. These nutrients can be provided by such foods as grain legumes (beans, peas, etc.), green leafy vegetables, and other fruits and vegetables that can be grown in intensive home gardens, if not generally available. Simple plans for crop rotation and storage can alleviate the "feast or famine" syndrome.

4. Fuel

Wood is by far the number one cooking fuel in the world, particularly in the "hungry half." Native forests are rapidly being cut down in many developing areas and are long gone in more ancient areas of civilization. The hope for renewable firewood production lies in several promising species of fast growing tropical trees including Eucalyptus, Leucaena, Melina, and Pinus species. Several of these are already widely used and are being replanted on hundreds of thousands of acres each year.

5. Health

Westerners are conditioned to think of health as a gift. Health care then is focused on curing diseases with expensive hospital and clinic complexes. In community development efforts, the stress should be in preventive medicine. Important components are teaching sanitation and public health, inocula-  tions, parasite and disease control, and nutrition training. These should be added to whatever curative medicine is present.

6. Shelter and clothing

These should be designed and provided by making maximum use of local crops, e.g., cotton for cloth and bamboo for buildings. Many other  plant materials can be used in addition to rock, clay bricks, etc., where available for buildings.

7. Income production

Cash crops are the pri-mary exports and cash earners for most develop-ing countries (except oil-exporting countries).  Typical cash crops include coffee, cocoa, sugar cane, rubber, tea, and palm oil, as well as some of the very food crops developing countries need most, such as beans. "Cottage" industries and village co-operatives can be encouraged. Using local labor and materials, these arrangements hold great promise with good marketing technique.

8. Education

In many needy countries there is insufficient educa-tion, and literacy rates are very low. Thus literacy often gets first attention in edu-cation improvement. Next comes the choice between so-called classical education to-  ward skills useful only at government desks (the biggest employer in many countries) or education toward meeting the needs of the people. The latter desperately needs expansion.

9. Communication and transportation

These two interacting factors are almost unbeliev-able in their negative effects on the welfare of the people in remote areas. The majority of the people in de-veloping countries live in these areas. Regional or national  programs are often necessary to make improvements, but the possibilities for local action should be thoroughly studied.

24. *Why must great care be taken when introducing innovations in a community where people live at a subsistence level?*

_____

_____

_____

25. *For each of the general areas above, list possible trained resource people who could be used to meet these needs (e.g., water—well driller, water analyst, water systems engineer).*

_____

_____

_____

_____

_____

_____

_____

_____

A team strategy

There are three kinds of gifts that are needed in Christian community development. One is the gift of bringing others to Christ and planting churches. Another is a gift in a needed technical area like food production, health care, literacy, or vocational training. The third is a gift of administration in order to design, implement, and evaluate programs to help the people.

A key strategy is to organize teams that have people with special gifts in these three areas of church planting, needed technical expertise, and management. While all these gifts may be found in one person, it would be more advisable to have these tasks assigned to specific members of a team.

Each committed Christian should strive to spread the gospel of Jesus Christ as his first priority. Each member of a team is best trained first as a "generalist" in addition to being trained as a specialist in a specific task. General training can be given to teach basic and practical skills and information that can be shared with the people. This can be on witnessing for Christ, small-scale family food production, health promotion, disease prevention, first aid, and simple treatment. Each member can also be trained to be more effective in planning and organizing his or her own work, in leadership, and in controlling (or getting the desired results). The latter means getting information on how the program is doing in order to improve areas that are not doing well.

The hungry half and the hidden people

Community development holds the most promise for the Christian worker desirous of promoting fundamental change in human societies. Community development is consistent with the posture of humility and involvement that Jesus modeled for His disciples. Community development revolves around vigorous yet sensitive evangelism. And the "hungry half" that are most in need of community development are more often than not the "hidden peoples" that are justly receiving increased attention by the church of Jesus Christ today.

26. *Why should an "unreached peoples" team seek to include the three basic types of gifted people mentioned above?*

_____

_____

The Bible strongly supports the concept of expressing Christian love through meeting basic human needs. Matthew 25:31-40 hardly allows us to treat this practice as "optional." The fact that meeting human need through Christian community development can also open the doors to unreached people should stimulate the church to actively pursue this channel for evangelization. It is not unreasonable to expect missionaries to develop a profession or skill of direct use in community development, in addition to obtaining Bible and church related training.

As we conclude this section (and this volume on strategy), we want to emphasize that mission is essentially God centered, not man centered. In the following article, Bob Moffitt eloquently brings us back to this focus with a biblical perspective of development.

❏ *Biblical Development* *

Bob Moffitt **

What is development? How is it defined? What are its characteristics? Secular and Christian development provide different answers to these questions.

Secular development is designed to improve living conditions. It supports and encourages a higher quality of life. It believes that people, individually and corporately, can improve their quality of life through intentional human effort. In the Two Thirds World, secular development works primarily to meet physical and social needs—health, water, housing, agriculture, economic enterprise, education, etc. Good secular development has two key characteristics: it helps people help themselves, and it is sustainable (it can be continued without ongoing external support).

> *Biblical development is God centered: from God, seeking to honor God, and relying on Him as the principal participant in the development process.*

Biblical development affirms much of this, but with a radically different orientation. This difference is critical. Secular development is man centered: for man, by man, limited to what man can do for him-

self. Biblical development is God centered: from God, seeking to honor God, and relying on Him as the principal participant in the development process. Biblical development does not exclude man, but sees him cooperating under God in the process of man's healing.

In biblical development, "quality of life" is determined by God's intentions for His people. It is not limited to the tangible and visible arenas of man's need, but includes the healing of areas of emotion and spirit. It is not limited to what man can do for himself, but is as limitless as God's power, love and mercy.

The goal of development is God's intentions

Development must have a goal, an objective, an agenda. The Christian objective and agenda is directed by God's intentions. Secular development asks, "What are your needs?" Biblical development asks, "What are God's intentions for you and this particular need?" The answer sets the goal for biblical development.

Felt needs are legitimate concerns in development works, but they are not the only concern. Heroin addicts feel the need for heroin. Some women ex-

* Moffitt, B. (1992). *Leadership development training curriculum.* Tempe, AZ: Harvest Foundation.

** Bob Moffitt is the founder and president of Harvest Foundation, an organization which is involved in curriculum development for leadership training in Two Thirds World churches. He is the author of *Adventures in God's Kingdom* and the *Leadership Development Training Program.*

press a felt need for abortion on demand. A teenager may express a need for a car. These represent real feelings; however, responding to them may actually hinder development. Therefore, the question must be, "What is the root need beyond the felt need?" Unless the felt need is life-threatening, such as food for a starving child, development work is best directed toward the root need.

Christians realize root needs are related to underlying spiritual causes. Scripture describes the relationships between all these needs, and God's solutions. Before setting goals, Christians ask, "Father, what is your perspective of this need, its root, and your solution?"

Jesus' development models God's intentions

Jesus, though divine, was also man, and He is our model for development. To understand God's intentions, Luke 2:52 is a good starting point. Luke, a medical doctor, described Jesus' development in four domains—wisdom, physical, spiritual, and social. "And Jesus grew in wisdom and stature, and in favor with God and men" (NIV).

If Jesus needed to develop in all these areas, so do all men. God is concerned about the *whole man*. Development must reflect this *holistic* or *balanced* concern to represent God's intentions. The purpose of Jesus' development was to honor God, to serve and give His life for others. Man also should grow in order to love and honor Him, to love and serve others. Biblical development will promote this.

It is well to note that Jesus' development was in the context of *adequacy* rather than *affluence*. God insured Jesus the necessary resources to grow in wisdom—a simple synagogue school in which the study of God's law was the focus. He had the necessary resources to grow physically—shelter, clothing, food, water, sanitation, physical labor, etc. He had the necessary resources to grow spiritually—a God-fearing home and ability to read the Scriptures. And, He had the necessary resources to grow socially—a loving, functional family who modeled appropriate relationships in the family and community. Jesus' development took place in an environment of *adequacy*, or even relative poverty, rather than in an affluent, technically advanced environment.

The primary resource for development is God

God is the originator of development. He created all things. He sustains all things. All resources come from Him. As stewards of talents and resources God provides, development workers prayerfully and courageously invest them to advance God's goals.

As Creator, God deals in the supernatural. He is not limited to the existing material world. His principles can and do produce blessing and change. Because development workers are servants of the Living God, they are not limited to visible material resources. In the face of insurmountable difficulties, they can take confidence in the biblical principle God has promised those who walk in His righteousness, that He will heal the people and their land.

Ten years ago I visited an impoverished village in central Mexico. Village leaders, recently converted, committed to live God's way. They weren't particularly interested in development. Yet, the village has been transformed from a place where families were killing each other in blood feuds to one where they serve one another in love. In a place where pigs once freely walked through mud huts, there are now tidy wooden houses. (The first seven houses were built for village widows.) In a place with a small stream and not one latrine, there is now running water and sanitation. In a place with an empty, deserted schoolhouse, children now go to school.

Ten years ago, the prospect for development in this village looked bleak. However, God's intervention was not limited to visible resources. The people of this village entered into a pact of righteousness with God—a pact in which they sought and followed His intentions. Leaders in the village regularly went to the forest to study Scripture and pray for several days. They stayed till they reached agreement on what God wanted them to do. Then they put their convictions into practice. I marveled as He moved to "heal their land."

27. Why isn't it enough for development to deal with "felt" needs?

_____

_____

_____

28. Why is the primary resource for development God Himself?

_____

_____

The local church should be an active participant in development

The local church is the most visible and permanent representation of God's kingdom in any community. More than any other institution, it can reflect God's concern in each domain of man's need. Other Christian institutions have a particular focus— evangelism, education, health, economic development. They are limited by organizational mandate in their ability to represent God's concern for the whole person.

Where there is a local church, it should be actively involved in servant leadership in development. Thereby, local churches grow their ability to proclaim and demonstrate Gods intentions for the people of their respective communities. The potential for sustainability of the work will increase, as well.

Development is required of the poor as well as the wealthy

The parable of the talents (Matt. 25:14-30) teaches that *no one* is exempt from the responsibility to courageously risk their resources for the kingdom of God. Damage results if the poor are regarded as too poor to play a part. Unless the issue is survival, the appeal to outside resources often reinforces a sense of powerlessness. If provided before local people learn to value and invest the resources God had entrusted to them, long-term dependency on outside financial, material, and technical aid may occur. The history of modern development is replete with examples of well intended effort which inhibited rather than advanced development.

God multiplies the gifts of the poor. In biblical accounts of the widow of Zarephath, the feeding of the 5,000, and the widow's mite, God acted in response to sacrificial commitment of resources. Even the poor must demonstrate God's love to those around them. This is their gift from God.

In India, a village church realized they had a responsibility to invest the little they had to demonstrate God's love to their Hindu neighbors. They went out to see what needs existed. They discovered that some Hindu women owned only one sari. Every other day, when the sari was being washed, they could not leave their homes for shopping or other necessities.

> *No one is exempt from the responsibility to courageously risk their resources for the kingdom of God.*

The pastor asked if any in the congregation with three saris would give one to the Hindu women's need. The result? All the saris needed (about 12) were given and delivered. At the same time, Hindu women requested Christians to come and pray for the protection of their unborn children. Matching needs with resources has become part of the Sunday worship experience of these Indian Christians. A church which had seen itself as too poor to make a difference, now entered a much fuller dimension of outreach.

Encouraging sacrificial stewardship for the poor in no way exempts those whose resources are abundant. In John 12:28 Jesus says, "You will always have the poor among you, but you will not always have Me" (NIV). This is often quoted to excuse indifference to the plight of the poor. In fact, Jesus was quoting Deuteronomy 15:11, which gives a very different conclusion: "Therefore I command you to be openhanded toward your brothers and toward the poor and needy in your land" (NIV).

God requires compassionate and liberal sharing with those in need. *All* people are to risk their resources for the kingdom. Isaiah 58, Matthew 25, Luke 10:25-37, James 2:14, and 1 John 3:16-18

make it clear that it is impossible to love one's neighbors without being open to promote all God's intentions for them.

The responsibility exempts no Christian. If the poor are held accountable for this, how much more will the rich be expected to use all they have to bless others, honor God, and expand the kingdom. Lovingly done, this is biblical development.

29. What is the role of the church in development?

_____

_____

30. Why should poor Christians as well as the rich participate in community development?

_____

_____

Summary

The 20th century evangelism vs. social action debate has moved evangelicals steadily towards a reconciliation of the two positions. While balance has been sought, evangelism is still recognized as the "leading partner." Notwithstanding, the biblical and practical reasons for engaging in social action are numerous and essential to contemporary mission strategy.

The breadth and intensity of human need around the globe are beyond comprehension. War, famine, and pestilence affect whole segments of humanity. All of these crises offer Christians a chance for involvement. The poorest of the poor socially are also the poorest spiritually. They also tend to be located in the most restricted access countries for Christian witness. Their needs, however, may become the open door to reaching them. Often, these same people become more accessible through migrations intended to escape their circumstances. Initially, these immigrants and refugees are particularly open to the good news shared by loving Christians.

Improving the lives of the poor in under-developed countries is a mission which has been attempted on a large scale by Western governments. Readdressing the issue through community development is only viable if the beneficiaries can also be transformed in their basic motivations. Only Christ can do that, and He must be the center of Christian community development. Christians are uniquely suited to engage in this activity, but they should recognize that teams with adequately equipped resource people provide the best framework for achieving holistic mission. God-centered development will encourage dependence on Him as the ultimate resource and will allow all the participants, rich and poor, to risk sharing their resources to the benefit of all.

Integrative Assignment

In this assignment, you will be drawing up a basic plan for implementing a mission to your targeted people group. You will attempt to answer the question: *How shall they be reached?*

WORKSHEET #4: THE PLAN

The Goal

Based on your previous research, you are now ready to attempt to formulate a *strategy* for reaching your targeted people group. Your planning must be based on a clear vision of what you are trying to achieve. We assume you have the "right" goal and plan to establish a "cluster" of reproducing churches within your people group. All plans and objectives must contribute to this end.

1. State your goal succinctly and in measurable terms. (Example: One thousand baptized believers in at least 20 viable groups in key locations throughout the Tbuli region by the year 2000.)

_____

_____

_____

The Process

You must now try to envision the steps that are required to reach your goal. These steps should be sequential and should be stated in general terms, such as, "recruit and equip a nonresidential missionary," "establish a missionary presence among the people," "train the emerging leadership," etc. Each step, in turn, may have its own objectives and may require an individual plan. Keep in mind, however, that an objective is not an end in itself but part of a harmonized process which leads to the final goal. This suggests a logical sequencing which begins with initiation of the mission and ends when the goal has been reached.

2. Based on what you know about the accessibility of these people and their felt needs, what general approach or methods will you use?

_____

_____

_____

_____

_____

3. What "partnerships" must be forged with others from the force for evangelization? What role does each partner play?

_____

_____

_____

4. How will you know when the first "church" is established?

_____

_____

_____

5. How will the leadership be selected (qualifications) and trained (process)?

_____

_____

_____

6. What needs to happen to initiate and support a "spontaneous multiplication" of churches in this region (and beyond it to unreached groups)? How will you support this movement?

_____

_____

_____

7. List your general objectives in sequential (chronological) order.

_____

_____

_____

_____

_____

_____

_____

_____

The Resources

Through your research, you should have identified people, churches, agencies, funding sources, and other resources for the evangelization of the targeted people. You will be using these resources to achieve your objectives. *The key to implementing your plans successfully is to anticipate the resources needed to carry out your plans, to pray faithfully, and to work towards applying the resources in achieving your goal.*

8. What resources will you need to carry out each of the general objectives you've listed above? Think in terms of people, tools, and money.* List your resource needs next to each objective.

_____

_____

_____

_____

_____

_____

_____

9. Which "partner" will fill each of the resource needs? Tag each resource need with the initials of the source or sources that may meet this need.

_____

_____

_____

_____

_____

_____

_____

_____

* This exercise does not replace prayer or dependence on the Holy Spirit. It does, however, help us to be specific in our prayer requests and hope in faith for expressed needs to be met.

Questions for Reflection

Have you developed a personal philosophy for meeting human need? Many Bible-believing Christians work harder at avoiding the issue than dealing with it—even missionaries! They may cross the street to avoid a beggar or not answer the door when such a person comes knocking. Fear of creating dependence or of being "overrun" by the needy often obscures Christ's simple injunction to "give to everyone who asks of you" (Luke 6:30). What "policy" will you follow when confronted with human need on a personal basis in your day-to-day activities? Define your thoughts; you may be tested in this area today!

_____

_____

_____

_____

_____

_____

_____

_____

_____

_____

_____

APPENDIX

Resources From
Adopt-A-People Clearinghouse

Adopt-A-People
Clearinghouse
721 N. Tejon, P.O. Box 1795
Colorado Springs, CO 80901 USA
(719) 473-8800 *Fax:* (719) 473-5907

People Group	Date	Source	Pgs	Qty x Cost=Total	AAPCCode
Afghanistan					
Baluchi	4/92	YWAM	2	$0.80	AFG BALU 1
Hazara	1/92	Perspectives	9	$1.50	AFG HAZA 1
Hazara		MARC	1	$0.70	AFG HAZA 2
Hazara	4/92	YWAM	2	$0.80	AFG HAZA 3
Kurd	2/91	YWAM	2	$0.80	AFG KURD 1
Nuristani		Perspectives	10	$1.60	AFG NURI 1
Pushtun		GMI	8	$1.40	AFG PUSH 1
Sanglechi	4/92	YWAM	2	$0.80	AFG SANG 1
Shugan	4/92	YWAM	2	$0.80	AFG SHUG 1
Tadzhik	4/92	YWAM	2	$0.80	AFG TADZ 1
Turkmen	4/92	YWAM	2	$0.80	AFG TURK 1
Uzbak	4/92	YWAM	2	$0.80	AFG UZBA 1
Albania					
Albanian	/91	MARC	1	$0.70	ALB ALBA 1
Gheg	5/92	Perspectives	2	$0.80	ALB GHEG 1
Gypsy	/92	Perspectives	15	$2.10	ALB GYPS 1
Algeria					
Arab		AOG	1	$0.70	DZA ARAB 1
Kabyle		CSI	14	$2.00	DZA KABY1
Angola					
Kongo	/92	WB 2000	1	$0.70	AGO KONG1
Argentina					
Quechua	3/92	Fuller SWM	20	$2.60	ARG QUEC 1
Armenia					
Kurd	2/91	YWAM	2	$0.80	ARM KURD1
Azerbaijan					
Azerbaijani	10/90	YWAM	2	$0.80	AZE AZER 1
Azerbaijani		MARC	1	$0.70	AZE AZER 2
Azerbaijani	3/89	Perspectives	10	$1.60	AZE AZER 3
Azerbaijani	/89	SCAN	8	$1.40	AZE AZER 4
Kurd	2/91	YWAM	2	$0.80	AZE KURD 1
Kurdish Jew	4/92	YWAM	2	$0.80	AZE KJEW 1
Oriental Jew	9/91	YWAM	2	$0.80	AZE OJEW 1
Talysh	9/91	YWAM	2	$0.80	AZE TALY 1
Bangladesh					
Bengali		MARC	1	$0.70	BGD BANG1
Bihari	/90	YWAM	2	$0.80	BGD BIHA 1
Bolivia					
Chipaya		GMI	2	$0.80	BOL CHIP 1
Quechua		Perspectives	1	$0.70	BOL QUEC 1
Botswana					
Bushmen	5/92	AEF	2	$0.70	BWA BUSH1
Kalanga	5/92	AEF	2	$0.70	BWA KALA1
Yeyi	5/92	AEF	2	$0.70	BWA YEYI 1
Brunei					
Malay	2/91	YWAM	2	$0.80	BRN MALA1
Bulgaria					
Sephardic Jew	9/91	YWAM	2	$0.80	BGR SJEW 1
Turk	/92	Perspectives	28	$3.40	BGR TURK 1
Burkina Faso					
Birifor		WEC	2	$0.80	HVO BIRI 1
Dagaari		WEC	1	$0.70	HVO DAGA1
Dioula	5/90	WEC	1	$0.70	HVO DIOU 1
Dogose	5/90	WEC	1	$0.70	HVO DOGO1
Gbadogo	5/90	WEC	1	$0.70	HVO GBAD1
Kaan	5/90	WEC	1	$0.70	HVO KAAN1
Komono	5/90	WEC	1	$0.70	HVO KOMO1
Lobi	5/90	WEC	2	$0.80	HVO LOBI 1
Cameroon					
Assumbo	5/92	Perspectives	9	$1.50	CMR ASUM1
Baka	6/92	Perspectives	9	$1.50	CMR BAKA1
Bulu	2/91	World Miss.	1	$0.70	CMR BULU1
Fulani	/91	Bapt.G.Conf.	1	$0.70	CMR FULA 1
Fulbe	12/91	GMI	3	$0.90	CMR FULB 1
Fulbe	12/90	Persp.	12	$1.80	CMR FULB 2
Canada					
Micmac	5/90	Perspectives	9	$1.50	CAN MICM1
Central African Republic					
Arab Traders	/92	AIM	1	$0.70	CAF ARAB 1
Central Asia					
Chaghatai	3/92	YWAM	2	$0.80	CIS CHAG 1
Dungan	10/91	YWAM	2	$0.80	CIS DUNG 1
Dungan	11/91		8	$1.40	CIS DUNG 2
Kazakh	10/91	YWAM	2	$0.80	CIS KAZA 1
Korean	/90	SCAN	2	$0.80	CIS KORE 1
Kurd	/91	SCAN	8	$1.40	CISKURD 1
Kurd	/91	MARC	1	$0.70	CIS KURD 2
Kyrghyz	10/91	YWAM	2	$0.80	CIS KYRG 1
Meskhetian Turks	10/91	YWAM	2	$0.80	CIS MESH 1
Mugat Gypsies	10/91	YWAM	2	$0.80	CIS MUGA 1
Osmanli	10/91	YWAM	2	$0.80	CIS OSMA 1
Persians	10/91	YWAM	2	$0.80	CIS PERS 1
Soviet Muslims	3/92	YWAM	10	$1.60	CIS MUSL 1

Comments:

1. The AAP Clearinghouse is still in the process of verifying the status of peoples reported to be unreached and adoptable. *Please Note: A people's inclusion in this list in not intended to be confirmation that it is unreached.*

2. Not all profiles are created equal! They vary widely in quality and length. Our prices are set to cover our office expense in distributing them to the public.

3. The AAP Clearinghouse is developing an electronic means of distributing profiles automatically via the fax. Also, in development is a software program that will assist researchers and prayers in developing their own profiles.

4. If you have a profile that is not included in this list, and would like us to distribute if for prayer and information sharing, please send us a copy. Thanks!

* NOTE: An order of all of the profiles will recieve more than 50% discount: **$230.00**

If you have a large order, use the profile list as your order form and only fill in the information below.

---

* AAPC pays U.S. ground shipping costs. All foreign (including Canada) will be billed actual shipping . Please allow 3-4 weeks for delivery. If you are in a hurry and wish Air Mail, UPS etc, please specify and we will bill you for the additional amount.

People Profiles Order Form *(Please fill in all info. requested)*

AAPC CODE	QTY x Cost = Total
I_I_I_I_I_I_I_I_I	_____
I_I_I_I_I_I_I_I_I	_____
I_I_I_I_I_I_I_I_I	_____
I_I_I_I_I_I_I_I_I	_____
I_I_I_I_I_I_I_I_I	_____

Customer Name:_____

Organization:_____

Mailing Address:_____

_____

Daytime Phone (if you have questions on your order):_____

Subtotal: = $_____

*Shipping & Handling: = $ 1.00

Colorado Residents Add 6.4% :   = $_____

Total Purchase: = $_____

Enclosed is my check or money order: = $_____

Payable to: *Adopt-A-People Clearinghouse*
(U.S. funds or I.M.O. only no C.O.D.)

People	Date	Agency	No.	Price	Code
Tadzhiks	10/91	YWAM	2	$0.80	CIS TADZ 1
Tatars	/90	SCAN	8	$1.40	CIS TATA 1
Turkmen	10/91	YWAM	2	$0.80	CIS TURK 1
Uighur	10/91	YWAM	2	$0.80	CIS UIGH 1
Uzbeks	10/91	YWAM	2	$0.80	CIS UZBE 1
Chad					
Alwa	/92	AIM	1	$0.70	TCD ALWA1
Bagirmi	10/90	WEC	2	$0.80	TCD BAGI 1
Bua	/92	AIM	1	$0.70	TCD BUA 1
Kanembu	5/92	TEAM	1	$0.70	TCD KANE 1
Kwang	12/91	TEAM	1	$0.70	TCD KWAN1
Kwong	/92	AIM	1	$0.70	TCD KWON1
Maba	5/90	WEC	2	$0.80	TCD MABA1
Massalit	5/90	WEC	1	$0.70	TCD MASS 1
Mbororo	/92	AIM	1	$0.70	TCD MBOR1
Miltou	/92	AIM	1	$0.70	TCDMILT 1
Ndam	/92	AIM	1	$0.70	TCD NDAM1
Niellim	/92	AIM	1	$0.70	TCD NIEL 1
Chile					
Mapuche	12/92	Fuller SWM	10	$1.60	CHL MAPU1
China					
Bai	/91	Perspectives	8	$1.40	CHN BAI 1
Buyi	/91	Perspectives	8	$1.40	CHN BUYI 1
Chinese	12/91	TEAM	1	$0.70	CHN CHIN 1
Dai	/88	Perspectives	10	$1.60	CHN DAI 1
Dai	1/90	Perspectives	9	$1.50	CHN DAI 2
Dai	1/92	Asia St. Inst.	13	$1.90	CHN DAI 3
Ewenki		AOG	1	$0.70	CHN EWEN1
Hakka	/91	Navigators	16	$2.20	CHN HAKK1
Hakka	4/92	Perspectives	24	$3.00	CHN HAKK2
Hani	1/92	AAPC	3	$0.90	CHN HANI 1
Hui	10/90	YWAM	2	$0.80	CHN HUI 1
Hui		MARC	2	$0.80	CHN HUI 2
Hui	/91	AOG	1	$0.70	CHN HUI 3
Hui			4	$1.00	CHN HUI 4
Jews	4/92	Fuller SWM	10	$1.60	CHN JEWS 1
Kazakh		AOG	1	$0.70	CHN KAZA1
Kazakh	1/92	AAPC	2	$0.80	CHN KAZA2
Korean	/90	YWAM	2	$0.80	CHN KORE 1
Manchu	/91	Perspectives	13	$1.90	CHN MANC1
Miao	2/92	AAPC	8	$1.40	CHN MIAO 1
Mongol	10/90	YWAM	2	$0.80	CHN MONG1
Pai		AOG	1	$0.70	CHN PAI 1
Tibetan	/90	YWAM	2	$0.80	CHN TIBE 1
Tibetan	6/92	Persp.	8	$1.40	CHN TIBE 2
Uigher	/91	AAPC	2	$0.80	CHN UIGH 2
Uigher	1/91	WEC	3	$0.90	CHN UIGH 3
Uigher	10/90	YWAM	2	$0.80	CHN UIGH 4
Uigher	/88	SCAN	12	$1.80	CHN UIGH 5
Uygur		MARC	2	$0.80	CHN UYGU1
Vietnamese Refugee		AOG	1	$0.70	CHN VIET 1
Zhuang	/90	YWAM	2	$0.80	CHN ZHUA1
Comoros					
Anjouanais	/92	AIM	1	$0.70	COM ANJO1
Comorian	/92	AOG	1	$0.70	COM COMO1
Mohelians	/92	AIM	1	$0.70	COM MOHE1
Cote d' Ivoire					
Barala	9/90	WEC	3	$0.90	CIV BARA 1
Mahou	5/90	WEC	3	$0.90	CIV MAHO 1
Mona	5/90	WEC	2	$0.80	CIV MONA 1
Nwan	5/90	WEC	1	$0.70	CIV NWAN1
Semufo	4/92	Perspectives	5	$1.10	CIV SENU 1
Yaoure	7/91	WEC	1	$0.70	CIV YAOU 1
Ecuador					
Cayapa	/91	GMI	8	$1.40	ECU CAYA1
Ethiopia					
Birale	/91		1	$0.70	ETH BIRA 1
Surma	/92	Perspectives	8	$1.40	ETH SURM 1
Europe					
Kurd	2/91	YWAM	2	$0.80	EUR KURD1
France					
Gypsies	4/92	Persp.	9	$1.50	FRA GYPS 1
Jew (Sephardic)	11/90	YWAM	2	$0.80	FRA JEW 1
Muslims	/90	WEC	2	$0.80	FRA MUSL 1
Gambia					
Fula	5/90	WEC	1	$0.70	GMB FULA1
Jola	5/90	WEC	1	$0.70	GMB JOLA 1
Mandinka	5/90	WEC	1	$0.70	GMB MAND1
Wolof	5/90	WEC	1	$0.70	GMB WOLO1
Georgia					
Adzhareli	9/91	YWAM	2	$0.80	GEO ADZH 1
Laz	9/91	YWAM	2	$0.80	GEO LAZ 1
Ghana					
Birifor	5/90	WEC	1	$0.70	GHA BIRI 1
Chumburung	7/91	WEC	1	$0.70	GHA CHUM1
Dagaaba	5/90	WEC	2	$0.80	GHA DAGA1
Dagomba	10/91	WEC	1	$0.70	GHA DAGO1
Dagomba	/91	Partners Int.	4	$1.00	GHA DAGO2
Frafra	5/90	WEC	2	$0.80	GHA FRAF 1
Gonja	5/90	WEC	2	$0.80	GHA GONJ 1
Hanga		WEC	1	$0.70	GHA HANG1
Konkomba	7/91	WEC	2	$0.80	GHA KONK1
Mamprusi	5/90	WEC	1	$0.70	GHA MAMP1
Namumba	5/90	WEC	1	$0.70	GHA NANU1
Nchumburu	5/90	WEC	1	$0.70	GHA NCHU 1
Vagla	5/90	WEC	2	$0.80	GHA VAGL1
Wala	5/90	WEC	1	$0.70	GHA WALA1
Guinea					
Susu	/92	PBT	12	$1.80	GUI SUSU 1
Susu	/91	World Partners	2	$0.80	GUI SUSU 1
Guinea-Bissau					
Biafada	/90	WEC	1	$0.70	GNB BIAF 1
Fula		WEC	2	$0.80	GNB FULA 1
Mancanha		WEC	2	$0.80	GNB MANC1
Manjaco		WEC	2	$0.80	GNB MANJ1
Nalu	5/91	WEC	1	$0.70	GNB NALU1
Guyana					
Akawaio		GMI	2	$0.80	GUYAKAW1
East Indian Sunni Muslim	5/92	Persp.	11	$1.70	GUYSUNN1
India					
Anavil Brahmans	6/92	YWAM	2	$0.80	INDANAV 1
Andhra Brahmans	6/92	YWAM	2	$0.80	INDANDH 1
Ayyar Brahmans	6/92	YWAM	2	$0.80	INDAYYA 1
Baghdadi Jews	9/91	YWAM	2	$0.80	INDBJEW 1
Bene Israel Jews	9/91	YWAM	2	$0.80	INDBIJE 1
Bengali	/91	Nat. Fellowship	2	$0.80	INDBENG 1
Bhil	3/92	AAPC	6	$1.20	INDBHIL 1
Bhil	/92	YWAM	9	$1.50	INDBHIL 1
Bhojpuri	3/92	AAPC	7	$1.30	INDBHOJ 1
Chenchu (Chenswar)		B. Savage	2	$0.80	INDCHEN 1
Chinese	/91	Nat. Fellowship	1	$0.70	INDCHIN 1
Cochin Jews	9/91	YWAM	2	$0.80	INDCJEW 1
Daudi Borhas	4/92	YWAM	2	$0.80	INDDAUD 1
Deccani	/91	AOG	1	$0.70	INDDECC 2
Deccani		MARC	1	$0.70	INDDECC 3
Deccani	10/90	YWAM	2	$0.80	INDDECC 1
Garasiyas	4/92	YWAM	2	$0.80	INDGARA 1
Garhwali	1/92	AAPC	2	$0.80	INDGARH 1
Gond		Perspectives	11	$1.70	INDGOND 1
Gond	10/90	YWAM	2	$0.80	INDGOND 2
Gujrathi	/91	Nat. Fellowship	1	$0.70	INDGUJR 1
Jain	10/90	YWAM	2	$0.80	INDJAIN 1
Jat	10/90	YWAM	2	$0.80	INDJAT 1
Jat	10/90	YWAM	2	$0.80	INDJAT 2
Kanarese	/92	Perspectives	23	$2.90	INDKANR 1
Kanarie	/91	Nat. Fellowship	1	$0.70	INDKANA 1
Karhada Brahmans	7/92	YWAM	2	$0.80	INDKARH 1
Kashmiri	2/91	CSI	18	$2.40	INDKASH 1
Kashmiri	10/90	YWAM	2	$0.80	INDKASH 2
Kashmiri		MARC	1	$0.70	INDKASH 3
Kashmiri	/91	CSI	1	$0.70	INDKASH 4
Kashmiri	/92	CSI	5	$1.10	INDKASH 6
Kashmiri Brahmans	6/92	YWAM	2	$0.80	INDKBRA 1
Kurichiya		AOG	1	$0.70	INDKURI 1
Labbai	4/92	YWAM	2	$0.80	INDLABB 1
Lambadi	/87	GMI	8	$1.40	INDLAMB 1
Lambadi	/91	AOG	1	$0.70	INDLAMB 2
Magahi Bihari	10/92	YWAM	2	$0.80	INDMAGA 1
Malakkara		AOG	1	$0.70	INDMALA 1
Malayali	/91	Nat. Fellowship	1	$0.70	INDMALA 1
Mapilla	6/92	YWAM	2	$0.80	INDMAPI 1
Marathi	/91	Nat. Fellowship	1	$0.70	INDMARA 1
Marwari	/91	Nat. Fellowship	1	$0.70	INDMARW 1
Mina	11/91	CSI	10	$1.60	INDMINA 1
Mohyal Brahmans	6/92	YWAM	2	$0.80	INDMOHY 1
Nagar Brahmans	6/92	YWAM	2	$0.80	INDNAGA 1
Nepali	/91	Nat. Fellowship	1	$0.70	INDNEPA 1
Oraon	2/92	AAPC	3	$0.90	INDORAO 1
Oriya	/91	Nat. Fellowship	1	$0.70	INDORIY 1
Parsi	10/90	YWAM	2	$0.80	INDPARS 1
Parsi	/91	Nat. Fellowship	1	$0.70	INDPARS 2
Punjabi	/91	Nat. Fellowship	1	$0.70	INDPUNJ 1
Purig-Pa		AOG	1	$0.70	INDPURI 1
Purig-Pa	4/92	YWAM	2	$0.80	INDPURI 2
Sarasvat Brahmans	6/92	YWAM	2	$0.80	INDSARA 1
Sindhi	/91	Nat. Fellowship	1	$0.70	INDSIND 1
Tamil	10/90	YWAM	2	$0.80	INDTAMI 1
Tamil	/91	Nat. Fellowship	1	$0.70	INDTAMI 2
Telegu	/91	Nat. Fellowship	1	$0.70	INDTELE 1
Tibetan	2/92	AAPC	6	$1.20	INDTIBE 1
Indonesia					
Achenese	/91	Perspectives	5	$1.10	IDNACHE 1
Batak-Angkola	10/90	YWAM	2	$0.80	IDNBATA 1
Betawi (Malays)	2/91	YWAM	2	$0.80	IDNBETA 1
Bima	10/90	YWAM	2	$0.80	IDNBIMA 1
Bugi	10/90	YWAM	2	$0.80	IDNBUGI 1
Dayak	/92	Perspectives	11	$1.70	IDNDAYA 1
Deli Malays	4/92	YWAM	2	$0.80	IDNDELI 1
Gayo	10/90	YWAM	2	$0.80	IDNGAYO 1
Gayo		AOG	1	$0.70	IDNGAYO 2
Gorontalo	10/90	YWAM	2	$0.80	IDNGORO 1
Iban	5/90	WEC	2	$0.80	IDNIBAN 1
Jagoi	3/92	CBFMS	4	$1.00	IDNJAGO 1
Javanese	10/90	YWAM	2	$0.80	IDNJAVA 1
Javanese	/91	Partners Int.	4	$1.00	IDNJAVA 2

Name	Date	Agency	Qty	Price	Code
Javanese (rural)	2/92	TEAM	1	$0.70	IDNJAVA 2
Kaur	8/90	WEC	1	$0.70	IDNKAUR 1
Kerinci	4/92	Perspectives	31	$3.70	IDNKERI 1
Kubu	10/90	YWAM	2	$0.80	IDNKUBU 1
Lampung	10/90	YWAM	2	$0.80	IDNLAMP 1
Madura		MARC	2	$0.80	IDNMADU 1
Madura	8/90	WEC	2	$0.80	IDNMADU2
Madurese	10/90	YWAM	2	$0.80	IDNMADU 3
Makasserese	10/90	YWAM	2	$0.80	IDNMAKA 1
Malay	2/91	YWAM	2	$0.80	IDNMALA 1
Malay	4/92	YWAM	2	$0.80	IDNMALA 2
Malay	4/92	YWAM	2	$0.80	IDNMALA 3
Malay	4/92	YWAM	2	$0.80	IDNMALA 4
Malay	4/92	YWAM	2	$0.80	IDNMALA 5
Manggarai Mulims		AOG	1	$0.70	IDNMANG 1
Minangkabau	10/90	YWAM	2	$0.80	IDNMINA 1
Minangkabau	/91	AOG	1	$0.70	IDNMINA 2
Minangkabau	/92	Pioneers	28	$3.40	IDNMINA 2
Minangkabau	5/92	Perspectives	9	$1.50	IDNMINA 3
Mongondow	10/90	YWAM	2	$0.80	IDNMONG 1
Mongondow		AOG	1	$0.70	IDNMONG 2
Mori	10/90	YWAM	2	$0.80	IDNMORI 1
Ogan	5/91	Perspectives	8	$1.40	IDNOGAN 1
Rejang	10/90	YWAM	2	$0.80	IDNREJA 1
Serawi	10/90	YWAM	2	$0.80	IDNSERA 1
Solorese		AOG	1	$0.70	IDNSOLO 1
Southern Toraja		AOG	1	$0.70	IDNTORA 1
Sundanese		MARC	2	$0.80	IDNSUND 1
Sundanese	10/90	YWAM	2	$0.80	IDNSUND 2
Sundanese	8/90	WEC	2	$0.80	IDNSUND 3
Timorese	/90	WEC	2	$0.80	IDNTIMO 1
KURDS					
Intro Kurd	2/91	YWAM	6	$1.20	INTKURD 1
Iran					
Jews	9/91	YWAM	2	$0.80	IRNJEW 1
Kurd	/91	YWAM	2	$0.80	IRNKURD 1
Kurd	2/91	YWAM	2	$0.80	IRNKURD 2
Kurd	2/91	YWAM	2	$0.80	IRNKURD 3
Kurd (Ahl-e-Haqq)	/91	YWAM	2	$0.80	IRNKURD 4
Mazandarani	9/90	Maz. Ministry	16	$2.20	IRNMAZA 1
Iraq					
Kurd	2/91	YWAM	2	$0.80	IRQKURD 1
Irian Jaya					
Auyu	1/92	TEAM	1	$0.70	IJAAUYU 1
Israel					
Alawites	4/92	YWAM	2	$0.80	ISRALAW 1
Beduin	4/92	YWAM	2	$0.80	ISRBEDU 1
Druze	/91	Perspectives	8	$1.40	ISRDRUZ 1
Druze	4/92	YWAM	2	$0.80	ISRDRUZ 2
Falasha Jews	9/91	YWAM	2	$0.80	ISRFJEW 1
Japan					
Deaf	8/91	CBFMS	4	$1.00	JPNDEAF 1
Koreans	10/90	YWAM	2	$0.80	JPNKORE 1
Kyushu	2/92	TEAM	2	$0.80	JPNKYUS 1
Jordan					
Bedouin	4/91	PSP	7	$1.30	JORBEDO 1
Kurd	2/91	YWAM	2	$0.80	JORKURD 1
Kampuchea					
Cham	10/90	YWAM	2	$0.80	KHMCHAM1
Khmer	/92	YWAM	13	$1.90	KHMKHME1
Kazakhstan					
Kazakh		AAPC	12	$1.80	KAZKAZA 1
Kazakh		MARC	1	$0.70	KAZKAZA 2
Kazakh	/83	SCAN	4	$1.00	KAZKAZA 3
Kurd	2/91	YWAM	2	$0.80	KAZKURD 1
Kenya					
Duruma	/92	AIM	1	$0.70	KENDURU 1
Duruma	/90	AIM	4	$1.00	KENDURU 2
Okiek	/92	AIM	1	$0.70	KENOKIE 1
Okiek	/90	AIM	6	$1.20	KENOKIE 1
Sakuye	/92	AIM	1	$0.70	KENSAKU 1
Somali	/92	AIM	1	$0.70	KENSOMA 1
Kirghizia					
Kirghiz	6/05	SCAN	8	$1.40	KIRKIRG 1
Kirghiz		MARC	1	$0.70	KIRKIRG 2
Kirghiz	1/92	Perspectives	8	$1.40	KIRKIRG 3
Kirghiz	/90	WEC	4	$1.00	KIRKIRG 4
Korea					
Chosun	10/90	YWAM	2	$0.80	PRKCHOS 1
Koreans		Confidential	11	$1.70	PRKKORE 1
Laos					
Hmong	10/90	YWAM	2	$0.80	LAOHMON1
Lao		GMI	10	$1.60	LAOLAO 1
Lao		SCBT	2	$0.80	LAOLAO 2
Phuan	5/92	Persp.	12	$1.80	LAOPHUA 1
Lesotho					
Basotho	/92	AIM	1	$0.70	LSOBASO 1
Liberia					
Mandingo	5/90	WEC	2	$0.80	LBRMAND 1
Malaysia					
Bisaya		AOG	1	$0.70	MYSBISA 1
Cham Refugees(Kampuchean)		AOG	1	$0.70	MYSCHAM1
Jahai	10/90	YWAM	2	$0.80	MYSJAHA 1
Jakun	10/90	YWAM	2	$0.80	MYSJAKU 1
Johore Malays	10/92	YWAM	2	$0.80	MYSJOMA 1
Kedah Malays	10/92	YWAM	2	$0.80	MYSKEMA 1
Kelantan Malays	10/92	YWAM	2	$0.80	MYSKEMA 2
Malay	/91	Perspectives	8	$1.40	MYSMALA 1
Malay	2/91	YWAM	2	$0.80	MYSMALA 2
Negritos (Orang Asli)	4/92	Perpsectives	10	$1.60	MYSNEGR 1
Sarawak Malays	4/92	YWAM	2	$0.80	MYSSAMA 1
Trengganu Malays	10/92	YWAM	2	$0.80	MYSTRMA 1
Maldives					
Maldivian	4/92	Persp.	10	$1.60	MDVMALD1
Mali					
Bozo	/91	Perspectives	8	$1.40	MLIBOZO 1
Bozo	/91	GMU	1	$0.70	MLIBOZO 2
Khassonke		Perspectives	8	$1.40	MLIKHAS 1
Soninke		Perspectives	19	$2.50	MLISONI 1
Mexico					
Aztec (N. Puebla)		AAPC	2	$0.80	MEXAZTE 1
Durango Aztecs	/91	Perspectives	25	$3.10	MEXDURA 1
Tarahumara	/87	GMI	8	$1.40	MEXTARA 1
Zoque		PCMS	8	$1.40	MEXZOQU 1
Mongolia					
Khalkha		Perspectives	8	$1.40	MNGKHAL1
Khalkha Mongol	3/93	CSI	2	$0.80	MNGKHAL2
Morocco					
Arab			6	$1.20	MARARAB 1
Jews	9/91	YWAM	2	$0.80	MARJEW 1
Rifi Berber	/91	Perspectives	11	$1.70	MARBERB 1
Mozambique					
Makonde	5/92	AEF	2	$0.70	MOZMAKO1
Makua	1/92	AAPC	9	$1.50	MOZMAKU1
Makua	5/92	AEF	2	$0.70	MOZMAKU2
Makua	/92	AIM	1	$0.70	MOZMAKU3
Ndau	/92	AIM	1	$0.70	MOZNDAU1
Myanmar (Burma)					
Mon		AOG	1	$0.70	BURMON 1
Khun	/92	Perspectives	9	$1.50	BURKHUN 1
Myen	10/90	YWAM	2	$0.80	BURMYEN 1
Shan	10/92	YWAM	2	$0.80	BURSHAN 1
Namibia					
Damara	5/92	AEF	2	$0.70	NAMDAMA1
Himba	5/92	AEF	2	$0.70	NAMHIMB 1
Mbukushu	5/92	AEF	2	$0.70	NAMMBUK1
Nepal					
Gurung	3/92	WCIU	8	$1.40	NPLGURU 1
Sherpa	/87	GMI	8	$1.40	NPLSHER 1
Tamang	12/91	AAPC: R. Wood	10	$1.60	NPLTAMA 1
Tharu	12/92	Fuller SWM	8	$1.40	NPLTHAR 1
Niger					
Fulani (Sokoto)	3/92	Benoit	8	$1.40	NERFULA 2
Songhay	3/92	SIM	2	$0.80	NERSONG 1
Toubou	3/92	SIM	2	$0.80	NERTOUB 1
Tuareg		AOG	1	$0.70	NERTUAR 1
Tuareg	3/92	SIM	6	$1.20	NERTUAR 1
Tuareg		34029	1	$0.70	NERTUAR 2
Zerma (Dyerma)	10/92	B. Benoit	9	$1.50	NERZERM 1
Nigeria					
Fulani	/91	EBI	8	$1.40	NGAFULA 1
Fulani	10/90	YWAM	2	$0.80	NGAFULA 2
Hausa	10/90	YWAM	2	$0.80	NGAHAUS 1
Pakistan					
Ahmadis	4/92	YWAM	2	$0.80	PAKAHMA 1
Baloch	/88	GMI	9	$1.50	PAKBALO 1
Baloch		MARC	2	$0.80	PAKBALO 2
Jat	11/90	YWAM	2	$0.80	PAKJAT 1
Oad	5/92	CBFMS	4	$1.00	PAKOAD 1
Od	/92		8	$1.40	PAKOD 1
Parsis	4/92	YWAM	2	$0.80	PAKPARS 1
Pathan (Pushtun)	5/92	Perspectives	2	$0.80	PAKPATH 1
Punjabi		AOG	1	$0.70	PAKPUNJ 1
Punjabi	5/92	Perspectives	10	$1.60	PAKPUNJ 2
Sansi Bhil	10/92	CBFMS	4	$1.00	PAKSANS 1
Sindhi	11/90	YWAM	2	$0.80	PAKSIND 1
Sindhi	1/91	CBFMS	5	$1.10	PAKSIND 2
Papua New Guinea					
Siane	4/92	Perspectives	14	$2.00	PNGSIAN 1
Peru					
Amahuaca	/87	GMI	8	$1.40	PERAMAH 1
Philippines					
Bontoc		AOG	1	$0.70	PHLBONT 1
Buwid		AOG	1	$0.70	PHLBUWI 1
Ilongot	1/92	Perspectives	8	$1.40	PHLILON 1
Maguindanao	4/92	Perspectives	12	$1.80	PHLMAGU 1
Maguindano		Confidential	1	$0.70	PHLMAGU 1
Mamanua		AOG	1	$0.70	PHLMAMA 1
Maranao	/92	Perspectives	8	$1.40	PHLMARA 1
T'boli		AOG	1	$0.70	PHLTBOL 1
Tawsug	/91	YWAM	2	$0.80	PHLTAWS 1
Waray-Waray	9/89	PMA	8	$1.40	PHLWARA 1

People	Date	Agency	#	Price	Code
Abaza	9/91	YWAM	2	$0.80	RUSABAZ 1
Adygei	9/91	YWAM	2	$0.80	RUSADYG 1
Agul	9/91	YWAM	2	$0.80	RUSAGUL 1
Akhwakh	9/91	YWAM	2	$0.80	RUSAKHW1
Andi	9/91	YWAM	2	$0.80	RUSANDI 1
Archi	9/91	YWAM	2	$0.80	RUSARCH 1
Ashkenazi "Core" Jews	9/91	YWAM	2	$0.80	RUSAJEW 1
Avar	9/91	YWAM	2	$0.80	RUSAVAR 1
Avar	/91	Perspectives	28	$3.40	RUSAVAR 2
Bagulal	9/91	YWAM	2	$0.80	RUSBAGU 1
Balkar	9/91	YWAM	2	$0.80	RUSBALK 1
Bashkir	2/92	YWAM	2	$0.80	RUSBASH 1
Bashkir	5/91	Perspectives	18	$2.40	RUSBASH 2
Bashkir	/91	World by 2000	1	$0.70	RUSBASH 3
Bashkir	4/92	Perspectives	29	$3.50	RUSBASH 4
Bezheta	9/91	YWAM	2	$0.80	RUSBEZH 1
Bik or Mountain Jew	9/91	YWAM	2	$0.80	RUSBIK 1
Botleg	9/91	YWAM	2	$0.80	RUSBOTL 1
Buriyat	/91	Perspectives	12	$1.80	RUSBURY 1
Chamalali	9/91	YWAM	2	$0.80	RUSCHAM 1
Chechen	/90	SCAN	2	$0.80	RUSCHEC 1
Chechun-Ingush	9/91	YWAM	2	$0.80	RUSCHEI 1
Chukchi	2/92	AAPC	5	$1.10	RUSCHUK 1
Chuvash		World by 2000	1	$0.70	RUSCHUV 1
Chuvash	2/92	YWAM	2	$0.80	RUSCHUV 2
Darghin	9/91	YWAM	2	$0.80	RUSDARG 1
Dido	9/91	YWAM	2	$0.80	RUSDIDO 1
Digiron Osset	9/91	YWAM	2	$0.80	RUSDIGI 1
Eskimo	12/91	LBC	13	$1.90	RUSESKI 1
Ginug	9/91	YWAM	2	$0.80	RUSGINU 1
Godoberi	9/91	YWAM	2	$0.80	RUSGODO 1
Kabardians	9/91	YWAM	2	$0.80	RUSKABA 1
Kaitak	9/91	YWAM	2	$0.80	RUSKAIT 1
Kalmyk	/92	Perspectives	8	$1.40	RUSKALM 1
Karachai	9/91	YWAM	2	$0.80	RUSKARA 1
Karata	9/91	YWAM	2	$0.80	RUSKART 1
Kasimov Tatars	2/92	YWAM	2	$0.80	RUSKASI 1
Khunzal	9/91	YWAM	2	$0.80	RUSKHUN 1
Khwarshi	9/91	YWAM	2	$0.80	RUSKHWA1
Koryak	2/92	A.A.P.C.	3	$0.90	RUSKORY 1
Krym Tatars	10/91	YWAM	2	$0.80	RUSKRYM1
Kumyk	9/91	YWAM	2	$0.80	RUSKUMY1
Kurds	4/92	YWAM	2	$0.80	RUSKURD 1
Lak	9/91	YWAM	2	$0.80	RUSLAK 1
Lezghian	9/91	YWAM	2	$0.80	RUSLEZG 1
Muslims	9/91	YWAM	10	$1.60	RUSMUSL 1
Nagaibaks	2/92	YWAM	2	$0.80	RUSNAGA 1
Nogai	9/91	YWAM	2	$0.80	RUSNOGA 1
Rutul	9/91	YWAM	2	$0.80	RUSRUTU 1
Tabasaran	9/91	YWAM	2	$0.80	RUSTABA 1
Tatar	/91	World by 2000	1	$0.70	RUSTATA 1
Tatar	2/92	YWAM	2	$0.80	RUSTATA 2
Tindi	9/91	YWAM	2	$0.80	RUSTIND 1
Tsakhur	9/91	YWAM	2	$0.80	RUSTSAK 1
Tuvinian	/91	Perspectives	3	$0.90	RUSTUVI 1
Western Askenazi Jew	9/91	YWAM	2	$0.80	RUSWJEW 1
Yakut	12/90	Perspectives	15	$2.10	RUSYAKU 1
Senegal					
Fula	5/90	WEC	2	$0.80	SENFULA 1
Jola	/90	WEC	2	$0.80	SENJOLA 1
Maure	5/90	WEC	2	$0.80	SENMAUR 1
Tukulor	5/90	WEC	2	$0.80	SENTUKU 1
Wolof	/88	GMI	8	$1.40	SENWOLO 1
Wolof	3/91	CBFMS	4	$1.00	SENWOLO 1
Wolof	5/90	WEC	4	$1.00	SENWOLO 2
Wolof		MARC	1	$0.70	SENWOLO 3
Sierra Leone					
Kono	/89	YWAM	10	$1.60	SLEKONO 1
Yalunka	/90	YWAM/Yoder	9	$1.50	SLEYALU 1
Singapore					
Malay	/91	YWAM	2	$0.80	SGPMALA 1
South Africa					
Gujarati	/92	AEF	1	$0.70	ZAFGUJA 1
Spain					
Basque	12/91	PSP	9	$1.50	ESPBASQ 1
Sri Lanka					
Buddhist Majority	5/90	WEC	2	$0.80	LKABUDD 1
Malay	2/91	YWAM	2	$0.80	LKAMALA 1
Sudan					
Beja	/90	Confidential	2	$0.80	SDNBEJA 1
Syria					
Alawite	4/92	YWAM	2	$0.80	SYRALAW1
Circassian	4/92	YWAM	2	$0.80	SYRCIRC 1
Druze	4/92	YWAM	2	$0.80	SYRDRUZ 1
Jew	9/91	YWAM	2	$0.80	SYRJEW 1
Kurd	2/91	YWAM	2	$0.80	SYRKURD 3
Kurd (Arabized)	2/91	YWAM	2	$0.80	SYRKURD 1
Kurd (Urban)	2/91	YWAM	2	$0.80	SYRKURD 2
Tadzhikstan					
Bartang	10/91	YWAM	2	$0.80	TADBART 1
Galcha	4/92	YWAM	2	$0.80	TADGALC 1
Ishkashim	10/91	YWAM	2	$0.80	TADISHK 1
Pushtuns	3/92	YWAM	2	$0.80	TADPUSH 1
Rushan	10/91	YWAM	2	$0.80	TADRUSH 1
Shugan	10/91	YWAM	2	$0.80	TADSHUG 1
Wakhan	10/91	YWAM	2	$0.80	TADWAKH1
Yagnobi	10/91	YWAM	2	$0.80	TADYAGN 1
Yazgul	10/91	YWAM	2	$0.80	TADYAZG 1
Taiwan					
Hakka	/91	AAPC	2	$0.80	TWMHAKK1
Hakka	5/90	WEC	2	$0.80	TWMHAKK2
Hakka	/91	YWAM	5	$1.10	TWMHAKK3
Tanzania					
Datooga	5/92	SIL	9	$1.50	TZADATO 1
Sandawe	/92	AIM	1	$0.70	TZASAND 1
Wazinza	/92	AIM	1	$0.70	TZAWAZI 1
Thailand					
Akha	4/92	Persp.	8	$1.40	THAAKHA 1
Lahu		AOG	1	$0.70	THALAHU 1
Lisu	/91	Perspectives	8	$1.40	THALISU 1
Malay (Patanni)	2/91	YWAM	2	$0.80	THAMALA 1
So		AOG	1	$0.70	THASO 1
Southern Thai	5/92	Persp.	6	$1.20	THATHAI 1
Togo					
Konkomba	/91	WEC	2	$0.80	TGOKONK 1
Tunisia					
Jew	9/91	YWAM	2	$0.80	TUNJEW 1
Turkey					
Kurd	2/91	YWAM	2	$0.80	TURKURD 4
Kurd	4/91	Perspectives	8	$1.40	TURKURD 1
Kurd	2/91	YWAM	2	$0.80	TURKURD 3
Kurd (Dimli)	2/91	YWAM	2	$0.80	TURKURD 2
Kurd (Yezidi)	2/91	YWAM	2	$0.80	TURKURD 5
Turk		MARC	1	$0.70	TURTURK 1
Turk	/91	WEC	2	$0.80	TURTURK 2
Turk	5/92	Persp.	9	$1.50	TURTURK 2
Turkmenistan					
Baluchi	10/91	YWAM	2	$0.80	TMSBALU 1
Kurd	2/91	YWAM	2	$0.80	TMSKURD 1
Turkmen		MARC	1	$0.70	TMSTURK1
Turkmen			8	$1.40	TMSTURK 2
Turkmen	/91	World by 2000	1	$0.70	TMSTURK 3
U.S.A.					
A:shiwi	4/92	Perspectives	35	$4.10	USAA:SH 1
Deaf	12/91	PSP	9	$1.50	USADEAF 1
Jews	9/91	YWAM	2	$0.80	USAJEW 1
Navajo	12/91	NG M	8	$1.40	USANAVA 1
Ojibwa	/91	Perspectives	8	$1.40	USAOJIB 1
Ukraine					
Karaim	6/92	YWAM	2	$0.80	UKRKARA 1
Tatar	/91	Perspectives	16	$2.20	UKRTATA 1
United Kingdom					
Jews	9/91	YWAM	2	$0.80	GBRJEW 1
Uzbekistan					
Fergana	10/91	YWAM	2	$0.80	UZBFERG 1
Karakalpak	5/91	Perspectives	8	$1.40	UZBKARA 1
Karakalpak	10/91	YWAM	2	$0.80	UZBKARA 2
Karapapakh	10/91	YWAM	2	$0.80	UZBKAPA 1
Uzbek	/91	Perspectives	7	$1.30	UZBUZBE 1
Uzbek		MARC	2	$0.80	UZBUZBE 2
Uzbek	/92	YWAM	3	$0.90	UZBUZBE 2
Uzbek		World by 2000	1	$0.70	UZBUZBE 4
Uzbek	11/91	WEC	4	$1.00	UZBUZBE 5
Venezuela					
Yanomamo	/87	GMI	8	$1.40	VENYANO 1
Vietnam					
Bahnar	6/92	YWAM	2	$0.80	VNMBAHN1
Bru	6/92	YWAM	2	$0.80	VNMBRU 1
Hainanese	6/92	YWAM	2	$0.80	VNMHAIN 1
Hakka	6/92	YWAM	2	$0.80	VNMHAKK 1
Hokkien	6/92	YWAM	2	$0.80	VNMHOKK 1
Jarai	6/92	YWAM	2	$0.80	VNMJARA 1
Khmer	6/92	YWAM	2	$0.80	VNMKHME1
Kwong-fu	6/92	YWAM	2	$0.80	VNMKWON1
Teochew	6/92	YWAM	2	$0.80	VNMTEOC 1
West Africa					
Fulani		Perspectives	14	$2.00	SOSFULA 1
Fulani		MARC	2	$0.80	SOS FULA 2
World					
Gypsy People Groups	/90	Euromission	28	$3.40	WORGYPS 1
Yemen					
Akhdam	1/92	Perspectives	10	$1.60	YEMAKHD2
Jews	9/91	YWAM	2	$0.80	YEMJEW 1
Yemenis	/90	WEC	2	$0.80	YEMYEME 1
Yugoslavia					
Albanian	/91	Perspectives	8	$1.40	YUGALBA 1
Montenegro	12/92	Fuller SWM	8	$1.40	YUGMONT1
Zaire					
Bamwe	/91	EFCA	2	$0.80	ZARBAMW1
Bamwe	12/90	Perspectives	8	$1.40	ZARBAMW2
Efe	/90	Perspectives	13	$1.90	ZAREFE 1
Nandi	/91	PCC	11	$1.70	ZARNAND 1
Pigmies	/91	WEC	2	$0.80	ZARPIGM 1

Finding Unreached Peoples in the Library

Adapted from "Finding Hidden Peoples in the Library" by Allan Starling, *International Journal of Frontier Missions,*
vol 2, no 2, April '85, pp. 141-150. (Also found in *Peoplesfile II Index,* 1989)*
*Note: Includes some adaptations and additional sources (L.L. Judd 11/27/90; S.G. Yoder 9/10/91)

Most single information sources can give you a little information about many groups. Most of the time you want much information about one or two groups. This paper is an attempt to help your search strategy. For example, look for information about the Danakil people. Assume that all you know is that there is a group called the Danakil somewhere in Africa that needs to be reached.

PART I — Before Going to the Library

Clues about the Danakil can be obtained through the *Peoplesfile II Index* and the three main sources it references.

Checking *Peoplesfile II* you discover these clues:

Clue #1 - All three source publications use AFAR as the *primary name*.
Clue #2 - The Afar (Danakil) are reported as being *unreached*.
Clue #3 - Gospel Recordings has made *recordings* of the Afar language.
Clue #4 - *Bible portions* are available in Afar.
Clue #5 - The group is found mainly in *Ethiopia*.
Clue #6 - *Other names*: Adal, Afaraf, Afarafa.

Checking the *Ethnologue,* you find:

Clue #7 - The Afar are a *Nomadic* people.
Clue #8 - *Saho* is a related, but distinct group.
Clue #9 - The following agencies are working among the Afar: SIM, CMML, OPC, RSM, ECMY.

Checking the *Unreached Peoples Annuals*:

Clue #10 - *Unreached Peoples '79* has an *expanded description* of the Afar.
Clue #11 - The Afar are a *Muslim* group.

Using some of the above clues, find more information about the group you are researching. The three publications mentioned above will not be found in most public libraries. Other references can either be found in Latourette Library (on the campus of the US Center for World Mission in Pasadena, California), obtained through inter-library loan, or purchased. Now you are finally ready for the library.

PART II — A Day at the Local Library

Spend plenty of time at the library. Finding unreached peoples isn't always easy. Look in several places. Break your search into a number of steps:

Step 1 - Determine the Search Procedure.

Use this procedure in each of the following steps. Unless you are looking for a large group, you may not find what you want immediately because the information will be hidden in some volume or periodical. Start with the specific and move to broader categories as necessary. The broader the term, the less likely you will be able to find relevant information. Here are the categories chosen in your sample search for the Afar:

a. Afar, Dankili (clue #1)   b. Nomads (clue #7)
c. Saho (clue # 8)   d. Muslim or Islam (clue #11)
e. Ethnology   f. Anthropology
g. Ethiopia (clue #5)   h. Other names for Afar (clue #6)

Step 2 - Check *National Geographic Magazine Index*.

The index of articles from 1947 to 1983 mentions an article, "The Danakil: Nomads of Ethiopia's Wasteland" in the Feb. 1970 issue.

Step 3 - Check *Encyclopedia Britannica, Index Volume*.

In the *Index Volume*, under Afar, there is an article entitled "Saho-Afar." There is also more information under "Ethiopia: The People." More information may be available under "Islam" and "Sunni Muslims."

Step 4 - Check *Muslim Peoples*, Richard V. Weekes, Editor *A World Ethnographic Survey, 2nd Ed*, Rev. (2 Vols.). Contains maps showing general location of Muslim groups. Documents 190 ethnic and/or linguistic groups, either totally or partially Muslim.

Step 5 - Check *Peoples of the Earth*, Danbury Press. Set of 20 volumes. Out of print, but Latourette Library (USCWM) has a set. Besides general articles, each volume contains thumbnail sketches and pictures of many people groups.

*continuing the quest for Afar information, note that Vol. 2, p. 22 has an article on the Danakil and Soho, (clue #8), together with maps and pictures.

Step 6 - Check the *Illustrated Encyclopedia of Mankind*, 20 volumes — more than 500 peoples and cultures are represented. The Afar are included. There is an article with color pictures on p. 12 of vol. 1.

Step 7 - Check the *Library of Congress Subject Headings*

Large bound volumes kept in most libraries, showing the subject headings used in the card catalog system. The classification system used is the Library of Congress (LC) system. Even if the Library you visit doesn't use the LC system, this step is useful. (The headings in bold type are those used in the card catalog. Other names in the volume are related topics.)

Under Afar, there is a heading *Afar Language* (PJ2421). Go straight to the "PJ" section in the shelves and look for related books under that section in the library, look under a broader topic. There are a number of headings under *Muslim*, under *Ethiopian Languages* (PJ8991-9). Even though you may be unsuccessful once again, keep a note of these headings to use in the next few steps (or in another library).

Step 8 - Check *Card Catalog File*.

Follow the procedure set up in step 1, aided by the subject headings found in the previous step. As soon as you find one volume, go to that section of the shelves and look for related volumes.

Step 9 - Check *Subject Guide to Books in Print*

Large bound volumes often in a reference area. Using your established procedure and your list of subject headings, find the names of several books in print related to the Afar.

Step 10 - Check *Machine Readable Catalog Fiche (MARC).*
If you are not familiar with fiche, they are a form of microfilm, but on 3x5 "cards". Libraries often have a microfiche reader or reader-printer handy. Don't confuse this "MARC" with the other MARC (Missions Advanced Research and Communication). Ask the library staff about the initial use of the MARC-fiche.

> *After checking the Author/Title index first and finding, "Afar Depression in Ethipia" #838e29, check microfiche number 838, column e, row 29, and see a description of a book which is not what you want. If it had been, you could have written down the LC and Dewey classifications which are given below the description, even if the item were out (using it in another library).

Step 11 - *Check Periodical Guides (Indexes).*
Step 12 - *Check Background Notes,* **US Department of State, Bureau of Public Affairs.**
Obtainable from Supt. of Documents, US Gov't Printing Office, Washingtion, DC 20402. Single copy by country name, or by subscription. The notes give an overview of the geography, government, policies, economy, history and people of the country.
Step 13 - *Check the Linguistic Bibliography.* J. Beyismit, Editor. This contains a listing of "all" the descriptions of known languages. Although the articles and books referred to may be technical in nature, many times they will include a section on the speakers of the language and give additional useful information.
Step 14 - Check Human Relations Area Files (HRAF).
This is only possible if you live in the USA and have access to certain major universities. The files contain detailed information on approximately 400 different cultures.
Step 15 - Talk to the Reference Librarian.
Before leaving the library, we talk to the librarian and explain what we are looking for and what we have already found. The more we know, the more the librarian can help us. (I got several of the clues for this treasure hunt from Harry Fuchiganmi at Latourette Library, USCWM.)

PART III — Back Home From the Library: What Next?
Check *Mission Agencies* working in/near the people group; have your questions ready before contacting the agency. Learn more about the areas where your group is located.
Step 1 - Check *Ethnologue* **for the missions working with your group (clue #8).**
To get their addresses and/or find other possible agencies, check the *Missions Handbook,* published by MARC (address in step 5); this handbook contains a listing by organization as well as by country.
Step 2 - Check *World Christian Series* **from MARC.**
A series of large paperbacks giving a survey of the status of the Christian faith in a particular part of the globe. Currently available: Central America and the Caribbean, Eastern Asia, Middle East, South Asia. Check for specific information on unreached peoples.
Step 3 - Check *Operation World,* **by Patrick Johnstone,**

STL Publications, P.O. Box 48, Bromley, Kent, England. A survey of the basic prayer needs of each country of the world is backed by information of population, ethinic groups, economy, religions and political situations.
Step 4 - Check *World Christian Encyclopedia.* Edited by David Barrett, Oxford University Press. "The heart of the *Encyclopedia* is a detailed, country by country survey of Christianity and other religions...including political, demographic, linguistic and cultural data," and much more.
Step 5- Check *Agencies doing research* **on unreached peoples.** Not only can you ask for specific information, but you can also help to update or correct existing data. Some groups have questionaires for use in gathering data.
  Some Addresses:
  Gospel Recordings - Field Div.; 122 Glendale Blvd., Los Angeles, CA 90026; ask for latest recorded language directory for a particular country; ask for catalog of available audio tools; obtain infomation on a specific recorded language.
  The Editor, Ethnologue - 755 Camp Wisdom Rd., Dallas, TX 75236; use its questionaire to supply information; order the *Ethnologue.*
  Global Mapping Project — P.O. Box 25399, Colorado Springs, CO 80936-5399, (719) 528-5891. Ask for both information and maps.
  Contact the following agencies at the US Center for World Mission, 1605 Elizabeth St., Pasadena CA 91104 (818) 797-1111.
  Zwemer Institute - Ask for information on Muslim seminars and specific information on Muslim groups.
  Institute of Chinese Studies
  Institute of Hindu Studies
  Institute of Tribal Studies
  Sonrise Center for Buddhist Studies
  Institutue of Latin American Studies
  Institute of Japanese Studies
  World Population Study Center
  Adopt-a-People Clearinghouse
Step 6 - Other References:
  Target Earth; From Every People ; *The World of Learning* Series; *World Directory of Mission Information and Research Centers; The World in Figures* from Lausanne II in Manila; *A People Prepared Series* from Lausanne II in Manila; Database Searches (search the *Dialog* database); *Orion* database (card cataglog for UCLA librairies); *Melvyl* database (card catalog for the UC system libraries).
  **Orion* and *Melvyl* are for both books and periodicals.
  Area Handbooks by the American University Foreign Affairs Studies Division. Each book deals with a separate country. Some studies are more recent than others.

ADOPT-A-PEOPLE ™
RESOURCE GUIDE

Help Your Fellowship Catch, Build and Act on the Vision of "A Church for Every People"
Raise Awareness, Excitement, Involvement and Funds for Your Adopted People!
These resources are financially accessible to most people at the retail price. You buy the resources at the quantity discount price and sell them at the retail price to your fellowship. The difference can be designated for your adopt-a-people emphasis.

"A Church For Every People"
A List of Unreached and Adoptable Peoples

Published By: **Adopt-A-People Clearinghouse**
Co-Published By: **AD 2000 and Beyond Movement**
MARC (Mission Advance Research & Communication)
Southern Baptist Convention - Foreign Mission Board
SIL (Summer Institute of Linguistics)
U.S. Center for World Mission

A Church For Every People — a reference guide, a work book and prayer guide with over 200 pages, listing the unreached and adoptable peoples. The listing includes the geographic location, language name, the stages of reachedness, 5 reasons to adopt a people and the Christian resources available. Resources available include: network, people profile, Jesus Film, audio recordings, radio/TV, evangelistic literature and Christ-centered relief and development. This book includes nearly 80 maps and timely written articles. **Retail $21.50 ea.**
Quantities of 3 or more $13.95 ea.   **Order #AAP-01**

An IBM compatible data file (DBF file format) not a program.
Data Diskette $100.00 *NOW! $25.00* Order #AAP-11

Adopt-A-People Prayer Cards
Beautiful full color prayer cards filled with moving information and prayer focus. Cards are available on the following peoples: Bihari, Fulani, Kashmiri, Thai, Turkmen, Uigher and Uzbek. Additional cards on the Wolof, Taureg, Moor, Kazakh, Kirgiz, and Tajik are being developed. In all 72 different prayer cards will be produced. Call for updates on new cards. **Retail $1.85 ea.**

Quantity Discount Available !

Quantity	Price per card	Quantity	Price per card	Order # AAP-02
10 -29	$1.09	30 - 99	$0.98	
100 - 1499	0.93	1500 - 2999	0.83	
3000 & up	0.63	(envelopes not included in discount price .10 ea.)		

Adopt-A-People Watch — attractive and beautifully crafted. Each time you look at your quartz watch it will remind you to pray for your "adopted" people. Comes with a Swaroski Crystal. Men's and lady's watches available!
Lady's AAP-12   Men's AAP-13
Retail $34.00 ea.   **Discount for 3 or more $29.00 ea.**

NEW An Appeal To Disciples Everywhere
All New! A bold appeal to the entire Church. A call for unity and action toward seeing a church for every people by AD 2000. This document is in a format that encourages you to sign and frame. Help make this truly an appeal to disciples everywhere.
Order# AAP-25
Retail $2.50 ea.   Qty Discount $1.25 ea. for 5 or more

NEW Adopt-A-People Certificate
All New! This beautiful certificate on parchment with a blue border is good for framing. Designed so individuals can proudly display their commitment to their "adopted" people. This certificate will help build commitment and accountability. A good way to involve pastors and leaders of your fellowship, their signature as witness.
Retail $2.50 ea.   Quantity Discount $1.25 ea. for 5 or more   Order #AAP-04

Send your order to:
Most Resources can be customized!
For more information or questions call:

Adopt-A-People Clearinghouse
P.O. Box 1795
Colorado Springs, CO 80901
(719) 473-8800   Fax: (719) 473-5907

574-7001

Adopt-A-People World Prayer Map

The world Christian's definitive prayer map. Details religions, languages, Bible status, unreached and adoptable peoples and peoples who are less than 1% Christian. Full color, dozens of original art illustrations, Each map is only $5.25. All New — with revision of the former Soviet Union complete!

Quantity	Price per map	
1 - 9	$5.25	
10 - 99	4.25	
100 or more	3.50	Order #AAP-03

NEW Adopt-A-People Pin

You can wear your love and dedication of your adopted people right on your clothing. Join the millions of dedicated prayer warriors who are praying for the unreached and adoptable peoples! This small and beautiful gold like crafted pin has a military clasp.

Retail $2.75 ea.   **Quantity Discount $1.75 ea. for 5 or more**   **Order #AAP-05**

Passports To The World — 42 pages of insightful analysis on world cultures with pictures and original artwork. A wholistic perspective on history, family, geography, the people, religion and more. Designed to focus prayer on the walls/barriers to missions on the country level. A must tool for prayer supporters, short-term missionaries and veterans alike. Each Passport comes with a *free* removable prayer guide. *Armenia, Mongolia, Myanmar, Spain, Thailand* available now. Look for more countries! *Indonesia, Laos, Ethiopia, Papua New Guinea and Tibet.*

	Order #
Armenia	AAP-06
Mongolia	AAP-07
Myanmar	AAP-08
Spain	APP-09
Thailand	AAP-10

Retail $3.50 ea.
Quantity Discount: $2.16 ea. for 10 - 999
$1.98 ea. for 1,000 or more

Adopt-A-People™ is a registered trademark of the Adopt-A-People Clearinghouse

* Shipping outside of USA billed actual amount

Adopt-A-People Video Series
(available in American VHS & European PAL)
(Call for quantity discounts)

Adopt-A-People Consultation II Series (AAP-15-AAP-23)

Milestones in the Development of the "Unreached Peoples" Concept, by Don Kammerdiener and **A Church for Every People by the Year 2000,** by Luis Bush   *AAP-15* **$18.75**

State of the World, by Ralph Winter and **World Evangelization: It Can Be Done! It Must Be Done! It Will Be Done!** by Dale Kietzman   *AAP-16* **$18.75**

The Peoples of the World: SHARE & PIN Networks, by Ron Rowland and **Unreached Peoples and AD 2000,** by John Robb and **A Church for Every People - The List!,** by Frank Kaleb Jansen and **Adopt-A-People Case Study in India,** by Gene Davis *AAP-17* **$18.75**

Adopt-A-People Case Studies for Churches, by Thomas Wolf, Joy Crawford, Stan Yoder   *AAP-18* **$18.75**

Non-Residential Missionaries, by Clark Scanlon and **Mission Strategies: Networks & Partnerships,** by Rick Stoller, **What Shall We Then Do?** A panel discussion by Dave Dougherty, Gary Corwin & Paul Filidis   *AAP-19* **$18.75**

What Will the Future Hold? The Trends Shaping Our Future, by Frank Kaleb Jansen   *AAP-20* **$18.75**

Debate & Input: Where Do We Go From Here? and **Ad Hoc Groups and Closing Challenge**
AAP-21 **$18.75**

Workshops:
Networking & Telecommunications, by Mark Patterson
  Adopt-A-People Database, by Marv Bowers *AAP-22* **$18.75**

Computerized Peoples Profiles, by Kent Schroder
  The Power of AD 2000, by Jay Gary *AAP-23* **$18.75**

Order #	QTY	Unit Price/Description	Total
		Add all Sub-Totals Here:	
		(Colorado residents add 6.4% Sales Tax)	
		* $2.00 shipping & handling	
		Cash or Check only-No C.O.D. Total Due	
		Name:	
		Organization:	
		Street:	
		City/State/ZIP:	
		Phone:	

The Complete AAP Consultation II Video Series
AAP-24 **$168.75** *NOW! $149.00*

(all prices subject to change without notice)

Subject Index

A

Abrahamic Covenant 7-12
AD 2000 Movement 7-22
Adam and Eve 7-17, 10-6
Allen, Roland 6-24
Ambcdkar, Dr. 9-13
American Board of Commissioners for Foreign Missions
    6-17, 6-19
American Indian missions
    See Native American missions
Anderson, Rufus 6-19
Animism 7-30
    See also Evangelization of tribes
Antioch church 9-31
Azariah, Bishop 9-12

B

Babel 7-17
Baptist Missionary Society 6-17
Barrett, David 7-13, 7-17
Berlin Conference 10-7
Bible translation 9-8, 10-1
Boniface 6-14 – 6-15
Brant, Albert 8-12
Bryant, David 6-13
Buddhist megasphere 7-19, 7-31 – 7-32, 7-34, 8-1
Bushmen
    See Han people

C

Carey, William 6-17 – 6-18, 6-27, 7-27
Catholic missions
    See Roman Catholic missions
China Inland Mission 6-8, 6-12
Chinese megasphere 7-4 – 7-5, 7-25 – 7-27, 7-34, 8-1
Christ
    and development 10-28
    and the poor 10-11 – 10-13
    example of identification 9-5
    strategy of 8-5 – 8-6
Church
    and development 10-29
    growth of 8-9 – 8-12, 9-6, 10-8
    indigenous 7-5 – 7-6
    role of 7-16, 10-9
    See also Church planting
Church Missionary Society 6-19
Church planting 9-3, 9-20 – 9-36, 10-8
    See also Evangelization
Closure 6-1
Comity 6-22 – 6-23

Community development
    See Development, community
Conferences 6-21, 6-23, 6-25, 7-1, 7-20, 10-7
Creative access 9-2, 9-36
Croft, Ann 8-27 – 8-28
Crusades 6-15
Cultural imperialism 9-1, 9-11
Cultural mandate 10-6 – 10-7
Culture
    and Bible translation 7-8
    and gospel 7-8 – 7-9, 9-20
    and social structure 7-9
    crossing barriers 7-8 – 7-11
    differences in 7-8

D

Danish-Halle Mission 6-11, 6-16
Davies, J. G. 9-11
Dawson, John 6-12
De Ridder, Richard 6-30
Development, community 8-23, 9-9, 9-24, 10-20 – 10-30
Diocese 6-26
Duff, Alexander 6-18

E

Edinburgh Conference 6-21, 6-23 – 6-24, 7-1
Engel scale 8-14 – 8-15, 8-29
Epochs of mission history 6-1
Eras of mission history 6-1
Evangelism
    See Evangelization
Evangelistic mandate 10-6 – 10-7
Evangelization
    and culture 6-14 – 6-15, 6-18, 7-10 – 7-11, 9-20, 9-36
    and development 10-20 – 10-23, 10-26 – 10-27
    and prayer 6-8 – 6-10, 6-12 – 6-13
    and social action 10-1 – 10-2, 10-6 – 10-9, 10-13, 10-30
    and social structure 9-16 – 9-17, 9-19
    and 10/40 window 7-17 – 7-22, 7-34
    barriers to 7-8 – 7-9, 9-1 – 9-2
    E-1, E-2, and E-3 7-5 – 7-7, 7-9 – 7-11, 7-34, 9-19
    forces involved 6-1
    goal of 7-12, 8-2, 8-9, 8-28, 9-10 – 9-12, 9-36
    of Buddhists 7-30 – 7-34, 10-15
    of Chinese 6-15, 7-19, 7-25 – 7-27, 7-30, 7-34,
        9-15 – 9-16, 9-19
    of Dorsas 8-12
    of families 9-15 – 9-16, 9-18, 9-32
    of Fulani 8-27 – 8-28
    of Han 10-2 – 10-5
    of Hindus 7-19, 7-27 – 7-30, 7-33 – 7-34, 9-16
    of Hondurans 9-21 – 9-35
        (continued on next page)

Evangelization (cont.)
　　of Karen　9-17
　　of Koreans　9-16, 10-8
　　of Lisu　6-9
　　of migrants　10-19
　　of Muslims　6-31, 7-19, 7-23 – 7-25, 7-30, 7-33 – 7-34,
　　　　8-21 – 8-24, 8-27 – 8-28, 9-17, 10-15
　　of people groups　7-16, 7-33 – 7-34, 8-13 – 8-19,
　　　　8-28 – 8-29, 9-19 – 9-20, 9-24, 9-36, 10-1, 10-11
　　of poor　7-20, 10-4, 10-15 – 10-17
　　of Quechuas　7-10 – 7-11
　　of Tongas　8-7 – 8-8, 8-20 – 8-21
　　of tribes　7-29 – 7-30, 7-33 – 7-34
　　of upper class　8-24 – 8-26
　　scope of　7-14 – 7-16, 10-8 – 10-9
　　structures for　6-25 – 6-29, 6-34
　　tactics for　9-12 – 9-14
　　vs. evangelism　6-7
　　See also Church
　　　　　　Gospel
　　　　　　Unreached peoples

F

Fenton, Horace　10-7
Foreign Missions Conference　6-23
Francis of Assisi　6-15
Frangipane, Francis　6-12
Fraser, J. O.　6-8 – 6-9
Friends Missionary Prayer Band　7-29
Frontier missions
　　See Missions, frontier
Fulani people　8-27 – 8-28

G

Garreau, Joel　7-8
Ghana Conference　6-23
Gill, Brad　6-7
Glover, Robert　6-11
God
　　kingdom of　6-1, 6-32 – 6-33, 9-10, 9-12, 10-1, 10-13
　　missionary purpose　7-16
Gospel
　　and culture　6-18, 7-8 – 7-9, 9-20
　　and identity　10-5
　　and social structure　9-15 – 9-19
　　content of message　10-12
　　point of contact for　8-8, 8-13 – 8-14, 8-20, 8-29, 9-23,
　　　　10-11, 10-17, 10-30
Gospel Recordings　7-12
Graham, Billy　7-31, 9-13
Great Commission　6-1, 7-21, 7-34, 8-1 – 8-2, 8-8, 9-10,
　　9-12

H

Hallesby, O.　6-9
Han people　10-2 – 10-3, 10-5
Hidden peoples　6-1, 7-1, 7-13, 7-22, 7-34, 10-26
　　See also Unreached peoples
Hiebert, Paul G.　6-31 – 6-32
Hindu megasphere　7-19, 7-27 – 7-29, 7-34, 8-1
History, meaning and purpose　6-1
Homogeneous unit principle　8-6, 8-8, 8-10 – 8-11

I

Identification
　　achieving　8-8
　　example of Christ　9-5
Immigration
　　See Migrations
India Mission Association　7-28
Indian Evangelical Mission　7-29
International Missionary Council　6-23
Islam
　　See Evangelization of Muslims
　　　　　Muslim megasphere

J

Jerusalem Conference　6-23
Jesuits　6-15
Jesus
　　See Christ
"Jesus" film　9-8 – 9-9
Jones, Stanley　9-11
Judson, Adoniram　8-12

K

Ko Tha Byu　9-17
Kraft, Charles　6-33

L

Lausanne Conference　6-24, 7-1, 7-17, 7-20, 10-2, 10-7
Lausanne Covenant　10-7
London Missionary Society　6-17
Lost, the　10-15 – 10-16
　　See also Unreached peoples
Lull, Raymond　6-15
Luther, Martin　6-26

M

Macrospheres   7-4 – 7-5
Madras Conference   6-23 – 6-24
Matthews, Arthur   6-10
McCurry, Don   6-12
Media ministries   9-8 – 9-9
Megaspheres   7-4 – 7-5, 7-22, 7-33 – 7-34
   See also Buddhist megasphere
            Chinese megasphere
            Hindu megasphere
            Muslim megasphere
            Tribal megasphere
Migrations   10-17 – 10-20, 10-30
Minispheres   7-4 – 7-5, 7-7
Mission agencies   6-17, 6-25, 6-27 – 6-28, 7-29, 9-19
   See also Evangelization, structures for
Mission movements
   partnerships   9-19
   student   6-17
   women's   6-22
Mission power
   See Spiritual warfare
Mission strategy
   See Strategy
Mission structures
   See Evangelization, structures for
Missions
   frontier   7-4, 7-7
   regular   7-4, 7-7
   See also Evangelization, E-1, E-2, and E-3
Modality   6-27 – 6-28, 6-34
Moravians   6-11, 6-16 – 6-17
Muslim megasphere   7-4 – 7-5, 7-19, 7-23 – 7-25, 7-34, 8-1

N

National Missionary Society   7-29
Nations
   See People groups
Native American missions   6-16
Needy
   See Poor, the
Nevius, John L.   6-20
Nietzsche   9-13
Nonresidential missionaries   9-6 – 9-9, 9-36

O

Otis, George, Jr.   7-17, 7-21

P

Pattaya Conference   6-24
Paul
   ministry of   7-3, 9-18, 9-26
   strategy of   6-3, 6-26, 9-4 – 9-6, 9-14
People groups   7-1 – 7-8, 7-16, 7-34, 8-1
   See also Macrospheres
            Minispheres
            Unreached peoples
People movements   8-8, 8-12, 8-24, 8-29, 9-17
Peregrini   6-26
Pierson, A. T.   6-10
Pietism   6-11
Poor, the   7-20, 10-1 – 10-2, 10-4, 10-11 – 10-17, 10-23,
   10-29 – 10-30
Poverty
   See Poor, the
Prayer
   and mission strategy   6-2, 6-8 – 6-13, 6-34
Prince, Derek   6-11
Protestant missions   6-1, 6-11, 6-14, 6-16 – 6-24,
   6-27 – 6-29
Puritans   6-16

R

Refugees
   See Poor, the
Regular missions
   See Missions, regular
Relief and development   9-2, 9-9, 10-2, 10-17
   See also Development, community
Religions
   distribution of   7-14 – 7-15, 7-19
Resistance/receptivity scale   8-16, 8-29
Roman Catholic missions   6-15

S

Satan
   and 10/40 window   7-20 – 7-21
   as god of this world   6-10, 6-30, 6-32 – 6-33, 7-21, 9-8
   See also Spiritual warfare
Schwartz, Frederick   6-16
Scroggie, Graham   7-18
Serampore Trio   6-18
Shearer, Roy   9-16
Social action   6-18, 10-1 – 10-2, 10-6 – 10-9, 10-13, 10-30
Social gospel   10-1

Social structure
    and gospel   7-9, 9-15 – 9-19
    and poverty   10-4 – 10-5
Sodality   6-27 – 6-28, 6-34
Spangenberg, Bishop   6-16
Spiritual warfare   6-8 – 6-9, 6-12 – 6-13, 6-29 – 6-34, 7-21
Stott, John R. W.   10-7
Strategy
    and Bible translation   9-8
    and prayer   6-2, 6-8 – 6-13, 6-34, 9-8
    case studies   8-7 – 8-8, 8-20 – 8-28, 9-15 – 9-16
    characteristics of   6-2 – 6-4, 6-6, 6-8, 6-34, 8-6,
        8-11 – 8-12
    formulating   8-1 – 8-6, 8-13, 8-17 – 8-19, 8-28 – 8-29,
        9-1 – 9-2, 9-8 – 9-9, 9-19 – 9-20, 9-36,
        10-9 – 10-11, 10-15 – 10-16, 10-19
    history of   6-14 – 6-24, 6-34
    types of   6-4 – 6-5, 6-34
    See also Development, community
            Nonresidential missionaries
            Tentmakers
Subbamma, B. V.   9-16

T

Taylor, Hudson   6-12
10/40 window   7-17 – 7-22, 7-34
Tentmakers   9-2 – 9-4, 9-9, 9-36
    example of Paul   9-4 – 9-6
Theological Education by Extension   9-21, 9-30
Tonga Team   8-7 – 8-8, 8-20 – 8-21
Toure, Sekou   6-12
Tribal megasphere   7-29 – 7-30, 7-34, 8-1
Two Thirds World missions   6-1, 7-29, 9-19

U

United Foreign Mission Society   6-17
Unreached peoples   6-1, 7-1, 7-11 – 7-13, 7-16, 7-18, 7-22,
    7-33 – 7-34, 10-1, 10-19, 10-27
    See also People groups
Untouchables   9-13

V

Van Der Post, Laurens   10-3
Venn, Henry   6-19 – 6-21

W

Walker, Alan   9-13
Warneck, Gustav   6-21
Warner, Timothy   6-30, 6-33
Waymire, Bob   7-13
Wheaton Conference   10-7
Whitby Conference   6-23 – 6-24
Willingen Conference   6-23
Wimber, John   6-33
Women's movements
    See Mission movements, women's
World Vision   10-4, 10-15, 10-21
Worldview   6-6, 6-31 – 6-32
Wycliffe Bible Translators   7-29

Z

Ziegenbalg, Bartholomew   6-16
Zinzendorf, Count   6-11, 6-16
Zwemer, Samuel   7-23

Author Index

Ali, Shah with Woodberry, J. Dudley
"South Asia: Vegetables, Fish, and Messianic Mosques"
    8-21 – 8-24

Beaver, R. Pierce
"The History of Mission Strategy"   6-14 – 6-24

Bush, Luis
"The 10/40 Window"   7-17 – 7-22

Dayton, Edward R.
"Evangelism as Development"   10-20 – 10-22
"How Do We Reach Them?"   8-13 – 8-19
"The Task at Hand: World Evangelization"   7-14 – 7-16

Dayton, Edward R. and Fraser, David A.
"Strategy"   6-3 – 6-6

Elkins, Phil
"A Pioneer Team in Zambia, Africa"   8-7 – 8-8,
    8-20 – 8-21

Filidis, Paul
"Worldwide Migration: Phenomenon and Opportunity"
    10-17 – 10-19

Garrison, V. David
"An Unexpected New Strategy: Using Nonresidential
    Missions to Finish the Task"   9-6 – 9-9

Hian, Chua Wee
"Evangelization of Whole Families"   9-15 – 9-18

Houston, Tom and Miller, Eric
"Is There Good News for the Poor?"   10-11 – 10-14

Johnstone, Patrick
"Unreached Peoples: How Many Are There?"
    7-11 – 7-13

Kane, J. Herbert
"The Work of Evangelism"   9-10 – 9-14

Mahoumet, Fatima
"Ann Croft and the Fulani"   8-27 – 8-28

McGavran, Donald D.
"A Church in Every People: Plain Talk About a
    Difficult Subject"   8-9 – 8-12

Moffett, Samuel
"Evangelism: The Leading Partner"   10-8 – 10-10

Moffitt, Bob
"Biblical Development"   10-27 – 10-30

Myers, Bryant L.
"Do We Have to Choose?"   10-2 – 10-5
"Where Are the Poor and the Lost?"   10-15 – 10-16

Patterson, George
"The Spontaneous Multiplication of Churches"
    9-20 – 9-35

Pickett, Robert C. and Hawthorne, Steven C.
"Helping Others Help Themselves: Christian
    Community Development"   10-23 – 10-26

Robb, John D.
"Prayer as a Strategic Weapon in Frontier Missions"
    6-8 – 6-13

Siemens, Ruth E.
"Tentmakers Needed for World Evangelization"
    9-2 – 9-6

Taylor, Clyde W.
"An Upper Class People Movement"   8-24 – 8-26

Wagner, C. Peter
"On the Cutting Edge of Mission Strategy"   6-30 – 6-34,
    10-6 – 10-7
Stop the World, I Want to Get On   6-2, 8-1 – 8-6

Winter, Ralph D.
"The Task Remaining: All Humanity in Mission Perspective"
    7-2 – 7-7
"The Two Structures of God's Redemptive Mission"
    6-26 – 6-29

Winter, Ralph D. and Fraser, David A.
"World Mission Survey"   7-23 – 7-32